THE PEN AND [

SAILOR

CASS SERIES: NAVAL POLICY AND HISTORY
ISSN 1366-9478

Series Editor: Holger Herwig

The series will publish, first and foremost, fresh quality manuscripts by research scholars in the general area of naval policy and history, without national or chronological limitations. Furthermore, it will from time to time issue collections of important articles as well as reprints of classic works.

THE PEN AND INK SAILOR

Charles Middleton and the King's Navy,
1778–1813

JOHN E. TALBOTT

University of California, Santa Barbara

FRANK CASS
LONDON • PORTLAND, OR

First published in 1998 in Great Britain by
FRANK CASS PUBLISHERS
Newbury House, 900 Eastern Avenue
London IG2 7HH

and in the United States of America by
FRANK CASS PUBLISHERS
c/o ISBS, 5804 N.E. Hassalo Street
Portland, Oregon 97213-3644
Website http://www.frankcass.com

British Library Cataloguing in Publication Data
Talbott, John E.
  The pen and ink sailor : Charles Middleton and the King's
  Navy, 1778–1813. – (Cass series. Naval policy and history ;
  no. 6)
  1. Middleton, Charles 2. Great Britain – History, Naval –
  18th century 3. Great Britain – Politics and government –
  18th century
  I. Title
  942'.073'092

ISBN 0-7146-4898-1 (cloth)
ISBN 0-7146-4452-8 (paper)
ISSN 1366-9478

Library of Congress Cataloging-in-Publication Data
Talbott, John E.
  The pen and ink sailor : Charles Middleton and the King's Navy,
1778–1813 / John E. Talbott.
    p.   cm. – (Cass series–naval policy and history, ISSN
1366-9478 : 6)
  Includes bibliographical references and index.
  ISBN 0-7146-4898-1. – ISBN 0-7146-4452-8 (pbk.)
  1. Middleton, Charles, 1726–1813. 2. Great Britain–History,
Naval–18th century. 3. Great Britain–History, Naval–19th
century. 4. Great Britain. Royal Navy–Biography. 5. Admirals–
Great Britain–Biography. I. Title. II. Series.
DA87.1.M53T35   1998
359'.0092–dc21
[b]   98-24026
                                                           CIP

Typeset by Vitaset, Paddock Wood, Kent
Printed in Great Britain by
Bookcraft (Bath) Ltd, Midsomer Norton, Somerset

To Amy, Annie, Matt, Sam and Molly

Contents

Illustrations

All prints courtesy of the National Maritime Museum, London.

Acknowledgements

Building sailing men-of-war often took longer than anyone expected, and so did writing about Charles Middleton. Many people helped me. R. J. B. Knight not only assisted in launching my research but eased my way at the National Maritime Museum and gave me a roof over my head each time I came to England to work in the Museum's unparalleled collections. To Roger, I am deeply grateful. Friends, colleagues and historians to whom I also owe thanks are George Baer, Dan Baugh, Hal Drake, Elizabeth Dubrulle, John Gillis, John Hattendorf, Sears McGee, Roger Morriss, Ken Mouré, N. A. M. Rodger and Paul Webb. The Committee on Research of the Academic Senate of the University of California, Santa Barbara, supported travel. The staffs of the British Library, Huntington Library, National Maritime Museum, Naval War College Archives, Public Records Office and Scottish Record Office helped me negotiate their collections. The Interlibrary Loans staff of the Davidson Library, University of California, Santa Barbara, brought me many books and articles from elsewhere. Chapter 4, 'Trying the Carronade', previously appeared, in somewhat different form, in *History Today* in August 1989, and I am grateful to the editors for permission to include it here. Thanks are also due to the Trustees of the National Maritime Museum for permission to quote from Charles Middleton's papers.

Series Editor's Preface

The British 'way of war' between 1665 and 1815, which Alfred Thayer Mahan used as the laboratory for his wildly popular *The Influence of Sea Power upon History* (1890), has been described and analyzed in detail with regard to its 'sea-fighting' facets. The great deeds of St Vincent and Nelson, the glorious battles of Aboukir and Trafalgar, have become the stuff of legends. Along the way, both contemporary naval officers and their biographers cleverly established a pervasive myth: that the great deeds were accomplished despite the abysmal performance of naval commands ashore such as the dockyards, the Victualling Office, the Sick and Hurt Board, the Ordnance Board and the Navy Office.

John Talbott of the University of California at Santa Barbara, an accomplished historian of the French 'way of war', much like Daniel Baugh before him, has offered a timely antidote to that view. Deftly interweaving sources from Great Britain (the National Maritime Museum, the Public Record Office and the British Library) as well as the United States (Huntington Library and the Naval War College Archives), Talbott provides a fascinating glimpse into the inner workings of what John Brewer has called 'the fiscal-military state' of Britain in the late eighteenth and early nineteenth centuries. In chapters devoted to 'Coppering the Fleet' and 'Thinking about War at Sea', 'Trying the Carronade' and 'Reforming the Navy Office', Talbott analyzes Britain's naval shore establishment and the prodigious efforts that it undertook to keep the fleet ready and at sea. At the heart of that enterprise stood the 'pen and ink sailor', Sir Charles Middleton. Variously called 'a prig and a bore of the first water' and 'that damned Scotch packhorse', Middleton had a hand in the great events of his times, first as serving sea officer and major investor in the East India Company, and later as reforming Controller of the Navy, naval adviser to William Pitt the younger, member of the Board of Admiralty, and First Lord of the Admiralty. In the latter office, Middleton reaped the rewards of decades of toil behind a desk in Nelson's success of Trafalgar, for, as Controller, he had had HMS *Victory* coppered in 1782 and recoppered five years later. In John Talbott, the 'pen and ink sailor' has found an eloquent and expert biographer.

Holger H. Herwig
Series Editor

Preface

For fully half the 150 years between 1665 and 1815 British men-of-war were at sea on a war footing. In nearshore waters and on the far side of the world they carried out orders to burn, seize, sink or destroy the enemy. Well into the twentieth century, naval historians of the era were preoccupied with events at sea. Alfred Thayer Mahan and Julian S. Corbett, to name the best known, were far more interested in ships as instruments of policy than as creations and extensions of a necessarily shore-based administration. Their books showed how peacetime navies defended far-flung economic and strategic interests and how, when war came, they engaged the enemy in decisive (or not so decisive) battles.

Mahan and Corbett took the one-hundred gun, first-rate ship of the line for granted. To them the *Victory*, Horatio Nelson's flagship, was largely the platform on which that admiral achieved apotheosis. So she was. But such ships were also the biggest, most complicated machines of their day (the *Victory* was launched in 1765). A first rate's crew of roughly 900 men was larger and more highly organized than any industrial enterprise of the time – except the one represented by the naval shore establishment itself, which ran to more than 10,000 employees.

Long after Mahan and Corbett, historians continued to accept uncritically the strictures of eighteenth-century sea officers and Opposition politicians against the dockyards, the Victualling Office, the Sick and Hurt Board and the Navy Office, to say nothing of the Ordnance Board. In their books, Britain triumphed at sea despite the woeful shortcomings of the shore establishment. Daniel Baugh's *Naval Administration in the Age of Walpole* (Princeton, NJ, 1965) demolished this older view. Scholarship since Baugh has reflected the chastened expectations of our times with respect to the performance of large-scale public organizations. Less confident of the prospects for improvement than their Victorian predecessors, historians also tend to be less censorious of the outlook and habits of eighteenth-century bureaucrats and politicians.

Increased tolerance for the inadequacies of the shore establishment may stem from our heightened awareness of the difficulties administrators and dockyard officers and workers faced. Take, for instance, the intractability of shipbuilding materials. Hard to preserve, hard to work, hard to repair, they were sometimes even hard to find. The dockyards' capacity for improving on what they took from nature was extremely limited. Wooden hulls, masts and spars, canvas sails, hempen cordage, were all subject to the flaws and irregularities of once living things. Introducing them to salt water accelerated the rate at which they decayed. Iron fastenings, anchors, blocks and other fittings were more durable, but they were expensive, and they rusted. Aside from tar and paint, slapped on everywhere they might do some good, the eighteenth century knew no effective preservatives. Wooden warships were heavy objects built without benefit of heavy machinery. Putting them together, the work of men and horses, was an exceedingly slow business. In such circumstances, Clausewitzian friction ran rampant. Things that could go wrong, did go wrong: supplies went astray and schedules awry; weather hampered repairs and ships sprang leaks. In short, many deficiencies that earlier historians put down to corruption, sloth, shoddy workmanship and other human failings, are now seen as corollaries of the iron constraints of nature.

Britain's prodigious naval effort was achieved at prodigious cost. Unlike the civilian enterprises that it dwarfed in size and complexity, the shore establishment was in business not for profit but for destruction. The King's ships went to sea to harm his enemies and keep them from doing likewise. Frigates and ships of the line, those ingenious, graceful, beautiful machines, carried on board the means of doing appalling violence. This combination of guns and sails has been offered as one explanation for Europe's brief ascendancy over the rest of the world.[1]

In Britain's case, the cost of guns and sails explains the rise of what John Brewer calls 'the fiscal-military state'. Finding the wherewithal for waging war – especially war at sea, in the case of an island nation such as Britain – was both the most pressing need and the *raison d'être* of the eighteenth-century state. Chiefly by means of the excise tax and the clever, economical and relentless methods by which it was extracted, the British government managed more efficiently than France, its chief continental rival, to tap the material resources necessary for war.[2] The British state may have been more 'enlightened' and less 'absolutist' than its contemporaries, to use terms historians have argued about for a long time, but its servants were no less eager than those of France, Prussia or Austria to increase the power of the state machine, and especially its potential for making war.[3] The most striking and visible proof of this ambition was the naval shore establishment.

This was the domain Charles Middleton, the subject of this book, ruled for a dozen years of war and peace. Middleton was by no means a typical or representative naval administrator, and he would be of less interest today if he had been. He strove to make the huge and ungainly machine in his charge (as an eighteenth-century man, he loved clockwork metaphors) run better. Middleton was a reformer of overwhelming energy and a near superfluity of ideas and projects. Called to office to deal with a war emergency, he stayed on in peacetime to prepare the navy for the next emergency – and also, there can be little doubt, because he vastly enjoyed the exercise of authority. Middleton has come in for only brief mention in many books. Usually he is described as 'formidable', as the greatest administrator the Royal Navy had known since Samuel Pepys, who achieved not merely fame as a government official but immortality as a diarist.

This book aims to show, in some detail, in what Middleton's greatness lies. I have more to say about the King's Navy than about the (private) life of Charles Middleton. As a diarist Middleton was, regrettably, no Pepys. The Middleton papers in the National Maritime Museum in Greenwich, voluminous as they are, have almost entirely to do with naval affairs. Of his boyhood almost nothing can be known. Middleton the sea-officer can be glimpsed only in his official guise, in the highly impersonal form of log-books, captain's letters and the proceedings of courts martial; the Middleton of the wardroom and great cabin – or the later Middleton of the drawing-room, for that matter – is lost from view. Yet the impersonality of official papers can be exaggerated. A temperament, a cast of mind, a view of the world – at least of the naval world – emerge from Middleton's always hurried scrawl. No flashes of wit illuminate his correspondence; at least, none caught my eye. Middleton was all business.

'A prig and a bore of the first water', Sir Oswyn Murray, a later First Secretary of the Admiralty, called him.[4] Perhaps Sir Oswyn was right. If by prig he meant 'a fellow who is always making you a present of his opinions', as George Eliot puts it in *Middlemarch*, Middleton's letters and memoranda offer abundant evidence to support the charge. Reformers may not infrequently seem to be bores: persons given to discourse only on the subject of their one, all-consuming passion. Or a bore may only be someone we find uncongenial. Plenty of Middleton's contemporaries found him tiresome; on this score Sir Oswyn agreed with them. He also conceded, however, that 'his sense of duty was unfailing and his courage, like his industry, had no limit'.[5]

PREFACE

In the course of Middleton's long life, Britain acquired control of most of India, lost control of much of North America, came into other imperial possessions, grew enormously in terms of overseas trade, went far toward becoming the first industrial nation, and nearly reached the end of the Napoleonic wars, last, longest and most brutal in the ancient series of Franco-British encounters. All these events had naval implications. Some came about through the direct application of naval force. In all of them Middleton played a lesser or greater role: as a serving sea-officer, as a major stockholder in the East India Company, as a reforming Controller of the Navy, as a naval adviser to William Pitt the younger, as a member of the Board of Admiralty, and, finally, as First Lord of the Admiralty during the Trafalgar campaign.

The role that best suited him takes up the most space in this book. As Controller of the Navy, Middleton served as animator of the vital link between the makers of policy in the Cabinet, about whom much has been written, and commanders at sea, who have also received a good deal of attention. He served a term as a Member of Parliament; he was not averse to bureaucratic in-fighting. Still, he was quintessentially a professional adviser, a man who applied his expertise to running and improving the machinery needed to keep the King's ships at sea. As such, he was a person of the second tier, a moderately influential man who had the ear of the most powerful men of the kingdom. Such persons are everywhere in modern government. They were much rarer in Middleton's day. He is sometimes said to have been ahead of his time, to have prefigured the great Victorian reformers. I disagree. He was as much a figure of Georgian society and culture as Samuel Johnson; he was thoroughly a man of the ships of the Georgian Navy, which Johnson compared to being in jail. But, then, James Boswell's great friend was not always as fair as he was amusing.

NOTES

1 Carlo Cipolla, *Guns and Sails in the Early Phase of European Expansion, 1400–1700* (London, 1965).
2 John Brewer, *The Sinews of Power: War, Money and the English State, 1688–1783* (New York, 1989), especially pp. 27–76.
3 Paul W. Schroeder, *The Transformation of European Politics, 1763–1848* (Oxford, 1994), pp. 50–1.
4 Oswyn A. R. Murray, 'The Admiralty', Part VI, *The Mariner's Mirror*, 24 (July 1938), p. 335. Murray's posthumous series of articles on the Admiralty appeared in *The Mariner's Mirror*, 23 (1937), pp. 13–36, 129–47, 316–31 and 24 (1938), pp. 101–4; 204–25; 329–52.
5 Ibid., p. 335.

1

Cruising the West Indies

'That damned Scotch packhorse', Lord St Vincent called Sir Charles Middleton.[1] In eighteenth-century England, where thoroughbreds were admired and Scots despised, St Vincent could hardly have contrived a more scornful remark. Scots were clannish and pushy, his generation believed; they were personally unreliable and politically treacherous; they spoke an incomprehensible dialect; they were stingy. Worst of all, perhaps, Scots immigrants to England seemed successful out of all proportion to their numbers: 'they were the top engineers, surgeons, and philandering biographers'.[2]

Middleton actually had the Jacobite ancestor that Englishmen imputed to every Scot. His namesake Charles Middleton, his grandfather's first cousin, joined James II in France soon after the last Stuart king was driven from the throne; he died there in 1719, loyal to the end.[3] Other Middletons eschewed lost causes in favor of higher education and the lower civil service. Charles's great-grandfather and grandfather were both principals of King's College, Aberdeen. As the youngest of 12 children, Charles's father Robert could apparently expect nothing in the way of academic preferment, so he joined the Customs and rose to the command of a revenue cutter. When Charles was born Robert was Collector of Customs at Dundee.[4]

Charles's mother Helen Dundas belonged to an important family of Scots lawyers and politicians. Her own father was a merchant-marine captain. But Charles's cousin Henry Dundas rose to become an important figure in the affairs of the East India Company, the Lord Advocate of Scotland (in less lofty terms, Scotland's political boss), a close confidant of the younger Pitt and incumbent, through the last quarter of the eighteenth century, of several important offices of state. The shrewd and able Dundas stood at the levers of a vast patronage machine and more than once Charles Middleton came to look to him for favors.[5]

Charles was born in Leith, Edinburgh's seaport, on 14 October 1726. He was lucky to survive infancy. For besides smallpox, diphtheria, tuberculosis, whooping cough and other commonplace diseases, he was also at risk from waves of deadly epidemics of typhus, malaria and unidentifiable 'fevers' then sweeping the British Isles.[6] Childhood was short-lived in the eighteenth century. Charles may have gone to sea as early as his eleventh year. At least the Navy credited him with three years' service (1738–41) aboard the merchantman *Loyal Jane*. He may have remained in school, however, while an obliging merchant captain, eager to do a customs collector's son a favor, carried his name on the *Loyal Jane*'s muster book. In any event, in April 1741 Captain Samuel Mead, a family friend, took Charles aboard the *Sandwich*, a 90-gun ship of the line, as a captain's servant. A few weeks later he followed Mead to the *Duke*, another 90-gun ship.[7]

A servant in the Navy's sense of the word was neither a domestic nor an employee; he resembled an apprentice, but in most cases had none of an apprentice's legal obligations. A servant was a boy undergoing training in the ways of the sea. Drawn from all social classes, such boys might become officers; they might become able seamen. In any case, so much was to be learned about sailing and fighting a man of war, that it was thought essential to begin at an early age. Regulations prescribed that officers' sons should be 11 and others 13, but these rules were often ignored, and many boys of 6 or 8 were to be found at sea. Charles was all of 14.[8]

Why did so many boys like Charles go to sea? Why did parents so eagerly commit their sons to a profession offering prolonged absences from home, poor pay, and a good chance of an early death? Customs officers despised the Navy as a gang of smugglers wearing the King's uniform; nevertheless, like Charles's father, they sent their sons into it in substantial numbers. The Middletons laid claim to distinguished ancestors, but in the 1730s they had little or nothing in the way of property, money or influence. The Navy was the only gentleman's profession requiring no capital or connections for entry. All parents could dream that their captain's servant carried an admiral's flag in his sea bag. Charles Middleton did. Horatio Nelson, a Norfolk parson's boy, became one of the greatest English sea officers who ever lived.[9]

Charles's real training in the ways of the sea came in the *Flamborough*, a sixth rate of 20 guns that he joined in Portsmouth in November 1741, near the outset of the War of the Austrian Succession, and served in for four years. The *Flamborough* had no room for the gang of Navy-supplied striplings that a boy found aboard a ship of the line; on a frigate a 15 year old grew up quickly. Based in Charleston, she cruised as far south as Cuba, protecting the trade between the mainland and the West Indies against Spanish privateers.[10] From captain's servant Charles advanced to midshipman and then to master's mate. None of these ratings had much to do with the actual tasks in which a young gentleman might be engaged. He was expected to learn the business of a warship, from working aloft, to navigation, to gunnery, to taking on stores, to conning, under the sharp eye of the master, a ship under way – all in the hope of one day passing the examination for lieutenant.[11]

The examining board, composed of senior officers and convened at the Navy Office, questioned candidates closely on all these matters. For the lives of seamen and the safety of ships depended on an officer's making right judgements in the face of wind, weather and the enemy. Admission ticket to the Navy meritocracy, the passing certificate qualified its holder to aim for command at sea, the great prize many reached for and many fewer grasped. Horatio Nelson was named a post-captain at the age of 20, little more than a year after passing his lieutenant's examination.[12] Charles Middleton, a far more typical junior officer, passed his examination on 4 November 1745 and waited a dozen years to command his own ship.

On receiving his passing certificate Middleton joined the *Chesterfield*, a 44-gun frigate moored at Deptford, as third lieutenant.[13] One incident in an otherwise routine cruise stands out. On 15 October 1748 most of the ship's officers, Middleton included, went ashore at Sierra Leone. In their absence, some of the crew overpowered their shipmates and made off with the *Chesterfield*. What the mutineers contemplated – possibly a life of piracy – is unclear. In any event, the boatswain, who must have been a persuasive talker, succeeded in retaking her. By the time he got the upper hand the ship was too far out to sea to make returning to her anchorage practicable, so he took her to the West Indies, where in March 1749 the officers abandoned in Sierra Leone finally rejoined her.

The Admiralty was, of course, curious to know why Captain O'Brien Dudley had been away from his ship with so many of his officers at once. At his court martial Dudley pleaded that his orders to survey the trading station required a large party to be on shore; he had not wanted to offend local officials who had extended their hospitality to him and his subordinates; and in any case no one had suspected that mutiny was afoot. The court martial acquitted Dudley, but the Admiralty nevertheless convicted him of poor judgement by relieving him of his command.[14]

The *Chesterfield* incident supports the revisionist argument that merely enforcing respect for officers was the least of the aims of naval discipline.

For a crew actually to make off with a ship was exceedingly unusual – one reason why the mutiny on the *Bounty* gained such notoriety. Unlike Fletcher Christian, acting lieutenant of the *Bounty* when he and his followers put Captain William Bligh and his loyalists over the side in a longboat, none of the *Chesterfield* mutineers was qualified either to navigate or to pilot, especially if Samuel Couchman, the first lieutenant, was the drunken bystander he claimed to be. Endangering a ship and her company was far worse, by the Navy's lights, than showing disrespect for her officers. And Couchman, who had the responsibility for preventing the mutiny if he did not connive at it, paid the price. The court martial sentenced him to be shot and John Place, the carpenter's mate, to be hanged.[15] Middleton never wrote about this episode of his youth, but his own later reputation as a stern disciplinarian suggests that he did not forget it.

By the time Middleton returned to England in the spring of 1749, the peace of Aix-la-Chapelle had put an end to the War of the Austrian Succession – without, however, resolving the Anglo-French antagonism. The Navy reverted to 10,000 men, its usual peacetime strength in the first half of the eighteenth century, reducing Middleton to half-pay. A Middleton on half-pay is always a Middleton lost from sight. He reappears in 1752, when he found employment as third lieutenant on the guardship *Culloden* (74). Moored in the rivers and near the dockyards with their masts and rigging up, their boats in service, and skeleton crews aboard, guardships formed a ready reserve. At least in peacetime, they were a coveted assignment – a comfortable berth making no very arduous demands and offering plenty of nights ashore.[16]

Middleton's longest and most eventful service as a lieutenant was aboard the *Anson* (60), which he joined in January 1753. As her second lieutenant he sailed to the West Indies, where he made his name and his fortune; on the *Anson* he made one of his closest naval friends. A great seaman as well as a great technical innovator, a brave and self-sacrificing officer driven by the most stringent conception of duty, Richard Kempenfelt remained first lieutenant until succeeded by his friend in January 1755.[17] Another shipmate was Samuel Wallis, who commanded the *Dolphin*'s circumnavigation of the globe in 1764–66 and served as Middleton's colleague at the Navy Board during the American War.

Aboard the *Anson* Middleton took part in one of the opening moves of a great war. In April 1754 a skirmish between French and British forces in the Ohio River valley sharply increased tensions between the imperial rivals for mastery in North America. Each side moved to strengthen its garrisons. In April 1755 the British government dispatched Vice-Admiral Edward

Boscawen's squadron across the Atlantic with orders to keep the French from landing reinforcements at their stronghold of Louisburg. Cruising off Newfoundland on 10 June, Boscawen intercepted three French 64s – the *Alcide*, the *Lys* and the *Dauphin Royal* – capturing the first two but allowing the third to escape. An encounter, the political repercussions of which far exceeded its military significance, gave Middleton what John Knox Laughton calls his 'nearest approach to war service on the grand scale'.[18]

This incident set in motion a diplomatic revolution that made old enemies into friends: France allied itself with Austria, Austria with Russia, Russia with Sweden. England and Prussia drew together to fight France and defend Hanover, the English king's hereditary electorate. Featuring land campaigns in Europe, North America, the Caribbean and India, and battles in every contiguous sea, the Seven Years War eventually drew in all the Great Powers. 'This wide geographical spread; this involvement of the major Powers; this loss of life and outpouring of treasure', General Sir Reginald Savory writes, 'marked the greatest upheaval the world had yet seen.'[19]

The *Anson* took Middleton to a vital theater of England's war with France. Even the poorest English worker of Middleton's time took sugar with his tea, a habit that assured a string of tiny, fever-ridden islands in the Caribbean a central place in British overseas trade. France had a comparable stake in the West Indies. Specks such as Barbados and Antigua, Guadalupe and St Lucia assumed gigantic proportions in the mental maps of English and French policy-makers.[20]

The sugar islands mattered not only for themselves. Around them pivoted the complicated machinery of the Atlantic trade. English ships brought supplies, especially food and finished goods, to the islands from England; they carried slaves from West Africa. The English settlements in North America furnished the West Indian planters with lumber and other materials in exchange for rum, molasses and less famous products. The islands shipped sugar, indigo, coffee, cocoa and cotton back to England and Europe. So dynamic was the Atlantic trade, and so dependent were the slaved-based sugar plantations on the mother country, that during the eighteenth century, English exports to North America and the West Indian colonies increased by 2,300 per cent.[21]

Vital to the trade of the two imperial rivals, each one's West Indian islands were also extremely vulnerable to the other's depredations. At the outset of the Seven Years War, England held an edge at sea and France in Europe. By making a military alliance with Prussia and sending British troops to support it, Britain aimed not only – or even primarily – to protect the Hanoverian territory of the British monarch but also to distract the French from their own operations at sea with an expensive continental war. By striking with naval forces at French trade and possessions in the Caribbean, Britain sought to cripple France's capacity for making war elsewhere.[22]

Sea officers had mixed feelings about serving in the Caribbean. Some went to great lengths to avoid it – feigning sickness, pulling strings, even resigning their commissions when all else failed. Not only were the sugar islands rife with malaria and other fatal diseases; colonial officials, planters and merchants could be counted on to heap a sea officer with complaints against the Navy. War, however, raised the prospect of a killing in prize money, and this helped alleviate the risks and nuisances of West Indian service. For in the eighteenth century, as Richard Pares pointed out, 'naval war was a branch of business, not only for the colonists who claimed protection of the navy, but for the strategists who planned operations and most of all for the sailors who carried them out'.[23]

On 27 April 1756, having succeeded Kempenfelt as first lieutenant of the *Anson*, the businesslike Middleton sailed for the West Indies. In company with the *Bristol* (50) and *Harwich* (50), his ship escorted the biannual outbound convoy, laden with essential English goods.[24] Such convoys tended to be small – the *Anson*'s had only 17 sail. Returning convoys were often huge, sprawling affairs of 100 sail or more, on whose stragglers French privateers fell like wolves on elderly elk. Providing convoy escorts was only one of the Navy's West Indian duties. Fearful of sea raiders swooping down and destroying everything they owned, the sugar planters clamored for a visible sign of England's commitment to protecting them. So the Navy kept a squadron on station in the Leeward Islands. The French government had a different approach to security in the Caribbean. Whenever a naval force was required in the West Indies one came out from home. If the French planters lived with an eye turned anxiously seaward, the French system nevertheless had its advantages. Owing to inadequate West Indian repair facilities, English ships were rarely sound – one of Middleton's ships proved so leaky that her pumps had almost continuously to be manned. Fresh from well-equipped dockyards, the French usually outsailed the English. Moreover, the stationing of squadrons in the Caribbean left them vulnerable to the occasionally disastrous effects of hurricanes.

The English system also had strategic drawbacks. The French system of sending out fleets from home kept the English guessing. Where were they? Would they remain concentrated, or would they disperse among the islands? The French did not have to guess the whereabouts of the English. Every colonial governor, imagining a French fleet lay just over his own horizon, insisted on the commander-in-chief's protection. His force scattered in little packets, no Leeward Islands commander could easily manage a concerted attack on the French. Concentrated or scattered, ships stationed in the Caribbean could not easily be sent elsewhere. No island politician wanted to hear that the West Indies were best defended from the French in the Channel and the Strait of Gibraltar.

Yet the English system worked well when it came to defending and intercepting trade. A compromise between conflicting political and military demands, it did have the considerable virtue of assuring the English squadrons of control of the sea for several months of every year.[25]

A ship as big as the *Anson*, however, was not well suited to intercepting trade, a point Middleton emphasized in one of his few surviving letters from this period. To Walter Pringle, a planter and merchant, he explained his views on the number and kinds of ship needed for suppressing privateers and protecting the Leeward Islands trade. Two ships of 40 guns were required, he wrote, and two of 20. But he emphasized the need for smaller vessels: eight brigantines of 16 guns and two sloops of ten, or a ratio of 5:2 in small ships over large. Brigantines, he stressed, 'are much cheaper to the government' (a theme he emphasized to the end of his days in public service), 'and full strong enough for the service they are employed upon'. Like brigantines, sloops 'can go into shoal water', where the small vessels that dominated the inter-island trade took refuge from two-deckers such as the *Anson*.[26]

Small ships would not only save the government money, they would also make money for whoever was lucky enough to sail them in the passages the French favored most. There were not enough of them to go around, however, 'and to prevent the cruizers being tempted to leave the bad and stretch into the good', Middleton told Pringle, 'I would have them shifted now and then'.[27] A captain assured that doing his duty would give him a fair chance to compete for prizes would be less inclined to forget what his duty was.

The *Anson* did not share in the excitement of these small-ship exercises. Middleton's lieutenant's log records weeks lying in St John's Road, the anchorage off Antigua, interspersed with shuttling trade convoys among the islands, in the company of the other big ships of the station, and escorting beyond the reach of privateers a homeward-bound convoy of 85 West Indiamen. The *Anson* took an occasional prize but also lost a brig under the shore batteries of Martinique, where no English ship dared venture. The weather proved a greater danger than the French. A September hurricane blew out all the *Anson*'s sails, carried away the foretop mast, fore topsail yard, main topmast and driver yard, and totally dismasted other ships on the station.[28] Such widespread and heavy damage the dockyard at English Harbour was hard-pressed to repair.

On 30 January 1757 Middleton wrote to his commanding officer Captain Robert Man, demanding a court martial on seaman John Dunbar for 'having treated me with a Contempt and Insolence tending to mutiny (in the Face of the Ship's Company) when in the Execution of my duty'.[29] At the court martial convened aboard the *Stirling Castle* (70), senior captains of the Leeward Islands station heard witnesses testify that Dunbar had accosted Middleton in the wardroom, demanding to know why his grog ration had been stopped. Middleton told Dunbar that they would take the matter up on the quarterdeck. Nevertheless, the seaman persisted and Middleton, striking him with a small stick, pushed him out of the wardroom. In the passageway Middleton reached to the overhead as if to take down a pike just as crewmen grabbed the vociferating Dunbar and hustled him forward.

The court martial did not press for details – except for asking how big Middleton's stick was (the thickness of a little finger) – but merely allowed each witness to give his version of events, passing without comment or query to the next. Witnesses for the Crown and the prisoner all agreed that they had heard Dunbar exclaim that a French jail was preferable to an English man of war. But did he say so before or after Middleton reached for the pike? Crewmen remembered that the gesture provoked the remark; officers believed the remark provoked the gesture. Seaman William Maddox swore that he heard Middleton say, 'You scoundrel, if I had a pike in my hand I would take your life.' His shipmate Thomas Still's version was, 'Damn your blood you rascal, if I had a pike in my hand I would run you through'; Alexander Linney testified that 'Mr Middleton said "you scoundrel, Rascal, I will run you through", and put his hand up in order to take down a pike.'

The Dunbar incident was thoroughly routine. Dunbar's behavior endangered neither the *Anson*, at anchor in an English roadstead, nor her company. Nor was such a man likely to have encouraged emulators. Sailors held drunkards in low esteem; none cared to share a maintop foot rope with one on a stormy night at sea. The senior captains of the panel had no doubt heard countless such run-ins recounted. They were curious to know only whether Dunbar behaved 'insolently' toward Middleton, the question on which the charge against the seaman stood or fell. Yes, he did, replied the master and purser, who alone witnessed the confrontation in the wardroom. By entering the wardroom without an invitation, Dunbar trespassed 'officers' country'. His complaint about his grog ration belonged only to the quarterdeck. Irked by the intrusion and further riled by Dunbar's back-talk, Middleton struck the intruder, pushed him, cursed him, threatened to impale him and finally kicked Dunbar in the backside as his mates dragged him away.

So the Dunbar episode reveals a Middleton of excitable temperament (in a later incident, he kicked one of his warrant officers in the crotch).[30] Perhaps the *Chesterfield* experience had made him wary of indulging the slightest infraction of shipboard etiquette. Not only was he quick-tempered – it did not take much to make him go for his stick; he was easily provoked to rage. Even a friendly witness, Jacobs the master, spoke of Middleton's being 'so much exasperated' that he reached for the pike; Thomas Still, a prisoner's witness, said 'Mr Middleton threw himself in a Passion'.[31] Had he made good his threat to skewer Dunbar, he surely would have lived to regret it. For the Navy did not hesitate to try officers for attempted murder, and such a charge would have ruined his career. But Middleton only threatened to run his antagonist through, he did not make good his threat. The court martial swiftly convicted Dunbar of 'having behaved contemptu-ously and insolently to his superior officer' and of 'having used reproachful and Provoking speeches, tending to make a Disturbance in the ship'. He was sentenced 'to receive Sixty Lashes on his bare Back, with a Cat of nine Tails'.[32]

No sooner had the court martial disposed of the Dunbar case than it tried Captain Richard Watkins, commander of the *Blandford* (24), on charges brought by Rear-Admiral Thomas Frankland, commander of the Leeward Islands station. Watkins unwisely 'by sundry letters and other written papers treated [the Admiral] in a highly contemptuous and disrespectful manner'. Frankland had only to produce the letters to see Watkins convicted and relieved of command.[33]

Watkins's disgrace gave Middleton the opportunity every sea officer waited for. Or so it briefly appeared. For on the morning of 27 February Admiral Frankland gave him command of the *Blandford* and ordered Lieutenant Darrock of the same ship to take Middleton's place on the *Anson*. But something happened to this economical swap, and the *Blandford* went to Lieutenant Penhallon Cuming instead.[34] Perhaps it was just as well. The *Blandford* appears to have been an unlucky ship, at least for commanding officers.[35]

Frankland gave Middleton the *Speaker* sloop (12) instead. This was quite a step down from the *Anson* (or from the *Blandford*, for that matter), but most sea officers would have preferred commanding the Navy's smallest ship to saluting, as first lieutenant, the captain of its biggest. And Middleton knew the advantages small ships had over large in pursuing war – and prizes – in the West Indies. The *Speaker*, however, was a leaky tub. By 13 May she was taking on so much water that keeping her afloat had to take priority over hunting prizes.[36]

Repairs in Barbados gave the *Speaker* a more profitable autumn. She took a small privateer in September, a slaver in October, and another small privateer in December. By the new year, however, no amount of island patchwork could stop the leaks in her hull, and in July 1757 Middleton relinquished command, without having taken another prize since the previous December.

The day after giving up the unlamented *Speaker*, he assumed command of the *Barbadoes* (14), which the Navy had ostensibly bought from a private West Indian owner. But the Navy Board later refused to recognize his claims for reimbursement for out-of-pocket expenses, on the grounds that the Admiralty had never confirmed that it had purchased the *Barbadoes*. With the Admiralty's help he finally settled his accounts, but not without learning that the naval bureaucracy could be as frustrating as a leaky hull.[37]

Next followed an odd interlude in Middleton's West Indian career. From 1 March 1759 through 14 July 1760 he was captain of the *Arundel* (24), but he evidently spent few of these 16 months at sea. Or if he did, he failed to apprise the Admiralty. Chided for not keeping their Lordships informed of his whereabouts, he rather feebly replied that he had received no inquiries from them until a few weeks before he surrendered command. But a man of his experience could not have been ignorant of the Admiralty's relentless curiosity. And when John Cleveland, the Secretary, demanded to know what he had been up to, Middleton replied that 'I commanded Arundel about 7 weeks – in Leeward Islands cruizing, convoying merchant ships and heaving down.' His reply left 14 months to account for, but Cleveland evidently did not press him for further explanation.[38]

If Middleton's conduct as captain of the *Arundel* met with mild reproof, his cruise in the *Emerald* (28) redeemed him. On 15 July 1760 Commodore James Douglas, commander in chief of the Leeward Islands station, named Middleton to succeed Captain Thomas Cornwall, incapacitated by gout at the age of 28.[39] The *Emerald* was just the sort of vessel Middleton and others had prescribed for war on trade in the West Indies: fast enough to

10

keep up with the enemy, small enough to pursue him into shoal water and well armed enough to take care of herself.

The tactics Middleton outlined for his friend Walter Pringle drew on practices dating from the time of Columbus. For in 1760 a reliable means of calculating longitude at sea had yet to be put into widespread use.[40] So a captain sailed down the latitude of his West Indian destination until he made landfall. Knowing this took much of the guesswork from meeting friendly convoys and intercepting enemy trade. As Middleton explained to Commodore Douglas, who had asked for his views on protecting the Leeward Islands trade, 'all our European, African, and [the] greatest part of our American trade' came down a channel running from 13 to 18°N. Of course, French privateers knew this as well as English merchantmen. To discourage the French, Middleton recommended putting two frigates in a zone a few degrees of latitude thick and to windward of Barbados and as many leagues wide as circumstances required. For the purpose of intercepting the swarming French privateers (which promised to be far more lucrative than protecting the incoming British trade), he advised cruising to windward between Martinique and Dominica, and watching the passages between Martinique and its neighbors. Middleton had no formula for looking after the inter-island trade. 'It is impossible', he told Douglas, 'to fix any certain plan for its protection. The vessels employed among [the islands] are very numerous, and they are running from one to another without interruption.'[41]

Middleton's policy of dispersal flew in the face of the principle of the concentration of force, but it was well suited to the West Indies, where the war at sea was an economic struggle, not the contest between battle fleets so dear to the Mahanians. England aimed to squeeze the life out of France's sugar islands, and by doing so to cripple its capacity to carry on the larger war. Lying in wait for their quarry in the known shipping routes of the Caribbean, Middleton and his colleagues adumbrated in method and purpose the submarine warfare of the twentieth century.

Between September 1760 and the end of May 1761, the *Emerald* took 16 prizes: 11 merchant vessels, mostly sloops and schooners loaded with coffee, sugar, lumber, wine and other goods; and five privateers. Most were captured off Barbados and the rich cruising grounds between Martinique and Dominica that Middleton recommended to Commodore Douglas. If only the value of these and other prizes in which Middleton held a share could be established! Whatever the *Emerald*'s prizes sold for – and it must have been a considerable sum – her captain had a right to one quarter of the profits. The merchants of Barbados expressed their gratitude to the scourge of neighborhood privateering by presenting him with a gold-hilted sword.[42] Indeed, following the mysterious *Arundel* episode, Middleton conducted with great energy the cruise that earned him the sword. The *Emerald* spent 56 per cent of her time in the West Indies at sea – far higher than the average of ships cruising home waters (39 per cent), higher than the average on the North American and East Indies stations (25 and 44 per cent, respectively), less than some Leeward Islands ships (78 per cent!), but still substantially higher than the average sea time of modern warships.[43]

Nearly as leaky as the *Speaker*, on 2 June 1761, Middleton's ship joined a homeward-bound convoy of 154 sail. Once again Middleton turned to a shepherd's tiresome work: 'Fired several shott at convoy to make them bear down', the log of 27 June noted, 'but little notice taken of it.' Off the Lizard by 23 July, on the 28th the *Emerald* came up the Medway to Chatham Dockyard.[44]

Middleton had not set foot in England for nearly five years. Eager to put the *Emerald* behind him, he asked for two months leave to look after his affairs in Scotland. Deaf to entreaties of how long he had been abroad and how far he remained from home, the Admiralty granted him a fortnight. When the two weeks expired he asked for three more, promising that 'I shall be ready to obey their Lordships commands at an hour's warning.' Their Lordships, having seen countless sea officers disregard similar assurances, granted him only 14 additional days.[45]

Surveying the waterlogged *Emerald* convinced the Portsmouth ship-wrights she was not worth repairing. Her crew was paid off, in October she was decommissioned and in November broken up.[46]

On 12 December 1761, at the church of St Martin-in-the-Fields, close by the Admiralty, Captain Middleton married Margaret Gambier, daughter of a prominent Huguenot family. The only surviving account of their courtship comes from John Deas Thomson's sketch for the Middleton biography he never managed to write. Middleton's long-time secretary tells a romantic story. Charles met the niece of Captain Mead, his patron aboard the *Sandwich*, when he was a 21-year-old lieutenant. Betrothed to someone else, she preferred the Scots sea officer to whomever her parents had chosen. For ten years, Thomson says, she and her father, an attorney and warden of the Fleet Prison, were at odds over Middleton. Finally Margaret's father disinherited her and she went to live with her schoolmate Elizabeth Bouverie, another Huguenot who owned large land holdings in Kent. When Middleton returned from his long tour of duty in the West Indies, Margaret was at last free to marry him.[47]

Pining away on the Leeward Islands station for his sweetheart back in England, Middleton came home and married for love. Nothing of this is even hinted at in his own writings. No letters between the Middletons survive. From Charles's return in 1761 until Margaret's death in 1792 they were evidently seldom apart more than a few days at a time, so they had little need to correspond. That they were inseparable, however, keeps much from being known about the most important relationship in Middleton's life. For 'the relations that are the most opaque [to historians]', as Paul Seaver observes, 'are those that were the most intimate – those between husband and wife and between parents and children'.[48]

Margaret proved to be inseparable not only from her husband but also from 'Mrs' Bouverie, as spinsters of a certain age were known. So Elizabeth joined the newlyweds. Charles outlived both Margaret and Elizabeth, but until the end of his days he kept the trio's habit of shuttling between the Middletons' townhouse in Mayfair and Elizabeth Bouverie's country seat at Teston. No ledger survives to reveal how they managed their domestic accounts, but the income from Mrs Bouverie's inherited wealth in land, combined with the fortune Middleton made from raiding French trade, would have produced a large sum indeed. The son of a Scots customs officer had made a big step in the world. Of course, Middleton was far from the only boy of modest means to do well out of the Navy. The prospect of striking it rich, it will be recalled, inspired countless parents to entrust their sons to a chancy profession.

Captain Middleton stood out from his fellow sea officers not for growing rich in the king's service but for holding deep religious convictions.[49] Charles, Margaret and their friend Elizabeth Bouverie were Evangelicals. Gathering influence as it collected adherents (and banked its fires) in the middle and upper classes, Evangelical religion afforded the later Victorian era the muscular energy, the cast of mind and the code of conduct summed up in the virtue of 'respectability'.[50] Already in 1808, as a contemporary Unitarian journal disapprovingly noted, '[Evangelicals] have invaded the Navy, they thrive at the Bank, they bear sway at the India House, they count several votes in Parliament, and they have got a footing in the Royal Palace. Their activity is incredible.'[51] When Charles Middleton married Margaret Gambier in 1761, however, Evangelicals were battling for a foothold in the Established Church; in the Navy they were a tiny flock of odd birds.

Evangelicalism was an intensely personal faith. Preoccupied with their relationship with Christ the Redeemer, Evangelicals tended to be unusually introspective, given to keeping diaries in which they enumerated their sins

13

and agonized over the state of their souls.[52] Middleton evidently kept no such diary. Nor did he apparently undergo the conversion experience that figured so prominently in the lives of Evangelicals such as John Wesley and William Wilberforce.[53] Huguenots were prominent in Evangelical circles. So it could be that Charles Middleton turned to a religion of the heart when he won the heart of Margaret Gambier. Yet the temperament that emerges from his surviving papers has closer affinities with the chilly spirituality of John Calvin than with the 'Enthusiasm' of the Wesleyans. Soon after meeting Middleton at a London dinner party in 1776 the writer Hannah More, in the midst of her own Evangelical awakening, described him to her sisters as 'the stern and simple Captain', and went on to lament that 'there are so few people [Middleton presumably being one of them] to whom one can venture to recommend sermons'.[54] Middleton's Evangelicalism more nearly fits Roy Porter's characterization: 'a stern, steely, clear-cut, personal creed to stabilize and energize the demanding calls of business, minimize insecurity and win respect'.[55]

Evangelicalism was so deeply imprinted on Middleton's character and his conduct as a public man that in his old age his enemies thought of him as an Evangelical first and a naval administrator second. 'A superannuated Methodist', Thomas Creevey sneered on hearing in 1805 that Middleton had been named First Lord of the Admiralty.[56] The same year, Lt Francis Beaufort, on station in the Mediterranean, expressed the wish to be delivered of 'Lord Barham and his Psalm-singers'.[57]

Middleton was not in fact a 'Methodist', as John Wesley's followers were called by their enemies and took to calling themselves. Like Wesley himself, Middleton was a lifelong member of the Church of England. Unlike Wesley, he neither challenged episcopal authority nor appeared to encourage anyone to think the last should be first. As sea officer, gentleman farmer and naval administrator, Middleton rubbed elbows with the lower classes. If he was in daily contact with sailors and artisans, farm workers and unskilled laborers, however, he never thought of fraternizing with them. Like Hannah More and William Wilberforce, younger and better known members of his Evangelical circle, he took the existing structure of church, state and society for granted – at least until the time came to defend them from the contagion of the French Revolution.

Middleton hewed to the old Puritan conviction that 'there could be no reason to doubt that the world was ruled by a divine Providence, mysterious though its workings might be to many at any given moment'.[58] Fearing God and trusting in Providence released him from the need to fear men. True, he deferred to others: his profession required deference; he lived in a deferential society. For all his respect for social convention, however, Middleton was utterly self-confident. As sometimes happens with such people, his belief in the superiority of his own judgement was not always well founded, and at least once it cost the Navy dearly. The Evangelical conviction that all work was God's work imparted a sense of urgency to everything he did. Enabling him to take up crushing burdens of work, his notion of acting as God's agent in the world also encouraged him to expect a wholehearted devotion to duty from others, and he did not hesitate to reprove even the First Lord of the Admiralty when his expectations were not met. In short, Middleton was a seagoing exemplar of the famous Protestant ethic. The same virtues of relentless toil, a preoccupation with effiency, innovation and the most profitable use of time, that have been said to have promoted the piling up of fortunes, also served to keep a navy at sea.[59]

An Evangelical's conviction that he had been saved by his Redeemer sometimes had a side that in Middleton's case was especially pronounced. Confident of his own righteousness, he was quick to pass judgement on sinners. A thick vein of censoriousness runs through his mountain of official correspondence. However much he strove to hold it in check, it nevertheless frequently broke the surface in spectacular outcroppings of anger and reproof. From Sandwich, the First Lord of the Admiralty, to Dunbar the seaman, no one who fell short of Middleton's exacting standards escaped his scolding tongue.

Wearing their convictions on their sleeves, Evangelicals made conventional Anglicans and unbelievers uneasy. They did not set the tone among sea officers, and they were often despised and scorned by those who did. Nevertheless, unlike the Dissenters, with whom they had temperamental and theological affinities, obeying their consciences did not bar Evangelicals from serving the state. They were not excluded from the universities. No laws prohibited them from practicing any of the professions. No religious inhibitions encouraged them to shun positions of power and influence.[60] Compared with the Quakers, their allies in the campaign against the slave trade, the Evangelicals were not outsiders. They were free to become sea officers and Members of Parliament, Controllers of the Navy and, in the days of Victorian triumph, prime ministers.[61]

In 1761, for the first time in more than a decade, Middleton found himself on half pay. But cruising in the West Indies had lengthened his purse since he last came on shore. Now he wrote to the Admiralty from Hertford Street, in newly-fashionable Mayfair.[62] As a newlywed and a man of means, perhaps he toyed with the idea of staying ashore. In late 1761, however, the war with France continued, and a sea officer who declined to serve in wartime jeopardized his prospects of being employed again. Besides, having already amassed a tidy sum in prize money, he probably hoped that another cruise would bring him more. When offered command of the *Adventure* (32), Middleton accepted.

Perhaps the prospect of Channel service appealed to a man who had been away from home so long. If so, disenchantment quickly set in. No sooner had Middleton taken command of the *Adventure* than he expressed to Charles Jenkinson his disappointment in his new ship and her cruising ground.[63] More heavily armed than the *Emerald*, the *Adventure* was not a good sailer, and Middleton recommended adding longer yards and more sail to his underpowered frigate.[64] After five years of war, the pickings off Le Havre promised to be far slimmer than they had been off Martinique.

The cruise began well enough. On her second day at sea the *Adventure* captured a 14-gun Dunkirk privateer. But in the following nine months she took only ten smallish prizes, including a small fishing boat and 'a vessel laden with oysters', a catch after the tastes of Samuel Pepys. A failed cutting-out expedition in the river mouth near Caen and weeks of fruitless cruising in St Malo Bay further depressed Middleton's spirits, and by February 1763 he was worn out.[65] Writing to the Admiralty to complain that he had been confined 'for some weeks past with a fever and Scorbutic Disorder', he asked for leave to recover.[66] A decade after Dr James Lind published his *Treatise on the Scurvy* (an essay in aetiology, not preventive medicine), the disease still ravaged crews on station a few days' sail from home.

The Admiralty's decision to pay off the *Adventure* gave Middleton more time to recuperate than he had bargained for.[67] Not long after he came ashore, however, their Lordships offered him command of the *Pearl* (32), a spanking new frigate. He declined, pleading, 'I have had no opportunity for these ten years past of settling my private circumstances on Shore, from a constant employment in service, and the greatest part of the time abroad.' The great war having ended, Middleton probably decided that it was safe to decline the *Pearl* without permanently injuring his career. But he knew he ran such a risk. 'I have likewise to entreat their Lordships Indulgence', he wrote, 'in hoping this request [to be excused from the proferred command] will not injure me in their Opinion as an Officer.'[68]

Without entirely closing the door on another appointment, Middleton had apparently decided that 20 years' naval service were enough. Instead of establishing their own household, the Middletons moved in with Mrs Bouverie. To be more accurate, Charles Middleton moved into the household the two women had long shared. Assuming the management of Mrs Bouverie's estates, he became a gentleman farmer. The property of Teston, where the Evangelical *menage à trois* took up residence, had a fine view of the Medway.[69] Close to Chatham Dockyard and near the London–Maidstone coach road, it enabled Middleton to turn his hand to farming without cutting himself off from either the larger world or the King's Navy.

As it turned out, Middleton never went to sea again. Compared with Nelson, who died of his wound in the cockpit of the *Victory*, or Collingwood, who worked himself to death in the great cabin of the *Ville de Paris*, he was a sea commander of limited experience, small responsibilities, and meagre accomplishments. In six years he commanded six ships, the largest a 32-gun frigate; many times he cleared his decks for action, and many times he was under the fire of an enemy, but he never took part in a great sea battle.

Yet measuring eighteenth-century sea officers against Nelson and Collingwood is like measuring eighteenth-century composers against Mozart and Haydn. Who would not be found wanting? Sailing and fighting a wooden man of war was a profession of nearly inconceivable complexity. By the time their Lordships entrusted a sea officer with the command of a ship, he had mastered a huge body of practical skills and theoretical knowledge. His employers expected him to pursue the enemy aggressively; to make life-and-death decisions in the blink of an eye; to keep his crew healthy and well disciplined and his ship's stores and equipment in good order; to represent his sovereign, should the need arise, on matters of the utmost sensitivity; to delegate authority to subordinates while acknowledging responsibility as his alone. All too often in such an exacting profession, failure, disgrace, unemployment and an early death fell to the competent and the incompetent alike. So a successful commanding officer required a substantial amount of luck, like the puff of wind that kept Captain Cook's *Endeavour* from driving on to the rocks of the Great Barrier Reef, or the single-ship engagement with the Spanish *Nuestra Señora de Covadonga*, laden with treasure valued at more than £500,000, that in 1743 made George Anson a rich man for life. Nothing like as great a seaman as Cook (indeed, he was apparently a rather clumsy shiphandler), nor as fearless a leader as Anson, nor even as lucky, perhaps, as some of his colleagues, Middleton nevertheless acquired a solid reputation as a wartime commander.

What inspired Middleton, after a dozen years ashore, to apply for active duty again? Did the improvement of agriculture lose some of its charms?

Did he yearn for companionship beyond the hearth at Teston and his small Evangelical circle? Did he miss the Navy? Did he long to go to sea again? At least this last seems doubtful, for his return to naval service was not exactly whole-hearted. In early 1775 he asked John Montagu, fourth Earl of Sandwich, the First Lord of the Admiralty, for 'one of the [royal] yachts', a plum reserved for distinguished or well-connected captains.[70] Ferrying the King about would have left Middleton time to pursue his private interests ashore. He did not get a yacht, but neither did he go away empty handed. On 11 March 1775 he took command of the *Ardent* (64), a Medway guardship moored just a few miles from Mrs Bouverie's estates.[71] Gentlemanly farming might as easily be pursued from a guardship as from a yacht. Farmers at Lexington and Concord, however, supervened to keep Middleton from enjoying this comfortable arrangement. Instead, he found himself Controller of the Navy at the moment of one of the greatest naval challenges England had ever faced.

NOTES

1 Quoted in C. Northcote Parkinson, *Britannia Rules: The Classic Age of Naval History* (New York, 1977), p. 50.
2 Roy Porter, *English Society in the Eighteenth Century* (London, 1982), p. 50; Paul Langford, *A Polite and Commercial People: England, 1727–1783* (Oxford, 1989), pp. 327–9. In the American colonies, Richard Pares pointed out, English settlers 'looked upon the Scots [immigrants], like the Jews or the Quakers, as a kind of epidemic – if you had one Scot, the next time you looked there were forty Scots, and soon after that four hundred. One Scot drew many others after him.' 'A Quarter of a Millennium of Anglo-Scottish Union', in *The Historian's Business and Other Essays* (Oxford, 1961), p. 95.
3 *Dictionary of National Biography*, vol. XIII (Oxford, 1921–22), pp. 339–41.
4 The scanty details of Middleton's early life come from the notes of John Deas Thomson, Middleton's secretary and factotum, who planned, but never wrote, a biography of his employer. National Maritime Museum (hereafter NMM) Middleton Papers MID/14/32/ Memoranda for Memoir, J. D. Thomson.
5 For biographies of Dundas, see Holden Furber, *Henry Dundas, First Viscount Melville* (London, 1931) and Cyril Matheson, *The Life of Henry Dundas, First Viscount Melville* (London, 1933). For an incisive sketch of Dundas's personality and character, see John Ehrman, *The Younger Pitt*, vol. I, *The Years of Acclaim* (New York, 1969), p. 132.
6 J. H. Plumb, *England in the Eighteenth Century* (London, 1950), p. 12.
7 John Knox Laughton (ed.), *Letters and Papers of Charles, Lord Barham* (hereafter *Barham Papers*), vol. I (London, 1907–11), pp. ix–xi.
8 N. A. M. Rodger, *The Wooden World: An Anatomy of the Georgian Navy* (London, 1986), pp. 263–4.
9 Ibid., pp. 252–4.
10 *Barham Papers*, vol. I, p. xi.
11 Rodger, *Wooden World*, pp. 263–4. Candidates for a lieutenancy were to have spent six years at sea, at least two of them as a midshipman or master's mate. Whether Middleton actually had six years afloat depends on whether he spent 1738–41 behind a school

desk, as Sir John Laughton, editor of his papers, believed, or on board the *Loyal Jane*, as the Navy credited him with doing.

12 Carola Oman, *Nelson* (London, 1947), pp. 22, 28.

13 NMM, Lieutenants' Logs, *Chesterfield*.

14 *Barham Papers*. vol. I, p. xiv.

15 Rodger, *Wooden World*, pp. 227, 229.

16 NMM, Lieutenants' Logs, *Culloden*, 3 November 1752.

17 For an excellent biographical sketch of Kempenfelt, see John A. Tilley, *The British Navy and the American Revolution* (Columbia, SC, 1987), pp. 133–6.

18 *Barham Papers*, vol. I, pp. iv–v.

19 Reginald Savory, *His Britannic Majesty's Forces in Germany during the Seven Years War* (Oxford, 1966), p. vii. A good recent account of the war is Jeremy Black, *Pitt the Elder* (Cambridge, 1992).

20 Sidney Mintz, *Sweetness and Power: The Place of Sugar in Modern History* (New York, 1985).

21 On the importance of the West Indies to European trade see Michael Duffy, *Soldiers, Sugar, and Seapower; The British Expeditions to the West Indies and the War against Revolutionary France* (Oxford, 1987), pp. 6–16.

22 See John Brewer, *The Sinews of Power: War, Money and the English State, 1688–1783* (New York, 1989), pp. 174–5; Daniel A. Baugh, 'Great Britain's "Blue-Water" Policy, 1689–1815', *International History Review*, 10, 1 (February 1988), pp. 33–58; Paul M. Kennedy, *The Rise and Fall of British Naval Mastery* (London, 1976), pp. 98–107; Richard Middleton, *The Bells of Victory: The Pitt–Newcastle Ministry and the Conduct of the Seven Years' War, 1757–1762* (Cambridge, 1985).

23 Richard Pares, *War and Trade in the West Indies* (London, 1936), p. viii. This remains the best book on the subject.

24 NMM, Lieutenants' Logs, *Anson*.

25 These paragraphs rely entirely on Pares, *War and Trade*, pp. 265–87.

26 *Barham Papers*, vol. I, pp. 5–6.

27 Ibid., p. 3.

28 NMM, Lieutenants' Logs, *Anson*.

29 The account of the court martial of seaman John Dunbar is based entirely on PRO, ADM 1/5296.

30 Rodger, *Wooden World*, p. 212.

31 PRO, ADM 1/5296.

32 On 26 February Dunbar received 20 lashes alongside the *Anson* and ten alongside each of the other four ships then in St John's Road. NMM, Lieutenants' Logs, *Anson*, 26 February 1757.

33 PRO, ADM 1/5296; also PRO, ADM 51/3788. Captains' Log, *Blandford*, 25 February 1757, in which Watkins's last entry states, 'I was dismissed from the command of the *Blandford* by the sentence of a court martial.'

34 NMM, Lieutenants' Logs, *Anson*, 28 February 1757; *Blandford*, 20 March 1757.

35 NMM, ADM L/B/103. Lieutenants' Logs, *Blandford*, 6 December 1758.

36 PRO, ADM 51/916, Captains' Log, *Speaker*, 13 May 1758.

37 PRO, ADM 1/2113, Captains' Letters, M. 10 August 1761.

38 PRO, ADM 1/2113, Captains' Letters, M. 17 and 21 September 1761.

39 N. A. M. Rodger (ed.), 'The Douglas Papers, 1760–1762', *Naval Miscellany*, vol. V, *Publications of the Navy Records Society*, vol. CXXV (London, 1984), pp. 254, 281n.

40 On the search for a means of finding longitude at sea see Dava Sobel, *Longitude* (New York, 1995); William J. H. Andrewes (ed.), *The Quest for Longitude* (Cambridge, MA, 1996).

41 *Barham Papers*, vol. I, p. 35.

42 Isaac Schomberg, *Naval Chronology; Or, An Historical Summary of Naval & Maritime Events, From the Time of The Romans, to the Treaty of Peace 1802*, vol. I (London, 1802), p. 295.
43 PRO, ADM 51/916, Captains' Log, *Emerald*; Rodger, *Wooden World*, pp. 38–9.
44 Captains' Log, *Emerald*.
45 PRO, ADM 1/2113, Captains' Letters, M.
46 PRO, ADM 51/295; J. J. Colledge, *Ships of the Royal Navy: An Historical Index*, vol. I, *Major Ships* (New York, 1969), p. 187.
47 NMM, MID/13/4, John Deas Thomson's notes for a memoir.
48 Paul Seaver, *Wallington's World: A Puritan Artisan in Seventeenth-Century London* (Stanford, 1985), p. 85.
49 M. G. Jones, *Hannah More* (Cambridge, 1952), p. 93.
50 G. M. Young, *Victorian England: Portrait of an Age*, 2nd edn (Oxford, 1953), especially pp. 1–6; Elie Halévy, *The Birth of Methodism in England* (trans. Bernard Semmel) (Chicago, IL, 1971); John Clive, *Not By Fact Alone: Essays on the Writing and Reading of History* (New York, 1989), pp. 128–9.
51 Leonore Davidoff and Catherine Hall, *Family Fortunes: Men and Women of the English Middle Class, 1780–1850* (London, 1987) p. 8.
52 In this they resembled Seaver's Puritan diarist: *Wallington's World*, *passim*.
53 Standish Meacham, *Henry Thornton of Clapham, 1760–1815* (Cambridge, MA, 1964), p. 14; Langford, *A Polite and Commercial People*, p. 243.
54 *The Letters of Hannah More* (London, 1925), p. 39.
55 Porter, *English Society*, p. 328.
56 John Gore (ed.), *The Creevey Papers* (London, 1963), p. 33.
57 Alfred Friendly, *Beaufort of the Admiralty: The Life of Sir Francis Beaufort* (London, 1977), p. 148.
58 Seaver, *Wallington's World*, p. 46.
59 Max Weber, *The Protestant Ethic and the Spirit of Capitalism* (trans. Talcott Parsons) (London, 1930). On the sheer busyness of members of the Evangelical movement see Joanna Innes, 'Politics and Morals: The Reformation of Manners Movement in Later Eighteenth-Century England', in Eckhart Hellmuth (ed.), *The Transformation of Political Culture: England and Germany in the Late Eighteenth Century* (London, 1990), pp. 57–118.
60 David Brion Davis, *The Problem of Slavery in the Age of Revolution, 1770–1823* (Ithaca, NY, 1975), p. 221.
61 Ford K. Brown, *Fathers of the Victorians: The Age of Wilberforce* (Cambridge, 1961); David Spring, 'The Clapham Sect: Some Social and Political Aspects', *Victorian Studies*, 5, 1 (September 1961), pp. 35–48.
62 PRO, ADM 1/2114, Captains' Letters, M. June 1762.
63 British Library, Add. Mss 38570, Liverpool Papers. Charles Middleton to Charles Jenkinson, *Adventure*, Spithead, 22 March 1762.
64 PRO, ADM 1/2114, Captains' Letters, M. Middleton to Admiralty, 22 March 1762.
65 PRO, ADM 1/2114, Captains' Letters, M. 15 July 1762, 9 August 1762.
66 PRO, ADM 1/2114, Captains' Letters, M. Middleton to Admiralty, 11 February 1763.
67 PRO, ADM 1/2115, Captains' Letters, M. 24 February 1763.
68 PRO, ADM 1/2115, Captains' Letters, M. 7 April 1763.
69 Edward Hasted, *The History and Topographical Survey of the County of Kent*, vol. V, reprint of 1798 edition (East Ardsley, 1972), pp. 126–36.
70 NMM, SAN/T 15 January 1775.
71 See Middleton's detailed Captain's Order Book, 1 August 1775, *Barham Papers*, vol. I, pp. 39–49.

2

The Mainspring of Everything Naval

When Charles Middleton came ashore in 1763, his pockets stuffed with prize money, his country was on the verge of the greatest victory it had ever won over France. By winning the Seven Years War, a mercantilist's dream come true, Britain enriched itself, increased its colonial holdings at the expense of its chief rivals, inflicted huge losses on French merchant and naval fleets, and restrained, by means of the alliance with Prussia, French military ambitions in Europe. The war left both Britain and France staggering under huge public debts, but the French monarchy, fiscally weaker to begin with, had been dealt a blow from which it eventually proved unable to recover.[1] Yet Britain's triumph was short-lived. France, smarting under the multiple humiliations sustained in the Seven Years War, resolved on a policy of *revanche* against its chief maritime and colonial rival, of which the most tangible – and worrisome – expression, was a naval rebuilding program.[2] Partly in an effort to overcome its own war-borne fiscal difficulties, Britain resorted to a series of schemes to squeeze revenue out of the American colonists. These misfired, and resistance to British authority deepened into rebellion against British rule. Between March 1775, when Middleton returned to active duty, and August 1778, when he assumed the Controllership of the Navy, Britain's prospects in America and security at home deteriorated dramatically. By the time Middleton assumed office 'the odds facing Britain were so overwhelming', as Paul Kennedy remarks, 'that only the bleak years of 1940–41 compare with them'.[3]

Conducting military operations and sustaining the British expeditionary force in North America depended on preserving Britain's superiority at sea. The British Army needed to be sustained by means of a supply line 3,000 miles long and subject to all the vicissitudes of wind, weather and bad planning as well as to the harassment of the Americans. Conducting military operations along the seaboard of a nearly roadless continent meant a heavy dependence on seaborne transport, not only for supporting amphibious raids and assaults and blockading rebel shipping, but also for moving troops and equipment from New York to, say, Philadelphia. From the outset, the war for America required the British Navy to exercise control of American waters.[4] The tiny American naval force posed no threat to this control, but Britain proved unable to run the rebels to ground in a timely fashion. Every campaigning season the Americans survived both multiplied and complicated Britain's military and diplomatic conundrums and diminished the likelihood of British success. By failing to smother the rebellion in its New England cradle, the objective during the first two years of war, Britain lost its best chance of forestalling foreign intervention. From the outset, the possibility of such an intervention was never far from the minds of British ministers, nor was the nightmare scenario it evoked: having to fight a world war at sea against the second-ranking maritime power – joined, in all likelihood, by the third – while continuing to pursue a major land war far from home.[5]

As recently as 1770, the Bourbon powers of France and Spain – the so-called 'Family Compact' – had joined forces against Britain in a diplomatic crisis over the Falkland Islands. Both powers saw in Britain's embroilment with a sprawling colonial rebellion an opportunity to settle scores with a distracted enemy. By mid-1776 British intelligence agents on the continent were reporting that France and Spain were each readying several additional ships of the line for sea.[6] Battleships devoured such huge amounts of dock-yard labor, naval stores, weaponry and seafaring men that mobilizing them was never undertaken lightly. Fearing worse to come, the British government instructed the dockyards to hurry forward numerous ships of the line.[7]

Commissioning more ships enlarged Middleton's prospects as an active-duty captain, but it cost him the comforts of commanding the *Ardent* from home. In November 1776 he was named captain of the Portsmouth guard-ship *Prince George* (90). Manning was always the most intractable problem of a naval mobilization, and raising even a guardship's skeleton crew was not easy, not when sea duty offered the promise of prize money, adventure and patriotic glory. As Middleton wrote to Captain Lord Mulgrave, 'She [the *Prince George*] is as well manned, my Lord, as the situation of a guard-ship under the temptation of active service going on under her boltsprit for these eighteen months past would admit.'

No sooner had Middleton assumed command of the *Prince George* than he incurred the First Lord's displeasure. In mid-January 1777 his ship's purser dropped dead. Responsible for victualling his ship and issuing or selling consumable articles to her crew, a purser with a good head for business could turn a handsome profit. But his obligations, especially his strict accountability to the government for goods and money passing through his hands, could drive an unlucky or incompetent purser into bankruptcy.[8] Middleton immediately wrote to Lord Sandwich recommending for the post his brother George, who years earlier had 'very unadvisedly relinquished' an Army commission.[9] He was a man with a large family and small prospects. Nothing recommended him for pursership. Sandwich's reply is missing, but Middleton's obsequious disavowal of his request makes clear that he was rebuffed. Pleading ignorance of the regulations respecting pursery – a curious lapse in a sea officer proud of his mastery of naval detail – Middleton assured Sandwich, 'I should not have occasioned your Lordship the trouble of an improper solicitation'.[10]

Patronage systems are bound to bring out the obsequious in many a petitioner. But not all such systems serve merely as engines of corruption, as Victorian reformers were disposed to believe.[11] The Navy's patronage system worked with a view to identifying and rewarding talent. Senior officers sponsored able junior officers; younger officers competed for the attention of the most influential senior men. Far more often than not, the talented were recognized and advanced and the incompetent ignored or shunted aside. True, well-connected but less than able men were found places, but usually they were put where they could do little harm. Too much money and too many lives were at risk when ships put to sea not to insist on competence in those to whom they were entrusted. Sandwich understood the difference between the Navy's customs and the far more latitudinarian conventions of politics (which in any case served different ends). In the case in question, the politician refused to countenance the sea officer's attempt to make his wholly unqualified brother the purser of the *Prince George*.[12]

The year 1777 was a poor season for making dubious requests of the First Lord. By the summer French ports from Bordeaux to Dunkirk were sheltering American privateers. The French reinforced a squadron in the West Indies and increased naval expenditures, actions Sandwich read as portents of French intervention in the American war.[13] In November came news of the disaster at Saratoga, where General John Burgoyne surrendered not only his army but the British hope of strangling the rebellion before it could win outside assistance. 'The defeat at Saratoga', Piers Mackesy remarks, 'is the clearest turning point of the war. It marked the beginning of a general war waged throughout the world.'[14] The news from Saratoga strengthened the resolve of Charles Gravier, Comte de Vergennes, the French Foreign Minister, to step up his interventionist policy. No longer would the French merely be running guns and other material support to the Americans and affording their privateers safe haven. Henceforth they would fight alongside them, and put to sea, against the common enemy, the world's second-ranking navy.[15]

Parliament and Cabinet were sharply divided over how to respond after Saratoga. Some politicians favored coming to terms with the rebels, or at least reducing the scope of military operations in America, the better to contend with France. Even Sandwich, formerly a staunch advocate of coercion, wondered whether America ought to remain at the center of his government's attention. The King, however, remained an adamant coercer and domino theorist. Overestimating loyalist sentiment and discounting rebel strength, he urged his wavering ministers to pursue a military victory in America. For the loss of the 13 colonies, he believed, would bring the loss of the sugar islands – an economic calamity, in view of their importance to British trade. The King's views prevailed. Britain continued to pour military and naval resources into America at the same time as it assumed the daunting challenge of a world war.[16]

Eighteenth-century turning points turned slowly. Not until five months after Saratoga (March 1778) did France actually come into the war, and Spain did not join France until the following year. But everyone knew that war between Britain and its old enemies would be fought at sea, so the Navy and its spies kept watch on the dockyards at Toulon and Brest, Ferrol and Cádiz. The naval initiative lay with the French. Britain had already committed large numbers of ships, especially frigates, to America; France had more ships of the line ready for sea and, as far as the British knew, free of commitment. Anxiety deepened in London when word arrived in March 1778 that Admiral Jean-Baptiste Théodat, Comte d'Estaing, who had taken command of the Toulon squadron, appeared to be putting to sea.[17] Where was he headed – to join the Spanish fleet at Cádiz or the Brest fleet in the approaches to the Channel? Either destination, the Admiralty believed, required Britain to keep many battleships close to home. Or did d'Estaing perhaps intend a descent on the West Indies, or a challenge to the English command of American waters?[18] Nothing worried the Admiralty more than not knowing where French squadrons were, or what they were up to.

In these circumstances of anxious conjecture and debate, Sandwich sounded out Middleton about his availability for the Controllership of the Navy. The incumbent, Captain Maurice Suckling, was a dying man. Like

Middleton, Suckling had distinguished himself in the West Indies, earned a fortune in prize money and bought a house in Mayfair. He held several peacetime commands, including the *Raisonnable* (64), in which his nephew, Horatio Nelson, served as a midshipman.[19] Unemployed at the outbreak of the American rebellion, he applied to Sandwich for shore commands in Newfoundland and Jamaica.[20] Nothing came of these requests, but a bigger plum soon fell into his hands. In 1776 he succeeded Rear-Admiral Sir Hugh Palliser, Sandwich's friend and political ally, as Controller of the Navy.

If not already in poor health when he took the job, Suckling soon fell sick. Sandwich evidently inquired whether he felt up to the demands of office, for on 28 January 1777 Suckling replied,

> Although I have been in much bodily pain for some days past it does not exceed what I feel in my mind on the idea that your Lordship should entertain the least thought that the Navy Board do not attend to the many great demands made on your Lordship for frigates, armed ships and transports, but that on the contrary, that we have been remiss do not, my Lord, add to the anxiety you must feel in the great department you so ably preside at by supposing any member of the Navy Board are not anxious not only for the public service but in their desires to forward with dispatch every wish of your Lordship.[21]

The First Lord surely feared that a sick man could not cope with the rising naval emergency, for in February he turned to Captain Middleton. Would he accept the Controllership? Middleton later remembered having to think it over. 'When Lord Sandwich proposed to me being Controller of the Navy', he wrote in 1804, 'I ... required some little time to consider it ... The truth was I felt myself unequal to the magnitude and consequence of the office and the confinement it would occasion me.'[22]

Sandwich had many able sea officers to choose from. Why did he single out a captain 'very little known to his Lordship'?[23] Attendance at the Concerts of Antient Music [*sic*] to which both subscribed may have made nodding acquaintances of the two men.[24] No politician exerted a greater influence on East India Company affairs than Sandwich,[25] and it is likely that Middleton's interest in the Company, not his grasp of naval affairs, brought him to the First Lord's notice. In 1767 Middleton invested some of his West Indian prize money (£500) in East India Company stock. Putting some of his sugar money into tea paid handsomely, for by the 1790s he owned enough stock to entitle him to three votes in the Company's meetings.[26] 'I have been an active well-wisher to government in India matters', he wrote Charles Jenkinson in 1777, 'and as far as my little influence has prevailed have employed it in their service; I may with truth add that I have both given time and money to forward their business.'[27] Sandwich was bound to feel obliged to a shareholder who so assiduously backed the government's candidates in Company elections.

Still, Middleton had 20 years' experience at sea. Controllers of the Navy were almost invariably drawn from the list of captains. The post demanded a competent, professional seaman. Sandwich knew this perfectly well; he would not have rewarded, on the grounds of political connection, a man unqualified for the job. Sandwich knew the Navy better than any civilian of his time. First Lord since 1771, he had first served at the Admiralty from 1744–51, including three and a half years as First Lord. Despite his long experience of naval affairs, however, his reputation as a libertine and political jobber, eagerly embellished by his enemies, impressed historians far more than his accomplishments at the Admiralty.[28] Not until his papers were published in the 1930s – and writers ceased regarding the moral climate of their own times as superior to that of the eighteenth century – did attention shift from Sandwich the rake to Sandwich the First Lord. Not all his contemporaries regarded him with hostility and suspicion. 'No man in the administration', the gossipy Horace Walpole wrote of Sandwich in his journal, 'was so much master of business, so quick or so shrewd, and no man had so many public enemies who had so few private.'[29] Typical of recent assessments is that of J. C. Beaglehole, who found that 'whatever might be said against his personal and political morals – his enemies said a great deal endlessly – [Sandwich] was a perceptive and able man, of knowledge and charm'.[30]

Sandwich was also a man of boundless curiosity. He liked to see for himself, to be shown how things worked. Paying annual visits to the dockyards probably taught him more about what they did and how they did it than any of his predecessors, sea officers included, had bothered to learn. Inviting Navy Board officials to join him on these tours not only eased their suspicions over what this outsider – and nominal superior – might be up to, but also won them to his plans for innovation. The American War curtailed his visits, but not before the First Lord managed to produce improvements in stores-keeping (the ingenious timber-curing sheds at the Chatham dockyard are an example),[31] maintaining ships in ordinary, and in the efficiency of dockyard labor.[32]

Sandwich knew how fleeting the salutary effects of such inspections were likely to be. His realism, as well as something of his charm, is manifest in his summary of his visitation of 1775, the last before the American War distracted him from the tidier pleasures of peacetime improvement.

> I hope I may flatter myself [he wrote] that my labor has not been thrown
> away in these expeditions, tho' I will fairly own, that as my Business is
> always my pleasure, they have afforded me great Amusement for the
> space of near two months every Summer; I shall certainly continue them
> as long as I have the honor of serving His Majesty in this Department
> [a resolution he proved unable to keep], and if my Successors do not
> follow my Example, I believe I may venture to Prophesy that many Abuses
> will creep in, and tho' their Abilities may be greater than mine, they will
> not know so well as I have done, how to administer the proper Remedies.[33]

Above all, Sandwich was a shrewd judge of humankind. It is hard to
conceive that he did not make discreet inquiries about Middleton among
his naval and political acquaintances before deciding that he had indeed
found Suckling's successor. The selection of Middleton attests to Sandwich's willingness to put the needs of the service ahead of his own comfort,
for the two were as dissimilar in temperament as men of similar aims could
be – the Controller as abrasive, self-assertive and unforgiving as the First
Lord was genial, diffident, and tolerant of others' shortcomings (as long
as he saw eye-to-eye with them politically). He could have picked from the
captains' list a far more tractable and congenial Controller than his Hertford
Street neighbor. Choosing such a cross-grained colleague does Sandwich
great credit. Indeed, in his definitive biography of the First Lord, Nicholas
A. M. Rodger calls the appointment of Middleton 'arguably ... the single
most important decision Sandwich took in his entire career'.[34]

Determined not to be denied, Sandwich enlisted Rear-Admiral James
Gambier, Middleton's unpopular brother-in-law and Dockyard Com-
missioner at Portsmouth, to cajole Middleton on his behalf. On 8 March
Middleton offered Sandwich a characteristically baroque reply:

> I am really, my Lord, so much more surprised at your friendship than
> captivated by its effects that I want words to express my sense of it, and
> I flatter myself however it may be determined, I shall never lose sight of
> the distinction your lordship has honoured me with. The Controllership,
> though superior to any pretensions on my part, has since Mr Suckling's
> decline been frequently mentioned to me by my partial sea friends as an
> office in which my turn to business and application might render me not
> unuseful, but as domestic and rural pursuits were, before this armament,
> my favourite objects, I never listened to their ideas, flattering as it might
> be to a man of more ambition than myself. Mr Gambier, however, having
> with friendly insistence, communicated to me some explanation of your

lordship's sentiments in my favour, I cannot but be desirous to take the first opportunity of expressing personally my gratitude, and hope to have that honour the beginning of the week.[35]

In short, he would probably accept.

Suckling lingered on, however, and Sandwich, a man of great warmth and delicacy of feeling, could not bring himself to thrust him aside, no matter how many ships of the line needed to be hurried to sea. In the meantime, as it appeared the *Prince George* would be designated a flagship, Middleton asked to be relieved of command. For one thing, commanding a flagship meant surrendering a good deal of independence to the admiral embarked, a prospect most senior captains did not relish. Perhaps he had also tired of the humdrum life of a guardship. In early January, before the matter of the Controllership arose, he wrote to Sandwich to say that he would be content with a large frigate, provided she were coppered, a task he even offered to undertake at his own expense.[36] He must have been willing to go to sea, for coppered bottoms remained too experimental, too expensive to waste on guardships.

Once the Controllership was dangled before Middleton, however, a sea command lost its appeal. He was offered and accepted just the type of frigate he had asked for – the *Jupiter* (50), still on the stocks at Deptford – but it is doubtful whether he took this assignment very seriously. He attended his ship's commissioning on 9 May and perhaps her launching on the 14th, when she got stuck in the mud just clear of the ways. But the next weeks, while shipwrights and caulkers swarmed over his new frigate, Middleton spent at Hertford Street. Maurice Suckling died on 14 July. The *Jupiter* came out of the dock a week later, and on the same day Middleton signed her log, a captain's last act on relinquishing command.[37] The King had approved his appointment as Controller of the Navy.

The shore establishment numbered nearly 10,000. A pocket of industrial organization in a predominantly agrarian society, it was by far the largest government enterprise in Britain; the dockyards' most impressive creation, the ship of the line, was the biggest and most complex machine of the pre-industrial era and the most destructive weapon, ton for ton and man for man, yet devised. Indeed, not until long after industrialization set in did any civilian factory employ as many as the 900 men required to sail and fight a 100-gun first rate such as *Victory*, let alone the hundreds who labored in the Navy's smallest dockyard.

Building or contracting for the building of ships; repairing, manning, supplying, and paying them off; managing the Royal dockyards; auditing accounts and preparing the Navy estimates, all fell to the Navy Board, whose struggles to keep control of this vast apparatus took place at the Navy Office, at the corner of Crutched Friars and Seething Lane, a few hundred yards north-west of the Tower. 'The principal Building', a handbook for sea officers explained, 'is extremely neat, regular and plain: it stands in the Centre of a handsome little pav'd Square, and looks like an eminent Mathematician with all his Apparatus about him; every side of the Square being furnish'd with Buildings appertaining thereto.'[38] Designed by Christopher Wren and Robert Hooke to replace buildings that burned to the ground in 1673, the Navy Office had already outgrown its quarters when Middleton took his Lieutenant's examination there in 1745. By 1774, the eve of the war for America, the Navy Board was warning the Admiralty that

> the number [of books and papers] now are so greatly increased, and are constantly accumulating, that the repositories will not admit of their being disposed of with any regularity, and more room cannot be had to contain them. Some of the buildings are in so bad a state as to be in danger of falling, ... and even if ... money was to be expended [for repairs] the Offices would be much too small and confined for trans-acting the business with convenience.[39]

Awash in seas of paper, naval administrators did not find their pleas for more room answered until they moved into Somerset House in 1786.

The Navy Board's rules for conducting its affairs also dated from the seventeenth century. In 1662, James, Duke of York, as able a Lord High Admiral as he was a foolish king, laid down a set of instructions for the Navy Board. Drafted by William Penn, the great sea officer whom Pepys jealously despised, the instructions were a model of ambiguity – one reason, no doubt, that they remained in force until the Navy Board went out of business in 1832 and its duties were divided up at the Admiralty.[40]

The instructions continued the four Principal Officers Henry VIII had established in 1546 – a Treasurer (whose office had removed to Broad Street), a Controller, a Surveyor and a Clerk of the Ships (later called Clerk of the Acts), to which were added several Commissioners.[41] In addition, a Commissioner resided at each major dockyard, but they rarely met their London colleagues and were not regarded as their equals.[42]

The instructions were especially ambiguous with respect to the Controller's relationship with his colleagues. He was meant to be an auditor checking his colleagues' accounts, keeping track of prevailing prices for goods and services offered to the Navy and the wages paid to labor, monitoring the estimates and the Navy Debt – in short, the one member of the Board in a position to be familiar with the work of the whole. Recognizing this, the instructions of 1661 called for the Controller 'to lead his Fellow-Officers as well as to comptrol their Actions'. The instructions went on to say, though, that his colleagues must 'be neither excluded from advising, nor yet from comptrolling him, when either from his Unexperience, Infidelity or otherwise, the Service … may be prejudic'd or his Majesty's Treasure without Ground given away'.[43] The tendency of the eighteenth century, however, was to erode the Restoration's check on the Controller's authority. Indeed, Middleton had no doubt that he was in reality chairman of the Navy Board – 'the mainspring', he wrote,'belonging to everything that is naval; no price can purchase a man fit for this extensive office; he must be in every part of it and know everything that is going on, in and out of it'.[44]

Each Commissioner had his own duties, his own clerks and his own rooms, but they met together daily, often for hours on end, to reach decisions for which, as the Navy Board, they assumed collective responsibility. A perusal of the Navy Board's minutes shows just how untidy its agenda was. On Tuesday, 25 August 1778, Middleton's first day on the job, he and his colleagues sent the dockyards instructions respecting cables, ropemaking and rigging; learned that Rear-Admiral Samuel Hood, the Commissioner at Portsmouth Dockyard, planned to advertise in his neighborhood for ten longboats to be purchased 'on best and cheapest terms he can'; informed Captain Adam Duncan of the *Suffolk* that George Owen had been appointed sailmaker; and waded through the day's flood of letters from the Admiralty and the dockyards, from the Navy's creditors and contractors, and from importunate captains and grievance-laden seamen's widows.[45] The Board's habits drove Middleton wild with frustration – just as they had Pepys, more than a century earlier – but he still had to put up with them.[46] He was at best *primus inter pares*.

The other Principal Officers joining Middleton at the Boardroom table were the Surveyor, in charge of designing, building and maintaining ships, the upkeep of the dockyards, stocking supplies at the yards, and supplying stores to the fleet; and the Clerk of the Acts, who managed the Navy Office itself, supervising clerks, attending to the torrent of correspondence and preserving voluminous records of the Board's transactions.[47]

The Surveyor, John Williams, erstwhile Master Shipwright at Sheerness Dockyard, had succeeded Thomas Slade, designer of the *Victory* and other great ships, in 1765. By the time of the American War, the infirmities his palsied signature betrayed were so marked that Edward Hunt, another Master Shipwright, was named to assist him.[48] George Marsh, the Clerk of the Acts, had been appointed a clerk in Deptford Dockyard in 1744 and arduously climbed through several dockyards and departments of the Navy Office until he finally became in 1772 a sort of clerk in chief. Like Marsh, the three Commissioners who looked after the financial side of Navy Board business had all risen from clerkships. Sir William Temple, the only Extra Commissioner serving at the outbreak of the American War, had managed the flow of paper at the Navy Office since 1761.[49]

So the neophyte Controller joined men of long experience. His colleagues shared 73 years of Navy Board employment among them. But they had spent their careers scribbling at a desk or roving about a dockyard. They had not been to sea, and in a sea-going service this counted against them. Middleton spoke as a typical sea officer when he disparaged the 'pen-and-ink gentlemen' even after he took up their tools himself.[50] Social and professional condescension mixed with the conviction that ignorance of life at sea disqualified these officials from carrying out certain Navy Board responsibilities.

Wartime strengthened the need for experience at sea in the highest reaches of the shore establishment, and so during the American War, as had been the case in previous conflicts, two Extra Commissioners with decades of sea duty between them were added to the Board. Captain Edward Le Cras joined in January 1778 from command of the *Russell* (74). Le Cras, with whom Middleton had served in the West Indies, was assigned to making sure that captains, lieutenants and masters kept their logs and journals correctly, a technical responsibility best left to someone who had kept them himself; to overseeing the supplying of ships at home and overseas with stores; and, most important in terms of the war emergency, to helping superintend the shipping for America.[51] Middleton came to regard him as indispensable.

LeCras's more famous counterpart was Captain Samuel Wallis, discoverer of Tahiti. Middleton's shipmate on the *Anson*, Wallis in 1766 commanded the *Dolphin* (24) on a celebrated circumnavigation of the world. Named an Extra Commissioner in late 1780, he came to the Navy Board from commanding the *Queen* (98) and assumed large responsibilities for all aspects of the American transports. Wallis was also a jack-of-all-trades with respect to examining midshipmen for the passing certificate, looking into deserters' claims for relief and assisting at the Pay Office.[52] The civilians had sat together at the Navy Office for years; the sea officers Middleton, Le Cras and Wallis, all veterans of the Seven Years War, had been friends for 20 years or more. Navy Board minutes yield no clues as to their alliances and alignments with respect to the issues that came before them; the sympathies and antipathies that meeting around the same table every day must have engendered among them have left no trace.

The establishment the Navy Board oversaw from Tower Hill stretched over southern England from the mouth of the Thames to Plymouth; reached north to Leith, and abroad to America and the East and the West Indies. This domain had grown haphazardly, in response to the shifting demands of naval war. The shoaling of the Thames and the Medway and Holland's decline as England's chief maritime enemy encouraged a division of labor among the dockyards. Deptford and Woolwich, the so-called 'River yards' as well as Chatham, on the Medway, concentrated on shipbuilding, major repairs and preparing naval stores for distribution to other yards. Portsmouth and Plymouth, whose fortunes rose as the principal strategic threat swung from the North Sea to the Atlantic, and Sheerness, readily accessible from the open sea, looked after routine maintenance, refitting and the repairing of battle damage.

Deptford, only three miles downstream from London Bridge, and Woolwich, a little farther on, were supervised direct from London. The other four domestic yards all had resident commissioners. Prohibited from giving orders on their own, they acted chiefly as go-betweens, conveying instructions downward to the senior officers of the dockyard and passing information upward to the Navy Board. This was a potentially troublesome arrangement, for it encouraged yard officers to play the local authority off against the distant one. But when a resident commissioner was as able (and as well connected locally) as Samuel Hood, at Portsmouth, it worked well.[53] The dockyard commissioners did carry one big stick: they shared with the Navy Board approval of all hirings and promotions in the yards.[54]

Each yard's senior officers composed a Navy Board in miniature, each answering for everything in his sphere to one of the Principal Officers in London. The yard officers were supposed to arrive at decisions collectively, but in practice the Master Shipwright, essentially the spider of the web, took the lead. The Master Attendant, almost invariably a retired master, had charge of everything afloat: ships in commission and in ordinary, yard craft and pilotage.[55] The Storekeeper, Master Rope-maker and Clerk of the Cheque, who looked after accounts, usually deferred to the builders and ship handlers. Except for the Masters Attendant, who came to their posts after years of sea duty, most senior officers entered the yards as boys and slowly rose to the top.[56]

Some two and a half miles upstream from the Navy Office stood the

Admiralty, a happenstance that nicely expressed the Admiralty's view of the relations of authority between them. Indeed, the Commissioners for executing the Office of Lord High Admiral represented the summit of the naval hierarchy.[57] The Navy Board kept the King's ships at sea, but the First Lord and his ministerial colleagues – the King in council – decided what to do with them.[58] The Navy Board seldom liked to be reminded of its subordinate status, however, and relations between Whitehall and Tower Hill sometimes took on the chilly tone of transactions between two not especially friendly sovereign powers.

On 27 July 1778 an English fleet of 30 ships of the line under Admiral Augustus Keppel engaged a French fleet of 29 ships under Admiral Louis Guillouet, Comte d'Orvilliers, in an inconclusive battle off Ushant. The first major encounter of the new naval war turned out neither as badly as Sandwich had feared nor as well as he had hoped. As Middleton readied himself for his new responsibilities, Keppel's fleet – masts and yards shattered, rigging shot away – struggled back to England for repairs.[59]

Wallowing in from their encounter off Ushant, Admiral Keppel's jury-rigged ships brought home the new realities of the war. In the first place, in previous wars with France Britain had always had at least one continental ally it could rely on to draw the great amphibian's attention, energy and resources toward central Europe. But in 1778 no Frederick II of Prussia, no Ferdinand of Brunswick, was willing, for his own purposes, to act in concert with Britain. Free of distractions on the continent, France could for once concentrate on a maritime strategy.[60]

The second circumstance piling up the odds against Britain was the link between France and Spain. Spanish finances were in good order and Spanish grievances against Britain were many. So in reckoning the hostile forces they might have to contend with, British naval authorities had to add the Spanish battle fleet to the French. Spain's ships of the line, some 40 in number, might never put to sea but Britain had to fear that they would; they always had to be taken into account (and in the event, to be sure, they did put to sea).[61]

The third major strand in the tangle of difficulties Britain faced was the American war itself. For in 1778 the lack of a European ally, French intervention, and the prospect of war with Spain, combined to put the American conflict in a new light. Never before had Britain (or any other great power, for that matter) found itself 'fighting a large-scale land campaign at the other end of the oceans',[62] while simultaneously facing threats to its security at home and to its naval supremacy world-wide.

Well might Middleton have thought the Controllership beyond him.[63] Nevertheless, his official duties did not keep him from attending to personal business. His third day in the job, Middleton once again solicited Sandwich on behalf of his brother, whom earlier in the year he had tried to make purser of the *Prince George*. Apparently, he had no better luck this time and had to go on supporting George and his numerous family from his own pocket. If his repeated efforts to find his brother an Admiralty niche came to nothing, at the end of September he received the consoling news that his captain's half-pay would be continued 'notwithstanding his being Comptroller of the Navy', and despite a regulation of 1713 against drawing two public salaries at once.[64]

Illness had kept Maurice Suckling from attending a Board meeting since March 1778, leaving Edward LeCras as the only sea officer on hand and the Navy Office without a Controller's guidance.[65] Nevertheless, the machinery of bureaucracy and dockyard continued to turn over, routine tasks continued to be carried out. When Middleton took up his duties in August, the mobilization against the French was moving forward, despite Suckling's mortal sickness. But the new Controller shared the view that not nearly enough was being done. By Middleton's count, Britain had no more than 40 battleships available for Channel service in autumn 1778; of these a good number were undergoing repair after the encounter off Ushant, and Admiral Keppel had regarded many of them as barely seaworthy even before his fight with d'Orvilliers took place.[66]

Middleton's first objective was to commission more line of battle ships, and 'in the end, to bring forward by degrees all that could be made fit for service'.[67] Just how far he was willing to pursue this objective will presently be seen. Over the longer run, he expected to encourage, by means of financial incentives, the merchant yards to build more ships of the line, freeing the King's yards to concentrate on repairing battle damage and other urgent tasks; to replenish stores, which, he charged, were woefully understocked; to increase the capacity of storehouses; to repair such docks as had fallen into decay; to recruit more shipwrights and caulkers, especially by the expedient of allowing each journeyman more apprentices; and to furnish stations abroad, especially at Halifax and in the West Indies, with greater supplies of stores.[68]

The Navy could keep ships at sea despite the shortcomings of the dockyards. The Army could not keep men and horses in the field, however, without feeding them, and when Middleton assumed office, hunger posed a greater threat to the expeditionary force in America than the rebels.[69] If the new Controller could have predicted that mobilizing more battleships would be one of his most urgent preoccupations, he could hardly have assumed that it would also fall to him to unsnarl the shipping on which the Army in America depended for food and supplies.

Why the Army was so dependent on Britain for sustenance takes some explaining. After all, the British conducted operations in America during the Seven Years War without logistical embarrassment. But the friendly settlers of the 1750s, from whom Army agents bought food for the troops and forage for their animals, gave way to the rebels of the 1770s. Bent on keeping the British hungry, they so successfully intimidated loyalists into going along with them that the expeditionary force could not meet its needs from local sources. Bread, beef or pork, oatmeal, butter, cheese, peas, rum and anti-scorbutics; hay and oats; boots, shirts, stockings, leggings, coats, weskits, shoe buckles, stocks, epaulets, sashes, muskets, bayonets, scabbards, cartridge boxes, sabers, pistols and carbines; saddles, limbers, caissons, harness and tackle; beds, bedding, stoves, lanterns, fireplace equipment; tents, camp kettles, axes, haversacks, knapsacks and canteens – virtually everything had to be brought from Britain.

Perhaps it is less surprising that the British expeditionary force in America was provisioned poorly than that it was provisioned at all. For the difficulties of supplying military forces across thousands of miles of ocean (not only in the eighteenth century but also in our day) can scarcely be exaggerated.[70] Even when contractors did their best to prevent food in cask from spoiling, their best, given the inadequacies of methods of preservation, was often not good enough, so a fair proportion of the rations shipped to America was bound to arrive inedible. Contrary winds kept ships from sailing for weeks at a time, and the notorious weather of the North Atlantic lengthened delays. If bacteria and the elements were formidable obstacles to supplying America adequately, administrative failings compounded the workings of nature. Private contractors had seen to the peacetime needs of the American garrison, but the demands of wartime proved beyond their capabilities, and in 1776 the Treasury superseded them. Under public management the supply service failed to improve. For one thing, inadequate statistics made supplying the expeditionary force a guessing game. Army commissaries in America failed to provide London with reasonably accurate head counts, and such information as they did receive London officials proved unable to interpret. The apparently unfathomable mystery of just how many troops, officers and horses needed to be supplied contributed to the great crisis of 1778, when storehouses in New York at one time fell to the perilous margin of four days' rations.[71]

The Treasury Board wanted desperately to rid itself of a business for which it rightly regarded itself as unsuited. In June 1777 George Marsh, the Clerk of the Acts, came over from the Navy Office to discuss taking over the transport service. The Navy Board, March told Treasury officials, was able to hire vessels at 11 shillings per ton – one shilling and sixpence less than the Treasury rate. Despite the savings that putting the transports under the Navy Board promised, these negotiations made little headway; they collapsed altogether when the Commissioners decided that they had their hands full in managing the naval build-up against France.[72]

Maurice Suckling's mortal illness also discouraged major initiatives on the Navy Board's part.[73] But soon after the bustling and self-confident Middleton joined the Board, he resumed negotiations over transports. In early February 1779 the Controller explored with Lord North and other Treasury officials the possibility of the Navy Board's taking over the transport business.[74] He liked to think of himself as a hard bargainer and on two points he was especially insistent. First, the Navy Board wanted to abandon the Treasury's practice of arming transports and sending them on their way as soon as they were loaded. Armed transports might have been able to scare off privateers and elude the tiny rebel navy, but French intervention had greatly increased the risk of capture at either end of the long supply line. No armed transport stood much chance against a frigate. Putting the transports under convoy would not only improve the odds on their reaching America but also make it unnecessary to arm them at public expense. Years of shepherding merchantmen among the islands of the West Indies no doubt inspired Middleton's confidence in the convoy system and insurance underwriters certainly shared his enthusiasm. Nevertheless, the system had drawbacks. Above all, it engendered delay. Assembling transports from widely separated locations and loading them at one depot; establishing a rendezvous between them and their naval escorts; making the ocean passage at the speed of the slowest member; unloading them in a port already thick with waiting ships, all took far more time than sending ships out singly or in twos and threes. Lord George Germain, the Secretary of State for America, was beside himself when he learned that putting the transports under the Navy Board's aegis also meant putting them under convoy.[75] Such a plan, he warned, was certain to aggravate the Army's operational problems. The Treasury, however, was too eager to get out of the transport business to heed Germain's admonition.[76]

In view of the Treasury's eagerness to come to terms, Middleton's second point required no circumlocution: 'Our trouble will require more pay.'[77] And as long as money was at issue, why not remind the Admiralty of the inadequacy of current Navy Board salaries? 'At the first Establishment of the Navy Office', according to the history lesson Middleton gave their Lordships, 'the Fleet was so small as to require the Board's sitting but two days in a week and continued in this state for many Years afterwards. But from the growing Progress and the immense Bulk it has now arrived at, six days close application and without intermission is absolutely necessary to carry on the business with proper dispatch.'[78]

The Navy Board's bid fell on deaf ears at the Admiralty; but the Treasury, conceding the need for extra compensation for extra work, proposed £300 a year for each Commissioner, £150 for the secretary, and £400 to be distributed among the Navy Office clerks.[79] No Commissioner complained about this schedule of salaries, but the clerks felt so underpaid for the additional work the transports required that they lodged a written protest with the Board. Middleton responded with characteristic vehemence. The clerks all 'ought to be discharged', he said, and if they did not care to do their duty, then he would find some who did. At that, one of them explained, the recalcitrants 'sunk under the grand hand of power'.[80] In such ways did the Controller's office echo the quarterdeck.

Having won the Treasury's agreement on the questions of compensation and convoy, Middleton insisted through private channels on the Navy Board's right to appoint all officials supervising the transport service.[81] Because in the power to make appointments resided the power to command loyalties, Middleton laid claim to such authority whenever he could. He did not always get his way, but this time he did. 'This Board', the Treasury informed him and his colleagues toward the end of March, 'now depends entirely upon your exertions for carrying on the service for victualling the Troops Abroad.'[82]

Henceforth it fell to the Navy Board to receive provisions from the contractors, inspect them and deliver them, in ships under its hire, to the Army in America. The experience of the first convoy conducted under its auspices shows how the system worked. On 17 March 1779 the Board asked the Admiralty to provide a naval escort for 24 transports destined for New York and Georgia with 7,200 tons of provisions. Within a month 6,000 tons of shipping had gathered at Spithead, but it took another three weeks – until 8 May – to assemble an additional 2,359 tons and send them, nearly 30 transports in all, to Cork, the principal victualling station for North America. The contractors in Ireland were slow to deliver the provisions they had promised, and the loading of the transports, hampered by a shortage of lighters, did not commence until 1 June. Two weeks later the Treasury anxiously inquired whether loading could be expedited, for '[the transports] are now much later than they ought to have been', but not until 16 July were the provisions for America stowed away.

On 19 July the convoy set sail from Cork: 8,045 tons of beef, pork, butter, flour and oatmeal aboard 28 ships – 19 of them bound for New York and nine for Georgia – escorted by the *Roebuck* (44). In a letter of 27 September, Lt Archibald Dow, the transports agent for New York, wrote to the Navy Board that the convoy, having arrived early in the month, was still unloading and would not be ready for sea for another two weeks; the voyage home would require several more weeks.[83] From start to finish, turning around this single convoy took more than six months. So despite the Treasury's high hopes, handing the transport service over to the experts of the Navy Board did not bring immediate relief to the expeditionary force. From the soldiers' perspective, 1779 was nearly as unsatisfactory as 1778 had been.

The optimists at the Treasury failed to take into account the relentless operations of Murphy's Law. After the transports came under the Navy Board's aegis, contractors continued to make late deliveries and indulge in fraudulent practices; victuals spoiled; transports caught fire, ran aground and were lost track of; customs officers meddled and pried; lightermen dawdled, the wind turned foul and the enemy picked off stragglers. Still, the crisis of 1779 also owed something to the convoy system itself. For instance, much time and effort was wasted in shipping to Cork for transshipment to America provisions that could more easily have been sent direct from England. The Admiralty sometimes proved as dilatory in providing naval escorts as Lord Germain had predicted (nor did Germain forbear from saying 'I told you so').[84]

Nevertheless, handing the victualling transports over to Middleton and his colleagues remained a sound decision. Never again did storehouses fall as short of supplies as they were in the early winter of 1779. Indeed, in the summer of 1782 a Hessian officer whose troops drew rations from the New York storehouses wrote in his journal, 'Our store of provisions has never been so plentiful as it now is'. Well over a year's rations for 27,000 men were on hand at New York in flour and pease, more than two years for beef, butter, rice and oatmeal.[85] These comfortable margins owed much to the Navy Board's improvements in the victualling service. Under Middleton's leadership the Board recruited able Agent Victualers such as John Cherry, who were intent on making contractors live up to their contracts; badgered the Admiralty into providing naval escorts in a timely fashion; unsnarled the confusion that attended the hiring of transports into the King's service; overhauled and simplified procedures for inspecting and loading provisions; eliminated the worst inefficiencies of the trans-shipment system between England and Ireland; moved a major victualling station from the overburdened docks and wharves of the Thames to more spacious and efficient facilities on the Isle of Wight; and reduced, if it did not eliminate, Customs' infuriating intrusions into the business of supplying America.

If Middleton and his colleagues were reasonably successful at tinkering with the transport service, Middleton had no luck at all with his ambitious scheme to establish, as part of the service, a kind of standing amphibious strike force. In an undated memorandum to Lord Germain, Middleton pointed out the inconvenience of embarking, from widely scattered ports, troops intended for the same operation. Not only did the practice cause delays sometimes fatal to the success of an amphibious expedition; it also ensured that the newspapers would discover that something was afoot, and the secrecy vital to many such missions would be lost. To get round such difficulties, Middleton proposed

> ten gunboats, thirty bateaux in frame, and as many flat boats, with every necessary material to be provided at leisure and lodged at Portsmouth; 10,000 tons of coppered transports, with a proportionate number of coppered victuallers, to be kept in constant readiness at Spithead, and as much provisions in store at Cowes as will serve 5,000 men for six months. To this preparation I would add every kind of artillery and ammunition that may be necessary for a distant expedition and lodged at the gun-wharf at Portsmouth. This preparation brings everything within a narrow compass and will enable you to embark six regiments in forty-eight hours.[86]

Beset by events in America, the distracted Germain apparently did not reply to Middleton's proposal. Perhaps the Controller never sent it to him. For sound as the idea of a standing amphibious force was (his claim that troops could be so speedily embarked deserves some skepticism, however), Middleton knew better than anyone that 10,000 tons of spare transports were nowhere to be found. Indeed, the shortage of transports was a difficulty – the most serious one of all, in terms of its consequences – that the Navy Board never overcame. There were several reasons for the scarcity of shipping. The Board never succeeded in chartering enough transports from private owners to meet the needs of the service. Army and Navy commanders in America could never be dissuaded from diverting to their own uses the transports that brought them provisions. Shipping detained abroad, however, was shipping lost to the transport service, and the Navy Board was helpless, despite its complaints, to do anything about it. But the main cause of the transport shortage, according to David Syrett, was the government's own strategy. By dispersing troops along the eastern seaboard from Halifax to Pensacola and by taking on responsibility for feeding, in addition to the expeditionary force, large numbers of Indians and civilians, the government assured that more and more victuallers, sailing to more places, would be required. The Navy Board could never keep up with the demand for more shipping.[87]

The government failed to heed the Board's ceaselessly reiterated warnings respecting the scarcity of transports. Instead, it laid plans for a world war as if a limitless supply of shipping were available to support its every scheme. Nothing could better have emphasized the Navy Board's status as a subordinate agency of the state than the confusing and contradictory orders pouring in from Whitehall to carry troops hither and yon at the same time as provisions were to be sent to and fro. Nor in fending off the Treasury's more unreasonable claims was the Admiralty much help. For what had a chore like victualling the land forces to do with war at sea? So the Navy Board was left to try to square the government's often fantastic demands for shipping with the realities of the shipping supply. Its duty was to react, not to initiate. In the view of the leading historian of the subject, 'the achievements of the transport service' – hence of the Navy Board – 'during the American War were prodigious … and [must] rank among the greatest military and administrative feats of the eighteenth century'.[88] Still, if Middleton would not have been reluctant to take credit for the feat, it was not his cup of tea. Supplying America covered a range of administrative problems too far beyond his own control to be congenial. Striking a bargain with Treasury officials over the victualling service was one thing; dealing with the frustrations to which the bargain inevitably led was another. As 1779 wore on, Middleton grew increasingly preoccupied with the growing threat the fleets of France and Spain posed at sea and with his own ingenious scheme for countering it.

NOTES

1 Paul Kennedy, *The Rise and Fall of the Great Powers: Economic Change and Military Conflict from 1500 to 2000* (New York, 1987), pp. 113–15; John Brewer, *The Sinews of Power: War, Money and the English State, 1688–1783* (New York, 1989), p. 175; Eric Robson, 'The Seven Years War', in *The New Cambridge Modern History*, vol. VII, *The Old Regime, 1713–1763* (Cambridge, 1963), p. 485.

2 Jonathan R. Dull, *The French Navy and American Independence: A Study of Arms and*

Diplomacy, 1774–1787 (Princeton, NJ, 1975), p. 11. As Dull points out, however, when the Duc de Choiseul, who combined the posts of foreign minister and naval minister, fell from office in 1770 his successors did not sustain his vigorous naval construction program.

3 Paul Kennedy, *The Rise and Fall of British Naval Mastery* (London, 1976), p. 107. See also Paul W. Schroeder, *The Transformation of European Politics, 1763–1748* (Oxford, 1994), p. 5.

4 The most recent account of all this is David Syrett, *The Royal Navy in American Waters, 1775–1783* (Aldershot, 1989).

5 On French plans to challenge British colonial and maritime supremacy, see Kennedy, *British Naval Mastery*, p. 110.

6 In early July 1776 agents reported a massive repair program under way in the French dockyards. In December 1777 intelligence reports counted 50 ships of the line ready for sea at Toulon, Brest and Rochefort. What is more, 11 36-gun frigates were under construction at Brest and Rochefort and two 32-gun frigates at Toulon. By July 1778, when war between France and Britain had begun, Spain had, according to intelligence estimates, 40 ships of the line in commission in Europe, another four nearly ready for sea at Cádiz and another six in America. Gathering intelligence on French readiness was not without risk. In 1769 the French hanged a Mr Douglas for spying on the dockyards. Nicholas Tracy, 'British Assessments of French and Spanish Naval Reconstruction, 1763–1778', *Mariner's Mirror*, 61, 1 (1975), pp. 73–85, especially pp. 74, 82–3.

7 Piers Mackesy, *The War for America* (Cambridge, MA, 1964), p. 171.

8 Mulgrave Castle Archives, vol. VI, pp. 10–249. Charles Middleton to Constantine John Phipps, Lord Mulgrave, 11 November 1776.

9 N. A. M. Rodger, *The Wooden World: An Anatomy of the Georgian Navy* (London, 1986), pp. 87–98.

10 Sandwich Papers [Notes of R. J. B. Knight], 13 January 1777.

11 Sandwich Papers [Notes of R. J. B. Knight], 16 January 1777. Middleton to Sandwich. Rebuffed by the First Lord, Middleton turned to his old Treasury acquaintance, Charles Jenkinson. Conceding that George was in no position to be choosy, he expressed his brother's willingness to go anywhere on behalf of 'his large and helpless family', adding a Uriah Heep-like assurance that 'however little you may rest on your own influence, yet to such as me who travel in a much humbler sphere, I cannot help looking up to it with respect and expectation'. British Library, Add. Mss 38209, Liverpool Papers.

12 Brewer, *Sinews of Power*, pp. 70–1.

13 Mackesy, *War for America*, p. 173; Dull, *French Navy*, pp. 72–82.

14 G. R. Barnes and J. H. Owen, *The Private Papers of John, Earl of Sandwich*, vol. I (London, 1932), p. 236.

15 Mackesy, *War for America*, pp. 135–44, 147.

16 Dull, *French Navy*, pp. 89–93.

17 Mackesy, *War for America*, pp. 192–6; David Syrett, *Royal Navy*, especially pp. 61–116.

18 Gerald S. Brown, 'The Anglo–French Naval Crisis, 1778: A Study of Conflict in the North Cabinet', *William and Mary Quarterly*, 3rd series, 13 (January 1956), pp. 3–25; Syrett, *Royal Navy*, pp. 96–7.

19 Carola Oman, *Nelson* (London, 1947), pp. 12–14; Julian S. Corbett, *England in the Seven Years War*, vol. I (London, 1907), pp. 365–7.

20 Sandwich Papers [Notes of R. J. B. Knight], 2 February 1775; NMM, SAN/T/3/. Appointments Books, vol. 3, 1776.

21 NMM, SAN/T/7, Maurice Suckling to Sandwich, 28 January 1777.

22 *Barham Papers*, vol. III, pp. 25–6.

23 Ibid.

24 William Weber, *The Rise of Musical Classics in Eighteenth-Century England: A Study in Canon, Ritual, and Ideology* (Oxford, 1992), pp. 147, 163.
25 Lucy Sutherland, *The East India Company in Eighteenth-Century Politics* (Oxford, 1952), p. 277.
26 *A List of the Names of the Members of the United Co of Merchants of England, Trading to the East Indies, Who Appear Qualified to Vote at Their General Courts, 1795* (London, 1795), p. 49.
27 British Library, Add. Mss 38209, Liverpool Papers, Charles Middleton to Charles Jenkinson, 5 July 1777.
28 For example John Fortescue, *A History of the British Army*, 13 vols (London, 1899–1930), vol. III, p. 172; Robert Albion, *Forests and Sea Power: The Timber Problem of the Royal Navy, 1652–1862* (Cambridge, MA, 1926), p. 282.
29 Quoted in Bernard Donoughue, *British Politics and the American Revolution* (London, 1964), p. 42; G.F. Russell Baker (ed.), *Horace Walpole, Memoirs of the Reign of King George the Third*, 4 vols (London, 1894), vol. IV, pp. 170–1.
30 J. C. Beaglehole, *The Life of Captain James Cook* (Stanford, CA, 1974), pp. 281–2.
31 The most recent book on the dockyards is Jonathan Coad, *The Royal Dockyards, 1690–1850: Architecture and Engineering Works of the Royal Navy* (Aldershot, 1989).
32 James M. Haas, 'The Royal Dockyards: The Earliest Visitations and Reforms', *Historical Journal*, 13, 2 (June 1970), p. 204.
33 PRO, ADM 7/662, Sandwich Dockyard Visitation, 1775, unpaginated.
34 N. A. M. Rodger, *The Insatiable Earl: A Life of John Montagu, Fourth Earl of Sandwich 1718–1792* (New York, 1994), p. 160.
35 Samuel Pepys and Charles Middleton were both beneficiaries of a Sandwich connection. Pepys had the good luck to be named as his cousin Edward Mountagu's personal secretary just before Mountagu helped engineer Charles II's restoration to the throne. A grateful king made Mountagu the Earl of Sandwich, and Sandwich in turn rewarded his secretary with high office. 'A young man of twenty-seven who a few months before had scarcely known one end of a ship from the other', Pepys was made Clerk of the Acts of the Navy in July 1660. Richard Ollard, *Pepys* (New York, 1974), pp. 37, 68–72. 'Pepys', says Arthur Bryant, 'was a member of the Navy Board because Lord Sandwich put him there.' *Samuel Pepys*, 3 vols (Cambridge, 1934), vol. I, pp. 112–13. Charles Middleton owed his appointment as Controller to John Montagu (as the name was spelled by then), the fourth Earl of Sandwich, great-grandson of Pepys's benefactor.
36 NMM, SAN/T/8, Middleton to Sandwich, 8 March 1778.
37 The coppering of the fleet is the subject of Ch. 3.
38 PRO, ADM 51/4229, Captains' logs.
39 *The Laws, Ordinances, and Institutions of the Admiralty of Great Britain, Civil and Military* (London, 1746), p. 385.
40 NMM, MID/2/54, Navy Board to Admiralty, 18 February 1774.
41 Bryant, *Pepys*, vol. I, p. 11; John Ehrman, *The Navy in the War of William III, 1689–1697* (Cambridge, 1953), p. 182; Ollard, *Pepys*, pp. 76–8; Bernard Pool, *Navy Board Contracts, 1600–1932* (Hamden, CT, 1966), pp. x, 4–5.
42 Michael Oppenheim, *A History of the Administration of the Royal Navy* (London, 1896), p. 85.
43 Daniel A. Baugh, *British Naval Administration in the Age of Walpole* (Princeton, NJ, 1965), pp. 32–8.
44 Quoted in Baugh, p. 47.
45 *Barham Papers*, vol. III, p. 33. Memorandum to Lord Melville (formerly Henry Dundas), May 1804.
46 PRO, ADM 106/2598, Navy Board Minutes, 25 August 1778.
47 Ollard, *Pepys*, p. 83.

48 Baugh, *Naval Administration*, p. 37.
49 *Barham Papers*, vol. II, p. 179.
50 William Palmer had been Controller of the Victualling Accounts since 1773; Timothy Brett, Controller of the Treasurer's Accounts since 1761; William Bateman, Controller of Storekeeper's Accounts since 1763. This paragraph relies on David Syrett, *Shipping and the American War, 1775–83: A Study of British Transport Organization* (London, 1970), pp. 24–8.
51 Barham Papers, vol. II, pp. 169–70.
52 NMM, *The Commissioned Sea Officers of the Royal Navy, 1660–1815* (n.p. 1954), pp. ii, 543.
53 Baugh, *Naval Administration*, pp. 262–5. On Portsmouth see R. J. B. Knight (ed.), *Portsmouth Dockyard Papers, 1774–1783: The American War* (Portsmouth, 1987).
54 Baugh, *Naval Administration*, pp. 289–93.
55 Ibid., p. 292.
56 Rodger, *The Wooden World*, p. 35.
57 Ibid., p. 30.
58 Ehrman, *Navy in the War of William III*, p. 186.
59 Baugh, *Naval Administration*, pp. 61–6; Ehrman, *Navy in the War of William III*, p. 305; Rodger, *Wooden World*, p. 32.
60 A. T. Mahan, 'Military History of the Royal Navy, 1763–1792', in William Laird Clowes (ed.), *The Royal Navy*, 6 vols (London, 1898), vol. III, pp. 412–22.
61 Dull, *French Navy*, p. 154.
62 Nicholas Tracy, 'British Assessments of French and Spanish Naval Reconstruction, 1763–1778', *Mariner's Mirror*, 61, 1 (1975), p. 83; Daniel A. Baugh, 'Why did Britain lose Command of the Sea during the War for America?', in Jeremy Black and Philip Woodfine (eds), *The British Navy and the Use of Naval Power in the Eighteenth Century* (Leicester, 1988), p. 152.
63 Kennedy, *Rise and Fall of British Naval Mastery*, p. 115.
64 NMM, SAN/T/7, Middleton to Sandwich, 15 August 1778.
65 NMM, ADM/A/2731.
66 Suckling's signature does not appear on any Navy Board warrants to the Portsmouth Dockyard after 3 March 1778.
67 *Barham Papers*, vol. III, p. 27.
68 Ibid.
69 R. Arthur Bowler, *Logistics and the Failure of the British Army in America, 1775–1783* (Princeton, NJ, 1975), p. 118.
70 Consider the extraordinary efforts required to supply the British expeditionary force to the Falkland Islands in 1982. Max Hastings and Simon Jenkins, *The Battle for the Falklands* (New York, 1983), *passim*. Or the even more extraordinary exertions, in view of the size of the force and the rapidity of the build-up, needed to supply the allied troops in the Persian Gulf in 1990–91. See Michael R. Gordon and Bernard E. Trainor, *The Generals' War: The Inside Story of the Conflict in the Gulf* (Boston, MA, 1995), pp. 57–66, 475–6. The best book on the subject is Martin van Creveld, *Supplying War: Logistics from Wallenstein to Patton* (Cambridge, 1977).
71 R. Arthur Bowler, *Logistics*, p. 118.
72 Syrett, *Shipping and the American War*, pp. 132–3.
73 Middleton later wrote to Lord Chatham: 'My predecessor was in a bad state of health and [the Navy Board's] own business more than they could get through.' PRO, 30/8/365. Chatham Papers, Middleton to Chatham, 10 January 1794.
74 PRO, T/24/48; T/64/200, Navy Board to Treasury, 3 February 1779.
75 PRO, T64/201, 27 March 1779.
76 Syrett, *Shipping and the American War*, pp. 137–8; Mackesy, *War for America*, pp. 118–19.

77 PRO, T64/200, 11 February 1779.
78 NMM, ADM/B/198, Navy Board to Admiralty, 11 February 1779.
79 PRO, T64/200, Navy Board to Treasury, 11 March 1779; PRO T64/201, Treasury to Navy Board, 13 March 1779.
80 Quoted in Syrett, *Shipping and the American War*, p. 137.
81 *Barham Papers*, vol. II, p. 153.
82 PRO, T64/201, Treasury to Navy Board, 27 March 1779.
83 This paragraph relies on PRO, T64/200 and T64/201.
84 Quoted in Syrett, *Shipping*, p. 179.
85 Ibid.
86 *Barham Papers*, vol. II, p. 46.
87 Syrett, *Shipping*, especially pp. 160–80, 245–7.
88 Ibid., p. 248.

3

Coppering the Fleet

When Keppel met d'Orvilliers off Ushant in the summer of 1778, Britain had a handful of copper-bottomed ships at sea, none bigger than a 32-gun frigate. By late 1780 most of the ships of the line had been sheathed with copper and, by the end of the following year, so had most of the fleet. This huge, complicated and expensive undertaking absorbed all the King's dockyards; for several months, coppering took precedence over all other work. For soon after taking office, Middleton recognized that mobilizing every serviceable frigate and ship of the line in the Navy would still not allow Britain to challenge the Franco-Spanish supremacy at sea. 'We were still deficient in strength', he later wrote. 'The enemy outnumbered us upon every station. Further exertions were still wanting to prevent our being overpowered by numbers.'[1] The coppering program was an attempt to counter by technological innovation the Franco-Spanish superiority in numbers. Coppering the fleet was Middleton's proudest achievement. He championed the idea from his first days as Controller, overcame the doubts of skeptics, held down costs and pushed the work to completion. But the program was not the unqualified success he remembered in later years.[2] In the interests of hurrying as many copper-sheathed ships to sea as quickly as he could, Middleton set aside the time-consuming techniques that had emerged from more than a decade of experiments with copper bottoms. At length, however, the Controller's short cuts threatened the seaworthiness of the ships in question; at great expense his methods had to be abandoned.

Copper sheathing was a new solution to the old problem of preserving a wooden hull from pests and the elements. Barnacles and marine vegetation were ancient enemies. Once British mariners began sailing tropical waters, their ships acquired the far more dangerous *Teredo navalis*, or shipworm, which could transform an oaken beam into a filligreed ruin. Fir sheathing laid over a mixture of hair, sulphur and tar was the common but far from effective remedy against the teredo.[3] Fir-clad cruisers needed to be docked for cleaning every six weeks; ships of the line came in three or four times a year. The yards worked efficiently – from start to finish a 74-gun third rate could be cleaned in two tides – but cleaning diverted the docks from other work. In wartime, repairing battle damage took precedence over maintaining ships' bottoms; meanwhile, the teredo chewed away undeterred.[4] So naval authorities had long been interested in finding an alternative to fir sheathing. Inventors and mariners recommended countless materials and techniques, and a few, such as lead, were tried out.[5]

During the Seven Years War the Navy turned to copper sheathing as a possible answer to the teredo.[6] In October 1759 the Navy Board adorned by Thomas Slade, the great naval architect, ordered Portsmouth Dockyard to copper the keels of two 74-gun ships of the line.[7] When the Board decided to try sheathing an entire ship's bottom – 'for an experiment of preserving it against the worm'[8] – it chose a much smaller vessel.[9] 'The sheathing of the *Alarm* frigate of 32 guns was finished', the *Gentlemen's Magazine* reported in November 1761: 'It is of copper, the first trial that ever was made of this kind of sheathing; it is very neat, not heavy, nor expensive. She is designed for the West Indies'[10] – where the teredo abounded.

When the *Alarm* returned from her West Indian cruise in August 1763, the Woolwich dockyard officers were gratified to discover that copper sheathing had kept her bottom free from both worms and weeds. But their careful inspection also brought disappointment.

> We were greatly surprized [they reported] to perceive the Effect the Copper had had upon the iron where the two metals touch'd; but it was most remarkable at the Rother [rudder] Irons and in the fastenings of the false Keel, upon the former, the Pintles and Necks of the Braces were so corroded and Eat, particularly the two lower ones, that they could not have continued of sufficient strength to do their Office many months longer, and with respect to the false keel it was entirely off ... the Nails and Staples that fastened it were found dissolved into a kind of rusty Paste ... The same effect, but not to so great a degree, was observable upon all the Bolts and Iron under water.[11]

Nevertheless, the inspectors were convinced that copper's benefits were great enough to warrant further trials, 'provided Methods can be fallen upon to obviate the difficultys we have before pointed out, the greatest of which is, the bad effect that Copper has upon iron'.[12]

The Admiralty was eager to put copper sheathing to additional tests. In March 1764 Philip Stephens, the Admiralty Secretary, asked the Navy Board to propose a 24-gun ship for 'some further Experiments to be made of the efficacy of Copper-Sheathing'.[13] On 14 May the *Dolphin* (24), newly sheathed with copper, emerged from a dock and went alongside the sheer hulk at Woolwich, to be masted and rigged for the first of two voyages around the world.[14] Like many sea officers after him – including Charles Middleton – John Byron, who commanded the *Dolphin* on her first circumnavigation, could not restrain his enthusiasm for the new technique. 'My opinion of Copper Bottoms', he wrote to the First Lord, John Perceval, Lord Egmont, from the Straits of Magellan in February 1765, 'is that it is the finest Invention in the world.'[15] Dockyard officers, who strode the quarterdeck only when ships underwent repair, were more circumspect. When the *Dolphin* came home from her second voyage in July 1768, the Deptford officers reported that copper's effectiveness against weed and worm had been amply confirmed. 'But it is also observable', they went on, 'that the bad Effect of the Copper in Corroding and destroying the Bolts and other Iron work under Water is also confirm'd in this and every other Ship that has been coppered, all the Bolts in the Dolphin being so much wasted as renders them unserviceable and must be drove out and replaced with new before the Ship can again proceed to sea.'[16]

With the results of the *Dolphin* trials in hand, the Navy Board ordered the Deptford officers to try copper bolts below the waterline of the 14-gun sloop *Squirrel*, building in their yard.[17] But this was strictly an experiment, for in 1768 every ship in the Navy, from 100-gun first rates to cutters, fireships and bombs, was held together with iron fastenings. Some yard officers doubted whether copper bolts could withstand the punishment to which the working of a wooden hull at sea would subject them. More important, rebolting iron-fastened ships promised to run up staggering bills for labor, materials and dockyard space, and in peacetime such a step was unthinkable. So the experiments that had begun with the *Alarm* petered out. Some lessons of the sea trials were put into effect. Copper-alloy braces and pintles (the hardware hinging rudder to sternpost) replaced iron ones on copper-sheathed ships; copper staples and scarph bolts were used to attach false keels to keels proper. Unless something could be done to offset 'the bad effect that copper has upon iron', however, its good effect upon the worm was likely to be lost to the Navy.

At the outbreak of the American War roughly a dozen ships had copper bottoms. The four largest were 32-gun frigates, the rest sloops. In 1777 an enthusiast at the Admiralty scribbled in the margin of an old Navy Board report on the *Alarm* experiment that '[copper sheathing] has been now brought to such perfection that a great number of Frigates are coppered, & it is found to answer extreamly well'.[18] By the time France intervened, another half dozen sloops and merchant-built, copper-fastened cutters had been coppered.[19] But a few small cruisers and auxiliary vessels were not enough to convince skeptics either of copper sheathing's economic value to the dockyards or of its strategic benefits afloat.

Charles Middleton came to office an enthusiast for copper sheathing. When the prospect of sharing his quarterdeck with a flag officer diminished the appeal of commanding the *Prince George*, Middleton asked Lord Sandwich for another ship. The captain of a 90-gun battleship was willing to make do with a 50-gun frigate on the Bristol station, he wrote to the First Lord in January 1778, provided that she were coppered (Bristol was a puzzling choice for a homebody like Middleton, unless he hoped that Margaret Middleton and Mrs Bouverie might take the waters at Bath while he cruised nearby). If the Bristol station were not available, Middleton continued, he would still like a coppered ship:

> The utility of such an improvement [as a coppered bottom] is so well known to your Lordship in particular, and so generally approved in the service that I have not a doubt but the next generation will see it universally adopted, and if such an advantage should meet with any difference of opinion, and I should be allowed to pay the difference of expence to Government, I would most readily do it, convinced of the sensible benefits the Service would reap thereby.[20]

Middleton did not get the Bristol station, but he did get the *Jupiter* (50), which in June 1778 (presumably at no cost to her commanding officer) became the largest copper-sheathed ship in the Navy.

Middleton later disparaged Sandwich's familiarity with copper sheathing,[21] but in fact the First Lord was well acquainted with its benefits and drawbacks. An enthusiast for technical innovation,[22] he had clambered over the copper-bottomed sloop *Hawke*, just returned from India, when he visited Sheerness Dockyard in 1775. He had seen for himself the effects of electrolytic corrosion: 'I also saw some of the Bolts that had been driven out of her [the *Hawke*], and which (tho' the heads of them which had been covered with lead were still sound and whole) were corroded and almost eat in two by the effects of the Copper.'[23] If anything gave the First Lord pause, it was surely Middleton's audacious intentions with respect to coppering the fleet.

48

The Admiralty took an extremely cautious approach to coppering ships of the line. On 19 September 1778 Philip Stephens queried the Navy Board as to 'whether Copper Fastenings cannot be made to Ships of the Line of Battle, as well as Frigates, in order to their being sheathed with Copper'. The Board should propose one ship of each class on which to conduct an experiment.[24] The Board replied that it was too soon to tell how copper-bolted frigates fared; no trial of copper fastenings had ever been made on a ship of the line. The *Europa* (50), building at Woolwich, might make a suitable experimental frigate; the *Goliath* (74), on the stocks at Deptford, might serve as the larger trial ship.[25]

Such a piecemeal approach stood little or no chance of meeting the war emergency. Ships built with copper fastenings could take years to reach the fleet and years more undergoing trials. In fact, the *Europa* was launched only in spring 1783 and the *Goliath* in autumn 1781.[26] Besides, the big ships on the stocks amounted to a token force. There was no getting around it: producing enough copper-bottomed ships of the line to meet the emergency required the sheathing of the iron-fastened vessels already afloat.

Sometime between the autumn of 1778 and the turn of the year a Liverpool shipbuilder named Fisher taught Middleton a new technique for coppering iron-fastened ships.[27] Essentially, Fisher's method aimed at establishing a watertight seal between a ship's copper overcoat and the iron bolts and nails holding its skin and skeleton together. Depriving the two metals of salt-water contact would prevent them from reacting to each other. Middleton convinced himself that the watertight seal offered the safe and expeditious means of coppering iron-fastened ships that had so far eluded the Navy.

By early January 1779 Middleton had convinced his fellow Com-missioners of the merits of the watertight seal (his old shipmate Samuel Wallis, erstwhile captain of the *Dolphin*, might have expressed some reservations, but he had yet to join the Board), for on the 8th the Ports-mouth Dockyard was instructed to carry out the new procedure on the next ship it sheathed.[28] A week later the Admiralty, having agreed to try the seal on a 44-gun frigate (possibly the *Roebuck*), asked the Navy Board to consider whether any ships of the line might be similarly sheathed.[29] The Commissioners had anticipated the Admiralty's query. Corrosion of iron fastenings, Middleton and his colleagues assured their Lordships, 'we have reason to believe will be prevented by covering the Bottom with Paper of about one eighth of an Inch thick, first dipped in hot tar, which being slightly tacked upon it, admit of the Copper Sheets (which are to be painted on the inside with white Lead being nailed and set on so closely that water can scarce get under them'.[30] During the life of the program the technique underwent many refinements, but its main components – paper, tar and coated copper sheets – remained essentially the same.

Middleton's version of how the Admiralty and Navy Board came to adopt the new technique makes him the lone hero of a campaign waged against vacillating superiors, skeptical colleagues and obtuse subordinates. His grandchildren must have heard many times of his visit to Buckingham Palace, where he and Sandwich showed the King a copper-sheathed model of the *Bellona* (74) and convinced him of the merits of coppering ships of the line. With the King in his camp, according to the story, all opposition to the new procedure fell away. The Controller may not have explained to the grandchildren, and he certainly did not tell his kinsman Lord Melville (formerly Henry Dundas), that he was not the first to instruct the monarch in the advantages – and drawbacks – of copper sheathing. The First Lord had kept George III well informed.[31]

Eager to press ahead, in late January 1779 the Navy Board submitted to the Admiralty a list of 27 ships of the line, mostly third rates of 64 and 74 guns, that the dockyards recommended for sheathing.[32] A circumspect Admiralty chose two 74s from the Board's list, and on 20 February Portsmouth yard received orders to sheathe *Russell* and *Invincible*.[33] In late May the Board ordered the dockyards to copper all ships, both in service and in ordinary, of 32 guns and fewer down to sloops. In early July came instructions to sheathe all 44-gun frigates and to supply with copper braces and pintles, as opportunities offered, all coppered ships.[34]

As the summer wore on, Middleton evidently concluded that the Admiralty needed some prodding, for in a memorandum probably composed in September 1779 he urged Sandwich to push to completion the coppering of the fleet. As the Controller's most comprehensive statement on the subject, it merits quoting at length:

> All my confidence in the practicability of [a plan for defending the West Indies] as well as every other success is founded on a supposition that the whole fleet of England is coppered with all possible dispatch. *This first of all naval improvements*[35] seems at this critical period the means which Providence has put into our power to extricate us from present danger, and it will be the height of imprudence not to make use of them. Such ships are ready at twelve hours notice for the most distant services. It is actually more than doubling our number of ships; and in point of activity there is no calculating the advantages arising from it ... We shall

have large ships enough, if coppering is made the first object, but it will be proper to double the number of frigates to act under them and to construct proper fireships to assist them. The hiring of armed merchant ships and purchasing privateers is an enormous and almost useless expence; such vessels do little service and are never lasting. If coppering is universal we shall be at liberty to build in our own yards; and one ship constructed there is of more real use to his Majesty than four purchased ones. Everything (under the direction of Providence) is still in our power towards humbling France and Spain, and very practicable with a coppered fleet under active officers. But if timid and prudential reasons should induce us to defer carrying the knowledge we have acquired in this branch into general practice till other powers have got into it, we might in any other light than an economical one have as well been without it …

The present times will not admit of delay in adopting, nor drowsiness in executing … Every hour that is lost may rob us of opportunities that will never return, and therefore I hope our equipment will begin early, and the three-decked ships be the first coppered after a sufficient number of the two-decks have been prepared for foreign service. When the whole of the Western Squadron is coppered it may defy the power of France and Spain; and we are not safe under their present superiority until that is completed.[36]

In a separate letter Middleton charted the path to safety. 'As soon as you can spare [the ships]', he wrote to the First Lord in mid September, 'we shall produce a useful coppered fleet early in the spring; … would propose coppering every ship, and we are laying in [supplies] accordingly.' Their speed and agility, he insisted, made coppered frigates well suited to keeping an eye on the French; adding to them a few ships of the line would be the best means of covering the mouth of the Channel; Sandwich's fears for the security of the West Indies would be eased were the islands to be sent 'nothing but coppered ships'. Finally, Middleton hinted, the program might serve to diminish the First Lord's political worries as well: 'I am very glad to see so many coppered ships proceeding down Channel, as I am hopeful they will equally defeat the purposes of the enemy abroad as well as those of your Lordship at home, who I am sorry to say are labouring very hard at this time to discover when an opening can be hit.'[37]

Middleton did not get everything he wanted. A blanket order to sheathe all ships of the line was never made,[38] but toward the end of 1779 an order went out to sheathe the entire Western Squadron.[39]

Usually the Navy Board issued orders – 'warrants' in Navy Office parlance – and left dockyard officers to decide how (and sometimes when) a thing was to be done. Their expertise gave them substantial autonomy – or, in the view of impatient officials such as Middleton, too much leeway to frustrate the will of the Navy Board. Coppering ships' bottoms, however, did not belong to the traditional body of dockyard expertise. Instead, the yards were required to follow the Navy Board's guidance to the letter. From the Navy Office poured a steady stream of 'Standing Orders' on coppering: instructions all yards were to follow at all times. Molds were to be made for copper-alloy braces and pintles; copper plates were to be painted three times on one side only; copper unfit for use was to be returned to Deptford Yard; at least 15 tons of sheathing paper were to be kept in store at all times; copper nails were to be countersunk; heavier copper was to be used in sheathing ships' bows; coppered ships should no longer receive a supply of fir sheathing boards; anchor stocks should be rounded off so as to prevent their damaging copper sheets; 22-ounce copper should be applied to clinker-built cutters; ships fitting for sea should be issued spare copper sheets in specified amounts. On and on the Standing Orders went.[40]

Binding instructions flowed from top to bottom; obligatory reports came back to London from the most far-flung yards. In the middle of it all sat the Controller, badgering the dockyards for more information on the amount of copper they held in store, on the progress of coppering, on the state of the copper on ships' bottoms, and on countless related matters. By making London the source of expertise, coppering turned the tables on the customary relationship between the dockyards and the Navy Board. Middleton shared with his great predecessor Samuel Pepys the ambition of tightening the Navy Office's control over its sprawling domain. The coppering program, for which all initiative arose at the center, afforded a means of turning the screws on the periphery.[41]

Middleton carried out the coppering of the fleet, he claimed, with an eye to strict economy. When the time came to procure large amounts of sheet copper, negotiations with the several companies in the business were 'executed so privately that we secured as much as would cover 40 sail of the line without any increase in price'.[42] It is hard to tell exactly what he meant by this, but it seems likely that keeping the copper merchants in the dark may have kept them from colluding to drive up prices. Statistics gathered in the course of a Privy Council inquiry of 1788 appear to bear out Middleton's claim – for the short run, at least. Between 1764 and 1775 the Navy bought relatively small amounts of sheet copper at an average price of £122 per ton. In the latter half of 1775 the price fell to £92 and drifted down to £76 in January 1780, despite the large purchases of 1779, the first year of the coppering program. Nevertheless, the inflationary pressures of the war as well as the Navy's appetite for sheathing pushed the cost of copper sheets to £91 per ton in June 1780 and to a high of £107 in August.[43]

At least six contractors, of whom William Forbes, yet another enterprising Scot, had the lion's share of the business, supplied copper sheets (as well as a variety of other brass and copper goods) to the yards. At the outset the sheets were transshipped from storage in Deptford; as the pace of the program accelerated, contractors delivered them by wagon direct from the smitheries and collected a surcharge stipulated in their contracts.[44]

Another handful of contractors furnished the reams of cartridge paper that insulated the copper sheets from iron fastenings. To complete the watertight seal the yards dipped into supplies of paint and tar in hand for other purposes – at least until William Dawson convinced the Navy Board to adopt his concoction of tar, linseed oil, rosin, beeswax and tallow. 'Mr Dawson's Composition', as the sealant was invariably called, must have sounded as if it would work; it was evidently never put to sea trials.[45] Relying on Mr Dawson and his composition conformed to the pattern of hopeful guesswork and wishful thinking that characterized the Navy Board's sponsorship of the watertight seal.[46]

With the war at sea straining yard facilities to the limit, finding a safe place to store and prepare the materials used in the coppering program was not easy. The Portsmouth Yard, whose records are the most complete, may serve as an example. The Portsmouth Storekeeper was given an extra clerk and shipwright to help him to keep dockyard workers from embezzling copper, which fetched a high price ashore. Inflammable materials such as tarred paper raised the danger of spontaneous combustion, when improperly stored, and offered tinder to incendiaries such as Jack the Painter, who had put Portsmouth Yard to the torch in 1775. Two entire floors of a new storehouse as well as the top floor of the Ropehouse (an odd choice, in view of the fire hazard) were given over to painting the copper sheets.

Between September 1779 and October 1780 Portsmouth sheathed 51 ships: 22 ships of the line, including one first rate (the *Victory* [100]), five 90-gun second rates, 11 74s (the most numerous class of heavy ships), and two 64s. The smaller vessels ran from frigates down to fireships and bombs. Forty-three of the ships sheathed at Portsmouth had iron fastenings under threat of corrosion if the watertight seal failed to work; only two were fastened with copper; the fastenings of the rest were not indicated. All coppered ships were furnished with copper-alloy braces and pintles.[47]

By 1 September 1780, 152 ships of between 20 and 100 guns had been coppered at all the yards, and 54 sloops, fireships and bombs, for a total of 206.[48] By the end of 1781, according to figures Middleton supplied to Lord Sandwich, the total had risen to 313: 82 ships of the line, 14 of 50 guns, 115 frigates ranging from 44 to 20 guns, and 102 sloops and cutters. Navy Board accounts show that for 1780 the coppering program cost £150,000 and for 1781, £122,416, for a total of £272,416. By way of comparison, the Navy spent £548,745 on transports in 1780 and £178,786 maintaining prisoners of war.[49] In terms of the direct costs of fighting the American war, the coppering of ships may have been something of a bargain.

The sheathing of so many vessels, in so brief a time, by artisans working without machinery in dockyards overloaded by the demands of war, was a truly remarkable achievement. What did these exertions contribute to meeting the war emergency? Such questions are not easily answered, for they entail speculation about events that never happened. The coppering program came too late to even, with faster-sailing and more maneuverable ships, the numerical odds favoring the Franco-Spanish battle fleet. For the great threat to the security of the home islands, about which more will be said later, came in the summer of 1779, only a few weeks after coppering began in earnest. The British squadron sent out to dog the combined fleet included only seven coppered ships of the line.[50] Sickness and hunger prevented the Franco-Spanish fleet from exploiting its domination of the Channel, however, and at length it sailed home. The combined fleet returned in smaller numbers in the campaigning seasons of 1780 and 1781, and by then far more coppered ships of the line were available to the British. In 1781, for instance, all 26 British ships of the line had copper bottoms; the 46 heavy ships of the combined fleet included Spanish ships that, Middleton pointed out, 'had been off the ground two or three years and … could not sail better than loaded colliers'.[51] In neither year did an engagement between the two sides take place. Nevertheless, in terms of the peculiar art of preparing for eventualities that never arise, the coppering program was a success. The French and the Spanish lagged years behind the British in coppering their fleets. It may be that coppered bottoms gave Admiral Rodney a decided tactical advantage over the French at the Battle of the Saints in April 1782. In any event, as Rodger has emphasized, 'Copper had transformed the performance of the British fleet and contributed enormously to restoring, or even reversing the balance of power at sea.'[52]

No amount of copper bottoms, however, would have kept the British from losing the initiative to Admiral François-Joseph Paul, Comte de Grasse, at Chesapeake Bay in 1781. A strategic disaster on land ensued from tactical blunders at sea, for French command of the waters off Virginia ensured Major-General Lord Cornwallis's entrapment on the Yorktown peninsula. His back to the sea, he surrendered to George Washington on 18 October 1781 and the war for America was as good as over. When news of the surrender reached London in late November, just before the opening of Parliament, the Opposition began howling for enquiries into Sandwich's management of the Admiralty. The First Lord's enemies (and some of his ministerial colleagues, who hoped by jettisoning Sandwich to save the North ministry) reasoned that the head of the Navy must take the blame for the victory of French sea-power in North America. Sandwich welcomed an opportunity to reply to his critics – unwisely, it turned out[53] – and over the Christmas recess he circulated among his friends his 'Observations upon the points it is supposed will be the subject of the Naval Enquiry in the House of Commons'. Most of Sandwich's points were drawn verbatim from another paper called 'Sir C. Middleton's Answers to Queries'. So under the First Lord's banner, the Controller advanced his claims.

'Is the coppering of the whole fleet of England no act of exertion?', Middleton–Sandwich asked. Taking his own advice, Middleton made the coppering program a chief answer to Opposition charges of naval unpreparedness. Only one or two frigates had been coppered when Sandwich came to office, he asserted, diminishing by several ships the experiments of the 1760s. The problem of corrosion had baffled everyone, he went on, severely limiting the usefulness of the new technique.

> But the industry and superior knowledge of the present Comptroller of the Navy adopted and recommended a preservative, well proved and attested to have answered every purpose expected for the space of nine years, which effectually preserves the fastenings of the ships from the corrosion of the copper sheathing; ... and as a conclusive proof of our conviction on this subject we are returned to iron bolts and have in a great measure laid aside the copper ones.

Furthermore, in the year just ending, Middleton–Sandwich averred, copper had on several occasions proved its worth at sea: in enabling Admiral Hood to elude de Grasse off the Chesapeake; in permitting Admiral Darby with his 26 coppered ships of the line to shadow the Combined Fleet at little risk to his own force; in allowing Admiral Kempenfelt to steal a considerable part of a French convoy from under the nose of its superior escort.[54] For once, technological determinism played a greater role than Providence in Middleton's philosophy of history.

Everything else – sweeping claims, unprovable assertions, self-promotion at the expense of worthy predecessors – was characteristic Middleton. Coppering was a remarkable innovation, an audacious response to a wartime emergency, a program on which, it could plausibly be claimed, the national security depended. In leading it, Middleton displayed something of 'the wide-ranging curiosity, the need to impose order and the instinct for business', that Richard Ollard ascribes to Pepys.[55] At the end of 1781, however, no ship of the line had been coppered and at sea for more than two-and-a-half years. It was too soon to tell whether the watertight seal 'effectually preserves the fastenings of the ships from the corrosion of the copper sheathing'. So perhaps it was just as well that Sandwich never brandished Middleton's claims on the floor of the House of Lords. The First Lord left office in March 1782. A year later evidence began coming in that Middleton's seal did not work.

NOTES

1 John Knox Laughton (ed.), *Letters and Papers of Charles, Lord Barham*, 3 vols (London, 1907–11), vol. III, p. 27 (hereafter *Barham Papers*).
2 Ibid.
3 J. R. Harris, 'Copper and Shipping in the Eighteenth Century', *Economic History Review*, 19 (1966), p. 550.
4 N. A. M. Rodger, *The Wooden World: An Anatomy of the Georgian Navy* (London, 1986), p. 142.
5 R. V. Saville (ed.), 'The Management of the Royal Dockyards, 1672–1678', in N. A. M. Rodger (ed.), *The Naval Miscellany*, vol. V, *Publications of the Navy Records Society*, vol. CXXV (London, 1984), pp. 98, 141n. In the 1670s, for instance, at Charles II's behest, the Navy tried lead sheathing, which soon proved unsatisfactory. Only the King continued to believe otherwise, long after his dockyard officers concluded that it was a mistake. In early 1770 the Navy Board ordered the bottom of the fir-sheathed *Resolution* 'to be payed with Dr MacBride's Composition, composed of plaster of Paris, turpentine and rosin in equal proportions, the two former being melted together and the latter ground to a very fine powder into it so as to make the other two of a sufficient body and hardness and as the same time very adhesive to the sheathing'. PRO, ADM 106/2895, Navy Board to Deptford Officers, 2 February 1770.
6 The best study of copper sheathing is by R. J. B. Knight, 'The Introduction of Copper Sheathing into the Royal Navy, 1779–1786', *Mariner's Mirror*, 59 (1973), pp. 299–309. See also Arthur L. Cross, 'On Coppering Ships' Bottoms', *American Historical Review*, 33 (1926–28), pp. 79–81; J. R. Harris, 'Copper and Shipping in the Eighteenth Century', *Economic History Review*, 19 (1966), pp. 550–68; Gareth Rees, 'Copper Sheathing: An Example of Technological Diffusion in the English Merchant Fleet', *Journal of Transport History*, 1 (1971), pp. 85–94; Maurer Maurer, 'Coppered Bottoms for the Royal Navy: A Factor in the Maritime War of 1778–1783', *Military Affairs*, 14 (1950), pp. 57–61.

7 PRO, ADM 95/17, Navy Board to Deptford Dockyard, 16 October 1759; Navy Board to Portsmouth Dockyard, 16 October 1759.

8 William L. Clements Library, Ann Arbor, Michigan (hereafter WLC), Shelburne Papers, 144:22. Navy Board to Admiralty, 31 August 1763.

9 In October 1761 a large quantity of copper plates measuring 4 feet by 14 inches and weighing 12 ounces to the square foot was ordered to be delivered to the Woolwich Dockyard. PRO, ADM 106/2895. Thomas Slade's Rough Minute Book, 16 October 1761. I owe this reference to Dr N. A. M. Rodger.

10 *Gentlemen's Magazine*, 31 (November 1761), p. 533.

11 WLC, SP, 144:22, Navy Board to Admiralty, 31 August 1763.

12 Ibid.

13 NMM, ADM A/2557, Stephens to Navy Board, 7 March 1764.

14 PRO, ADM 51/4535, Log of the *Dolphin*, 14 May 1764.

15 Robert Gallagher (ed.), *Byron's Journal of His Circumnavigation, 1764–1766*, Hakluyt Society Publications, 2nd series, vol. CXII (Cambridge, 1964), p. 160. Egmont was First Lord of the Admiralty.

16 PRO, ADM 106/2895, Navy Board to Admiralty, 29 July 1768; PRO, ADM 106/3315. Deptford Officers to Navy Board, 25 July 1768. The Navy Board estimated the cost of repairing the *Dolphin*'s hull at £3,602.6s.4p, 'arising chiefly from being Obliged to Drive new Bolts and work that will be occasioned thereby'. ADM 106/2895, Navy Board to Admiralty, 29 July 1768. But consider the fate of the *Endeavour*, which Captain James Cook commanded on his first voyage of exploration to the Pacific. Fitted out in May 1768, she was not sheathed with copper. Off Tahiti (discovered on the *Dolphin*'s second voyage), her anchor stocks were 'eaten away to destruction by the worm'. Inspection of her hull in the Dutch yard in Batavia in October 1770 revealed that near the keel 'two planks and a half near 6 feet in length were within 1/8 of an inch of being cut through, and here the worms had made their way quite into the timbers, so that it was a Matter of Surprise to every one who saw her bottom how we had kept her above water; and yet in this condition we had sailed some hundreds of Leagues in as dangerous a navigation as in any part of the world, happy in being ignorant of the continual danger we were in'. Quoted in J. C. Beaglehole, *The Life of Captain James Cook* (Stanford, CA, 1974), pp. 130, 192, 262–3. The copper-sheathed *Dolphin* was in far better condition after completing two voyages to the Pacific than the fir-sheathed *Endeavour* in the middle of one such voyage. On this voyage, at least, the greatest of navigators was also one of the luckiest.

17 PRO, ADM 106/2895, Navy Board to Deptford Dockyard Officers, 25 July 1768.

18 WLC, SP, 144:22, Navy Board to Admiralty, 31 August 1763.

19 This is an estimate pieced together from PRO, ADM 180/4. Abstract of Progresses; ADM 95/84, A List of His Majesty's Royal Navy, When and Where Built, etc. See also John Fincham, *A History of Naval Architecture* (London, 1979) pp. 95–100.

20 NMM, SAN/T/8, Middleton to Sandwich, *Prince George*, Portsmouth Harbour, 6 January 1778.

21 *Barham Papers*, vol. III, p. 29.

22 Beaglehole, *Life of Cook*, pp. 281–2, 295–6. On Sandwich and coppering see N. A. M. Rodger's superb biography, *The Insatiable Earl: A Life of John Montagu, Fourth Earl of Sandwich, 1718–1792* (London, 1994), pp. 97, 295–9.

23 PRO, ADM 7/662, Sandwich Dockyard Visitation, 1775.

24 PRO, ADM 2/559, 19 September 1778; NMM, ADM/A/2731. 19 September 1778.

25 NMM, ADM/B/197, Navy Board to Admiralty, 29 September 1778.

26 J. J. Colledge, *Ships of the Royal Navy; An Historical Index*, 2 vols (Annapolis, MD, 1987–89), vol. I, pp. 196, 237.

27 'This method of sheathing was communicated to us', the Navy Board informed the

Admiralty, 'by Mr Fisher, a Ship Builder of Liverpool, who assured us that he covered the bottom of a merchant ship using the Guinea Trade from that port in this manner, which after being on for nine years was taken off, when the Iron Work was found to be unimpaired.' NMM, ADM/B/198, Navy Board to Admiralty, 27 January 1779.

28 NMM, POR/A/29, Portsmouth Dockyard Warrants, 8 January 1779.

29 PRO, ADM 2/561, Admiralty to Navy Board, 16 January 1779.

30 NMM, ADM/B/198, Navy Board to Admiralty, 27 January 1779. Instructions to Portsmouth Dockyard put the matter in considerably more detail. Copper sheets were 'to be painted with white lead on inner side and strips of painted cartridge paper cut to about one inch and a half broad are to be laid under the Nails at the Edges to prevent water getting in'. In the middle of the sheets, nails were to be driven 3 inches apart, and a 'small mallet to be used in driving punches, which are not to exceed the size of the pattern to be sent you. In laying on sheets, being from abaft, that all the Edges may lap over to the after part of the Ship, taking care to close them over with the Mallet, as much as may be … P.S. A piece of plank covered in the manner above described will be forwarded to you as a pattern.' On 13 January the *Sybil* (28), a brand-new sloop built in the famous Adams yard at Buckler's Hard, was ordered sheathed according to the new procedure. NMM, POR/A/29, Portsmouth Dockyard Warrants, 8 and 13 January 1779. Adams had already fitted the *Sybil* with copper-alloy braces and pintles, as presumably became standard practice on ships that merchant yards built on contract for the Navy. NMM, POR/A/28, 29 October 1778.

31 *Barham Papers*, vol. III, p. 29. According to his secretary J. D. Thomson's version of this interview, 'The great and important measure of coppering the Whole Navy in extending it to Line of Battle Ships was the result of a private interview between His Majesty, Lord Sandwich and Sir Charles at Buckingham House, as Lord S altho in every way friendly to the measure conceived it to be one of too bold a nature and so of too much importance to be carried into effect without H[is] M[ajesty's] direct Sanction'. NMM, MID/13/4, J. D. Thomson's memoir on Lord Barham. The model of the *Bellona* remained in Middleton's family until the National Maritime Museum purchased it in 1977. NMM, A. H. Waite, 'Catalogue of Ship Models', part I, 'Ships of the Western Tradition to 1815', looseleaf binder, p. 119. 'This model, commissioned to demonstrate the practice to the King, is the earliest known example of coppering on a contemporary model.' In December 1777 Sandwich sent the King, an avid naval buff, 'three bolts in the corroded state in which they were taken out of the *Jason* (32), which had had a copper bottom for about ten years'. John Fortescue (ed.), *The Correspondence of King George III*, 6 vols (London, 1967), vol. III, p. 509. Lord Sandwich to the King, 9 December 1777. In early 1778 the King witnessed the sheathing of the *Centaur*, which he pronounced, 'quite compleat, though begun only at five in the morning it was finished by twelve at Noon'. *Correspondence of King George the Third*, vol. IV, No. 2324, Memorandum of the King relative to a Journey to Portsmouth, 5 May 1778. On the *Bellona* see Brian Lavery, *The 74-Gun Ship Bellona* (London, 1985).

32 NMM, B/198, Navy Board to Admiralty, 27 January 1779.

33 A curious incident marked the transition to an operational program. On 10 February 1779 Captain Sir John Jervis wrote to the Navy Board urging the coppering of his ship the *Foudroyant*, a captured French 80. On Jervis's letter Middleton scribbled the endorsement 'Coppering of Ships is not left with this Board but lies with the Admiralty. We have no orders to Copper Line of Battle Ships.' PRO, ADM 106/128, Jervis to Navy Board, 10 February 1779. Strictly speaking this was true, but at the moment he rebuffed Jervis, Middleton was strenuously urging the Admiralty to issue just such orders. Evidently the sea officer later celebrated as Lord St Vincent should not have expected favors from the Controller known to him as the 'Scotch Packhorse'.

34 NMM, POR/A/29, Portsmouth Dockyard Warrants, 25 May and 9 July 1779.

35 Emphasis added.
36 G. R. Barnes and J. H. Owen (eds), *The Private Papers of John, Earl of Sandwich, First Lord of the Admiralty, 1771–1782*, 4 vols (London, 1932–37), vol. III, pp. 174–5 (hereafter *Sandwich Papers*).
37 *Sandwich Papers*, vol. III, p. 178, Middleton to Sandwich, 15 September 1779.
38 Navy Board warrants, however, frequently named several ships at once. On 11 January 1780, for example, Portsmouth dockyard officers were instructed to 'clean, sheathe with copper, refit and store for Channel service' no fewer than 11 ships of the line, including the *Victory* (100), *Duke* (90), *Namur* (90), *Union* (90), *Princess Amelia* (80), *Prince George* (90), *Thunderer* (74), *Centaur* (74), *Culloden* (74), *Valiant* (74) and *America* (64). NMM, POR/A/29, 11 January 1780.
39 NMM, POR/A/29, 20 November 1779.
40 These examples are among the countless references to copper in the standing orders of the Navy Board, on which Dr R. J. B. Knight kindly lent me his notes.
41 In his friend Captain Samuel Hood, Dockyard Commissioner at Portsmouth, Middleton had an eager and able ally. 'Your Majesty may firmly rely', Hood wrote to the King in December 1779, 'on the utmost exertion of every person in the department of the Dockyard, in carrying on the Equipments of Your Majesty's Ships, and I have full belief Sir, that the expedition that was used in coppering the *Sandwich* was never exceeded by any Artificers and I can venture to assure your Majesty, the same active and zealous disposition will ever prevail, not only in the Master Shipwright and his assistants, but in every subordinate person.' Samuel Hood to the King, 3 December 1779. *Correspondence of King George III*, vol. IV, No. 2866, p. 508.
42 *Barham Papers*, vol. III, p. 29.
43 NMM, ADM/BP/8, Navy Board to Admiralty, 4 February 1788. Prices paid for copper – for information of Lords of the Committee of the Privy Council appointed to inquire into the state of the coin of the realm. Numbers rounded off to the nearest pound.
44 Shipping by sea would have been far cheaper, of course, but the relative locations of copper smitheries and yards, as well as considerations of security – the fear that a seaborne strategic material might fall into enemy hands – apparently made land transport preferable. Between 26 February and 4 August 1779 one contractor made 21 shipments of copper sheets 'by land carriage'. NMM, POR/A/29, Portsmouth Dockyard Warrants, 9 August 1779.
45 PRO, ADM 106/1256, Chatham Dockyard Officers to Navy Board, 9 January 1780.
46 Dawson not only supplied the Navy with his composition; he and his brother, who served as his only helper, themselves applied it to the entire stock of copper sheets issued to the Portsmouth and Plymouth yards. NMM, POR/A/29, 14 February, 7 March 1780.
47 NMM, POR/J/2, Progress, etc.
48 NMM, MID/9/5, Lists of Ships. Middleton's mistaken arithmetic gave him a total of 226.
49 NMM, ADM/BP/2, 22 February 1781, 'An Account shewing the increas'd Debt of the Navy on 31st December 1780 with the Reasons for the said Increase'; ADM/BP/3, 13 February 1782, 'An Account shewing the Increase of the Debt of H. M. Navy on the 31st December 1781'.
50 According to a list kept in the King's own hand, these included the 74s *Invincible*, *Hector*, *Courageux*, *Defence*, *Bedford* and *Shrewsbury*, and the 64-gun *Bienfaisant*. *Correspondence of George III*, IV, No. 2724, p. 401. The much greater speed of the seven coppered ships may have made a fleet in company even more difficult to handle. Rodger, *Insatiable Earl*, p. 296.
51 *Sandwich Papers*, vol. IV, p. 286.
52 Rodger, *The Insatiable Earl*, p. 298.

53 Charles James Fox, who led the parliamentary attack on Sandwich, was much too clever to engage the First Lord on ground so favorable to him – or so boring to the country gentlemen – as administration; instead, Fox limited his offensive to the conduct of recent naval operations, blaming Sandwich for consequences the head of the Admiralty could neither have foreseen nor controlled. Piers Mackesy, *The War for America* (Cambridge, MA, 1964), pp. 460–8.
54 *Sandwich Papers*, vol. IV, pp. 285–7.
55 Richard Ollard, *Pepys: A Biography* (London, 1974), p. 81.

4

Trying the Carronade

'In this war', Napoleon I wrote to his minister of marine in 1805, 'the English have been the first to use carronades, and everywhere they have done us great harm. We must hasten to perfect their system, for the argument is all on one side for sea service in favor of the system of large calibers.'[1] An expert artilleryman, but never at home in naval matters, the Emperor may have allowed himself to be too impressed. During Middleton's tenure at the Navy Office the carronade provoked argument on all sides. Some questioned its merits, others doubted its usefulness, still others disagreed over its purposes. It remained an experimental weapon as the American war drew to a close. Debate over the carronade's contribution to Britain's wars at sea continues to this day.

The carronade was a bulldog of a naval gun: short, squat, ugly and extremely effective at close range. Much shorter and lighter than the artillery piece – the long cannon – generally in use in the Navy, it used less powder, owing to a better fit between ball and bore, to fire a bigger and heavier shot. Instead of the small-wheeled carriage that cradled the long cannon, the carronade nestled in a low, slotted platform called a slide.

Several kinds of Scots enterprise figured in the carronade's introduction into the Navy. A Scot invented the gun, a Scottish company made it, and the Scot Charles Middleton championed its adoption by the naval service. Credit for inventing the carronade usually goes to the soldier and polymath Robert Melville, who in the 1750s turned his attention to the improvement of ordnance.[2] Putting Melville's invention into production, however, awaited other inventions, especially John Wilkinson's cylinder-boring machine. Previously cannon had been cast in a mold surrounding a core – the bore of the gun – that molten iron invariably distorted and displaced. No two of them were quite alike. Wilkinson's machine bored out barrels cast as solid pieces of iron.[3] The new technique enabled guns to be made with the thin casing and truer bore essential to the carronade.

The cylinder-boring machine promised obvious military benefits not only at sea but on land. For instance, the gargantuan proportions of older cannon, owned and serviced by civilian contractors, largely confined them to siege warfare. Lighter, more uniform guns opened new tactical vistas, and in the middle decades of the eighteenth century forerunners of Wilkinson's machine spread across Europe. For no eighteenth-century government was willing to concede a competitive edge to its likely antagonists. Such ambitious newcomers to the armed rivalries of the continent as Prussia and Russia believed that they could not be without the new invention.

The improvement of artillery followed two patterns. In France, for instance, the state took the lead. In the 1760s Jean-Baptiste de Gribeauval combined the new technology with new forms of organization to create field units capable of keeping up with the infantry. Internal army quarrels delayed until the late 1780s the implementation of Gribeauval's reforms, but Napoleon came to wield with devastating effect the instrument a soldier of the Old Regime had created. And Gribeauval's state-sponsored program of weapons development foreshadowed a far more distant future.

The other – and far more widespread – pattern of eighteenth-century improvement saw private entrepreneurs assume the risks of research and development, in the hope of winning from governments big contracts for big guns and other weapons. This pattern prevailed in Prussia, Russia, in seventeenth-century France, and in the production of the carronade.

The Carron Iron Company assembled a cylinder-boring machine – apparently without asking John Wilkinson's permission – not long after the great ironmaster acquired his patent in 1774. Indeed, the company was up to date in every way. On the banks of the Scottish estuary whence the firm and its gun took their names, invention met entrepreneurship. Established in 1760 with a view to exploiting the munitions market generated by the Seven Years War, the Carron foundry was meant from the outset to be a big operation. Combining mining, smelting and forging in one enterprise, it was the first in Scotland to smelt with coke and the first successfully to use native iron ore (its skilled gunfounders, however, were initially imported from Sussex). Soon it established itself as the leading foundry in Europe.[4]

However, the Carron company got off to a shaky start. Badly undercapitalized, it drove William Cadell and Samuel Garbett, two of its three founding partners (along with Dr John Roebuck), into bankruptcy. Aggressive price-cutting landed the Carron works early contracts, but the poor quality of its wares caused it frequent embarrassment. In 1767, for instance, some cannon from Carron were landed in London. Samuel Garbett reported home, 'I was ashamed to see them because they are a disgrace to the works … I fear the [Ordnance] Board will have nothing to do with us.'[5] Garbett's fears soon came true. In 1771 the Ordnance Board complained that too many Carron guns burst when fired. After 36 of 133 of them – 27 per cent – failed to pass trials at Woolwich in May 1773, the Carron Company was ordered to cease casting cannon; Carron guns were removed from all naval vessels.[6]

So the cylinder-boring machine came along in the nick of time. Indeed, since the carronade promised to deter small-time privateering, the huge British merchant fleet offered a better market than the government did.[7] The new weapon could serve a merchant ship as a shotgun serves a chicken farmer. A privateer, like a fox, had to get close to its prey; neither predator was likely to risk serious injury for the sake of one victim.

Charles Middleton saw the carronade's promise as a shipboard weapon. Middleton knew Charles Gascoigne, manager of the Carron works and an entrepreneur of shady reputation, and their acquaintanceship raises the question – to which there is no answer – whether Middleton's professional interest in the carronade was amplified by a financial stake in the Carron Company. In any event, in making the case for the carronade, Middleton employed the same line of argument that he used in urging the coppering of the fleet: like coppering, carronades would compensate for the Franco-Spanish advantage in ships of the line. In early July 1779, on the eve of the Combined Fleet's appearance in the Channel, the Ordnance Board[8] conducted carronade trials at Woolwich Arsenal, giving Middleton a chance to make his case.[9] On 8 July Lord Sandwich forwarded to the King a memorandum setting forth 'the Comptroller's ideas concerning the Canonades'.[10]

Never hesitant to jump to broad conclusions, the Controller read the Woolwich experiments as evidence that the carronade would make an excellent auxiliary weapon for '*all* ships'.[11] For one thing, it could be installed on forecastles and poops, the uppermost fore and aft decks of a naval vessel, which could not bear the much heavier weight of long cannon. For another, a carronade required a crew of only two men, Middleton (under) estimated, as opposed to a long gun's 11 or 12. Moreover, it never over-heated, despite firing twice as rapidly as a conventional cannon. In short, the carronade offered a means of quickly and cheaply offsetting the superiority in numbers of ships, manpower and firepower of the combined Franco-Spanish fleet. 'They are the best Improvement hitherto proposed',

Middleton insisted, 'and if added to the guns already established on our smaller ships, they will be rendered superior in force to any of the same Size belonging to the Enemy, without the necessity of other ways augmenting their Sizes, and adding to their Numbers of Men.'[12]

The gun would be most useful, Middleton believed, in depriving ships of their ability to maneuver. Loaded with canisters filled with a mixture of small balls and langridge (a kind of scrap-metal shrapnel capable of inflicting horrendous wounds), the carronade would shred sails and rigging, rather than holing them, leaving the enemy dead in the water. Not incidentally, langridge would also sweep sharpshooters down from the enemy's tops.

> Upon the whole [the Controller concluded], this seems the moment for embracing every Improvement that can be offered in the Naval line, and as far as my Judgment reaches, these Carronades if properly used with grape, case, or langrage shot, on our Quarter Decks and Poops, and Howitzers in the Tops, will if not too long delayed give us a great Superiority over the Enemy in all Naval Actions.[13]

If the Admiralty did not entirely share Middleton's enthusiasm (Lord Mulgrave, who was serving at sea, especially had doubts),[14] on 15 July 1779 it simultaneously asked the Ordnance Board to acquire carronades and ordered ships to be furnished with them as they came in for refitting. Middleton apparently had the Navy Board solidly behind him. For no sooner had the Woolwich trials been completed than the dockyards were supplied with a table showing the number of carronades to be established on each class of ship, from first rates down through sloops. With the exception of 28-gun frigates, which for some reason were limited to six of them, all were to have between eight and ten 12-pounders. Frigates carrying between 32 and 44 long cannon were to be fitted with beefier 18-pounder carronades, perhaps an expression of Middleton's idea – never carried into effect – for putting at least the 44s in the line of battle.[15]

As it turned out, in the early days most ships carried about half as many of the still-experimental weapons as the Navy Board recommended. For one thing, many ships had less space available than the Board realized. Some frigate captains reported that a few of their carronades were so placed as to risk shooting away their own rigging.[16] For another, the slides made in the dockyards often split, causing the carronade to jump from its mount and risk serious injury to its crew. Muzzle flashes sometimes set stowed hammocks afire or scorched gunport sills.[17] No two captains agreed as to how many carronades their ships could carry, so the Board soon gave up trying to establish numbers for each rate and ordered the dockyards to comply with all 'reasonable requests' to carry fewer than was first proposed.[18]

Soon, however, commanding officers besieged the Navy Board with requests for more and bigger carronades. In a society as small and insular as the Navy, word travelled fast, and competition among sea officers was fierce, so the new gun must have benefitted from favorable reports. In December 1779 the Navy Board gave the coppering of the Western Squadron's ships of the line precedence over fitting them with carronades, but countless smaller vessels had already been equipped with the weapon. Confident of seeing its own good judgement vindicated, the Board urged the Admiralty in March 1780 to petition the Ordnance Board for additional trials on 24-, 18-, and 12-pounder carronades – 'in presence', it added, 'of some Sea Officers of Experience'.[19] Evidently the Navy Office felt that the artillery officers who conducted such tests bore watching. The Ordnance Board's tendency to believe that it knew best respecting all matters under its purview infuriated sea officers, who felt similarly about their own sphere of competence, in which they included the guns they employed at sea.

If the Navy Board expected the Ordnance Board merely to confirm its own high opinion of carronades, it was badly disappointed. The trials, which commenced at Landguard Fort on 18 July 1780, matched 6-pounder, 4-pounder, and 3-pounder long cannons against the carronades in question. It was not a great day for the Carron Company. The 24-pounder carronade cracked on firing its first round and had to be replaced. The breeching (restraining ropes running from a gun carriage through ring bolts on either side of a gunport) of the 18-pounder parted under the strain of firing a second round.[20] Toward the end of October 1780 the Ordnance Board informed the Admiralty that 'these Experiments have confirmed our opinion that Carronades are of little use in the Royal Navy'. In mid December Philip Stephens asked the Navy Board whether it agreed with the artillery experts that 'the guns have greatly the preference and that Carronades are of little use in the Royal Navy', and 'whether it may not be adviseable to retrench so heavy and unnecessary an expense'.[21]

The artillerymen, the Navy Board angrily replied, had compared apples with oranges. No one questioned the superiority of cannon over carronades at long range. But the Navy Board was interested in the carronade's qualities as a close-in, auxiliary weapon. Nothing was like them for slashing rigging and sails, generating splinters and killing men. The Commissioners had requested Ordnance Board trials in the first place, the memorandum explained, because several captains of smaller vessels – cutters and brigs – had asked to exchange all their guns for carronades (hardly an argument for auxiliary weapons, the chief emphasis of their reply to the Ordnance Board). The real question, the Navy Board went on, was not whether guns were better than carronades but whether the latter 'are any addition to the present strength of our ships'. Carronades, it insisted, 'ought not to be condemned on account of their inferiority to cannon, which cannot be added if these are taken away, and particularly at this juncture when the enemy are so strong and numerous at sea'. Knowing that on discrediting the Ordnance Board's report the carronade's future probably depended, the Navy Board went for the clincher. Experience with the carronade at sea, under the real conditions of naval warfare, it declared, was far more telling than experiments contrived on land. The advantages of carronades 'have been so frequently confirmed by the Reports of Officers who have tried them in action and are so strongly corroborated by the increased Number of applications made in consequence of them that We continue firm in our first Opinion [here Middleton's voice can be heard], that they are the best improvement hitherto proposed for increasing the strength of Frigates and Sloops and rendering them superior to those of the Enemy without the necessity of adding to their complement of Men'. Perhaps the captain of every ship furnished with carronades should be directed to send the Navy Board reports on his experience with them in close action – the implication being that the opinions of sea officers in such matters were far more trustworthy than those of landbound artillerymen.[22] The Admiralty could hardly be expected to demur.

In the clash between Ordnance Board and Navy Board, preconceived opinions collided. The Ordnance Board admitted that the experiments at Landguard Fort 'confirmed' its low opinion of the weapon. When these same tests failed to produce the results the Navy Board counted on, the Commissioners denounced them. The Ordnance Board did not let the matter drop without hinting that it suspected the Navy Commissioners of soliciting reports only from known partisans of the carronade. 'We beg leave to assure your Lordships', they concluded, 'that we entertain no Prejudices for or against the Carronade any more than the Commissioners of the Navy but make our Experiments most impartially and transmit them as faithfully described.'[23]

Insinuations of bad faith did not keep the Navy Board from parrying the Ordnance Board's challenge to the carronade. Endorsements from commanding officers were plentiful enough to convince the Admiralty of

Middleton's and his colleagues' sound judgement. Middleton liked to point to the testimonial of Captain John MacBride, of the *Bienfaisant* (64), whose 12-pounder carronades, loaded with grape, kept the *Artois* from using small arms. 'No musquetry on the Poop, Gangways, or Tops', MacBride reported, 'can withstand them in Close Action and even out of Musquet Shot.'[24] Experiences such as MacBride's, as Middleton expected, no doubt encouraged captains to ask for carronades for their own ships. In April 1782, the Carron works reported that it was casting and finishing between 60 and 80 carronades a week, having devoted nearly its entire productive capacity to the gun. By the end of July 1782, when the American war was virtually over, 157 vessels, including 36 ships of the line and 63 frigates, had been equipped with the new weapon.[25]

Nearly all these ships mounted only a few carronades, reflecting their status as auxiliary weapons. Some people, however, began suggesting that if a few carronades were good, a lot would be even better. They pushed for using them as a main battery. Middleton initially had his doubts about this, chiefly owing to their low muzzle velocity, but he soon came round to thinking there might be something to the idea. Reports of the carronade's effectiveness in action probably helped encourage the thought that a ship fitted with many such large-caliber guns would be capable of inflicting even greater damage, not only on sails, rigging and personnel, but also against hulls. Indeed, in such a role the carronade earned its reputation as 'The Smasher', the famous nickname for which William James's classic *Naval History* credits General Robert Melville himself.[26]

Carron Company officials knew a good business opportunity when they saw one. A paper comparing a 74-gun ship of the line armed entirely with carronades with a conventionally armed 74 found its way from the Carron works to the Controller. In place of the conventional 74's array of cannons, the hypothetical ship would mount 30 68-pounder carronades, 30 42-pounders and 14 32-pounders. The guns of the conventional 74 weighed 158 tons, required 744 men to work them and consumed five barrels of gunpowder firing a 1,400-pound broadside. The all-carronade 74's guns would weigh 94 tons, require 368 men to work them and use up three barrels of powder in firing a 3,300-pound broadside. So to Middleton's correspondent, at least, an all-carronade 74 looked superior in every way: a main battery weighing less, demanding a smaller crew and burning up less powder would hurl a broadside twice the weight of a long-cannon 74's at twice the rate of fire.[27] In short, the carronade would produce what in a later time and place would be called 'more bang for the buck'.

Economy and efficiency impressed Middleton as much as firepower did, and with a view to making better use of Britain's scarcest resources – men and ships – he pushed for arming some ships of the line entirely with carronades. The occasion was the fear that France and Holland, its recently acquired ally, threatened in the spring of 1782 to dominate the North Sea. How was a navy already spread too thin to meet this new challenge? The Navy Board proposed countering the Franco-Dutch threat with some old 74s equipped with carronades. Its light weight and small crew, not its heavy shot, recommended the carronade. For carronades would lessen the strain on the timbers of the barely-seaworthy ships the Navy Board designated for this duty and, by requiring half the usual complements, merely skim a dangerously shallow pool of manpower. Despite generating much correspondence and some work in the dockyards, this scheme apparently never went as far as putting all-carronade ships to sea – perhaps because Sandwich, who strongly supported it, had left office.[28]

If making the most of scarce resources seemed to recommend the carronade for emergency purposes, the Navy Board emphasized firepower when it turned to the question of long-term employment. Recommending that two 68-pounders (the Carron Company was already urging 130-pounders on the Navy) be installed in the forecastles of all ships capable of bearing them, the Board in December 1781 asked the Admiralty to approve the testing with the *Rainbow* (44) of Middleton's notion that armaments consisting entirely of carronades might 'increase … the number of ships capable of acting in a line of battle'.[29]

The *Rainbow* experiment took place at the Nore, the fleet anchorage at the mouth of the Thames, at the end of July 1782, in the presence of Commander Charles Stirling and six captains (including Middleton's good friend Adam Duncan). The Navy Board spared itself the Ordnance officers' tiresome objections to the carronade by neglecting to invite them to attend. A few of the 46 carronades on board – 20 68-pounders, 20 42-pounders and six 12-pounders – were fired at flagged casks moored at ranges of between 600 and 1,500 yards; the new weapon's accuracy, the report said, 'surprized all present'. Only once, though, were all the *Rainbow*'s carronades fired simultaneously. Indeed, an Ordnance officer might have found something odd in an experiment that withheld the test of brute firepower – a broadside of 1,238 pounds as opposed to the 318 pounds of the frigate's conventional armament – for which it had ostensibly been arranged.[30]

The *Rainbow* soon got her chance at sea, however. Under the command of Captain Henry Trollope, she encountered the *Hébé* (40) off the Ile de

Bas on 4 September 1782. According to Charles Duncan, the *Rainbow*'s master, her carronades as good as intimidated the French frigate into striking her flag. Firing from the forecastle only one 32-pounder, the *Rainbow* landed several shots on board as the *Hébé* crossed her bow, killing the first lieutenant and helmsman and evidently taking the fight out of the French. Amazed and disheartened to see such heavy shot fired from a forecastle gun, they fired a face-saving broadside and surrendered to Trollope.[31]

Firing one 32-pounder no more made the case for an all-carronade ship than sighting one swallow makes the case for summer. As it turned out, the war came to a close without providing any more opportunities for testing such an armament in action. With an eye to the return of peace, the Admiralty in March 1783 ordered carronades removed from the forecastles and quarterdecks of such ships as were to be kept in commission, so as to ease the strain on their timbers.[32] Not until a decade later, when Middleton had left the Navy Office and war with France broke out once again, did experiments with carronades resume.

Middleton's sweeping claims for coppering and the carronade exaggerated their merits. Impatient of criticism, he brushed aside the reservations of superiors and subordinates who worried about corroded bolts and Ordnance officers skeptical of the carronade's promise. He was a convincing advocate and he prevailed against his critics. Constantly reiterating his warning that the risk of losing a major encounter at sea outweighed the dangers of innovation, he persuaded the Navy to adopt, at the height of a great war, an untried technique for preserving ships' bottoms and an untested weapon. The great encounter Middleton warned against never took place. Nevertheless, his persistence helped to ensure that when the last great naval war with France came along in 1792, coppered bottoms and the carronade were established equipment.

A postscript is in order. For British naval victories in the wars of the French Revolution and Napoleon by no means stilled the debate over the carronade. Such a light, powerful, rapid-firing and easily manned gun, one advocate wrote in 1801, deserved to find wide employment as the main armament of two- and three-decked ships.[33] So Middleton had argued during the war for America. In 1804 Rear-Admiral Henry Trollope, erstwhile captain of the *Rainbow*, proposed a North Sea fleet fitted out entirely with carronades – the same scheme the Navy Board had put forward in 1781. And to such arguments the Ordnance Board continued

THE PEN AND INK SAILOR

to object. Conceding the carronade's value as an auxiliary weapon, the Board nevertheless had no use for it as the main armament of ships of the line. Prone to causing fires aboardship, firing less rapidly than its proponents claimed, the carronade offered less versatility than cannon, at greater risk to guncrews. Such plans as Trollope's, the Ordnance officers insisted, encouraged the sending of unsafe ships to sea.[34] Nothing could have been more irksome to sea officers than landsmen passing judgement on their seamanship. In any event, the Ordnance Board's strictures did not cause the Navy to cease arming ships of the line entirely with carronades. As a primary armament, the 'smasher' worked to best advantage when commanding officers followed Nelson's celebrated tactical advice: 'No captain can do very wrong if he places his Ship alongside that of an Enemy.'[35] Indeed, captains may have taken Nelson's counsel too much to heart. Neglecting the subtler arts of gunnery in favor of the carronade's devastating close-range power may have contributed to the relatively poor showing the British made in single-ship actions against the Americans in the War of 1812.[36] As has often been the case in the history of weaponry, obsolesence, not lessons gained in warfare, finally ended the debate over the carronade. Steam power diminished its role as a disabler of sails and rigging. Armor plate left the low-velocity 'smasher' with nothing to smash.

NOTES

1 Quoted in John Terrain, *Trafalgar* (London, 1976), p. 29.
2 *Dictionary of National Biography*, vol. XIII, pp. 246–7; Henry Hamilton, *The Industrial Revolution in Scotland* (London, 1932), p. 159n, discusses the controversy over inventorship.
3 For a discussion of eighteenth-century innovations in gun-making, see William H. McNeill, *The Pursuit of Power; Technology, Armed Force and Society since AD1000* (Chicago, IL, 1982), pp. 166–77.
4 Patrick H. Campbell, *The Carron Company* (London, 1961); Patrick H.Campbell, *Scotland since 1707: The Rise of An Industrial Society*, 2nd edn (Edinburgh, 1985), pp. 55–6; Henry Hamilton, *An Economic History of Scotland in the Eighteenth Century* (Oxford, 1963), pp. 193–6.
5 Hamilton, *The Industrial Revolution in Scotland* p. 158.
6 Campbell, *Scotland since 1707*, p. 56; Hamilton, *Economic History of Scotland*, p. 199. The Admiralty's suspicions of the Carron Company died hard. On learning from the *Bedford*'s captain that he believed her guns had been made by the Carron Company, their Lordships on 17 January 1778 ordered the Navy Board to 'inspect [them] immediately and exchange for others if they are found to be of the Carron Foundry'. Advised that the *Martin* sloop's guns were supplied by Carron, the Admiralty on 3 February ordered others to be supplied. PRO, ADM 2/556.
7 Bruce Lenman, *An Economic History of Modern Scotland, 1660–1976* (London, 1976), p. 130, makes this suggestion.

8   Responsible for testing and supplying guns and ammunition employed on land and sea, the gentlemen of the Ordnance were independent of both the Army and the Navy; they took their independence very seriously indeed.

9   A 9-pounder long cannon and a 9-pounder carronade were each fired at two bulkheads, 2-feet thick and 15 yards apart, meant to represent the sides of a 74-gun ship. NMM, ADM/B/199, Navy Board to Admiralty, 28 June 1779. The report of Captain Daniel Grose, Royal Artillery, is included among Middleton's papers. NMM, MID/9/2.

10 John Fortescue (ed.), *The Correspondence of King George III from 1760 to December 1783*, 6 vols (London, 1927–28), vol. IV, No. 2704, p. 389.

11 NMM, MID/9/2, Middleton's emphasis.

12 Ibid.

13 Ibid.

14 G. R. Barnes and J. H. Owen (eds), *The Private Papers of John, Earl of Sandwich, First Lord of the Admiralty, 1771–1782*, 4 vols (London, 1932–37), vol. IV, pp. 413–22, including dispute with Mulgrave (hereafter *Sandwich Papers*).

15 The table of carronades is in NMM, ADM/B/199, Navy Board to Admiralty, 13 July 1779; the directions to the yards are in NMM, POR/A/29, 16 July 1779.

16 NMM, POR/A/29, 28 Dec 1779.

17 NMM, POR/A/30, 9 November 1781.

18 NMM, ADM/B/200, Navy Board to Admiralty, 22 January 1780; POR/A/29, 24 January 1780.

19 NMM, ADM BP/1, Navy Board to Admiralty, 20 March 1780.

20 PRO, ADM 7/940, 'A General Comparative Abstract of the Round Shot Experiments with Carronades and Sea Service Iron Guns carried on at Landguard Fort in July and August 1780 under the direction of Lieut Colonel Abraham Tovey'.

21 NMM, BP/1, 18 December 1780; NMM MID/9/2, Ordnance Board to Admiralty, 21 October 1780; Philip Stephens to Navy Board, 15 December 1780.

22 NMM MID/9/2, Navy Board to Admiralty, 18 December 1780.

23 PRO, ADM 1/4013, Ordnance Board to Admiralty, 30 December 1780.

24 NMM, MID/9/2, MacBride to Navy Board, 12 January 1781. Middleton was so taken with MacBride's letter that he copied it out in his own hand.

25 NMM, MID/9/2, 'List of Ships Supplied with Carronades as of 22 July 1782'.

26 William James, *The Naval History of Great Britain, from the Declaration of War by France in 1793 to the Accession of George IV*, 6 vols (London, 1837), vol. I, p. 33.

27 NMM, MID/9/2, undated, but probably 1781.

28 'As it is of the utmost consequence to the King's Service that every Ship that can be brought forward should be employed on Home or Foreign Service', the Navy Board wrote to the Portsmouth Yard, 'We direct you to consider [whether] the Ships named in the margin [*Royal William, Elizabeth, Grafton, Essex, Modeste* and *Firm*] … might not be made capable of going into the North Sea for the Summer Season, to carry Carronades instead of their proper guns', NMM, POR/A/30, 12 February, 23 February, 9 March, 19 March, 27 May 1782. In early autumn Portsmouth Yard was ordered to put cannon back on board *Elizabeth*, NMM, POR/A/30, 9 October 1782.

29 PRO, ADM 106/2209, Navy Board to Admiralty, 28 December 1781.

30 NMM, MID/9/2, 'Report of Trials made at the Nore the 31st day of July 1782 on Board the Rainbow'.

31 NMM, MID/9/2/. The copy of Duncan's letter in Middleton's file is dated Plymouth, 11 September 1782. On the engagement see also James, *Naval History*, vol. I, p. 37.

32 PRO, ADM 106/2210, Admiralty to Navy Board, 11 March 1783; NMM POR/A/30, Navy Board to Portsmouth Yard, 18 March 1783.

33 Scottish Record Office (SRO), GD/51/2/167/2, Bentham to Melville, 22 February 1801.

34 SRO, GD51/2/167/1, Ordnance Board to Lord Melville, 29 May 1804.

35 From the so-called '1805 Cádiz Memorandum', quoted in Nicholas Tracy, *Nelson's Battles: The Art of Victory in the Age of Sail* (London, 1996), p. 208, as it appears in William Beatty, *Authentic Narrative of the Death of Lord Nelson* (London, 1807), pp. 89–93. Beatty was Nelson's personal physician.
36 Such a suggestion is made by the author of the entry 'guns, naval' in Peter Kemp (ed.), *The Oxford Companion to Ships and the Sea* (Oxford, 1976), pp. 363–4.

5

Thinking about War at Sea

As a decidedly junior post-captain, Charles Middleton did not hesitate to give tactical advice to the commander-in-chief of the Leeward Islands station.[1] Surely, the horseback ruminations of Mrs Bouverie's estate manager occasionally strayed from crops and livestock to tactics and strategy. Returned to active duty, Middleton engaged in a voluminous correspondence on the conduct of the American war with a wide circle of friends serving at sea. But, it was one thing to exchange views privately with old shipmates; it was another for the Controller of the Navy to urge on the First Lord of the Admiralty a particular line of strategy. For Middleton's authority ran only to the civil side of the Navy. The military side, the responsibility to 'advise the Government on the use of the navy as an instrument of policy',[2] lay with the Admiralty Board. Middleton had an ampler notion of his duties.[3] 'The office I am in is of that nature as to see every branch of the service and how it is conducted', Middleton claimed. 'My zeal for its success', he confessed, 'often carries me out of my own line.'[4]

Middleton's bustling self-confidence, his conviction that he owed amateurs in sea affairs the benefit of his professional judgement (never mind that Lord Sandwich had been in and out of the Admiralty since 1744), drove the Controller to proffer advice that had not been asked for. Whatever Middleton liked to think, however, it was less as landsman to sailor that Sandwich listened to him than as a master politician always careful to solicit a variety of views. On at least one occasion the First Lord made this plain. Locked in a tiresome and seemingly interminable struggle with the Controller over dockyard appointments, an exasperated Sandwich finally wrote,

> I shall continue to ask information from you, as I have done ever since you have been comptroller of the navy, in matters *both within and without*

the cognisance of the navy board. This has been my method, in every branch
of business in which I have been concerned, to gain knowledge from
men of ability who I thought were likely to give me useful instruction.
No one comes more fully under that description than yourself.[5]

As every politician knew, listening to advice differed from acting on it.

The war at sea, already going badly when Middleton went to the Navy
Office in late summer 1778, worsened as the French readied more big
ships. In March 1779 came news of Spain's intervention. 'We have no one
friend or ally to assist us', Sandwich wrote to the King. 'On the contrary
all those who ought to be our allies, except Portugal, act against us in
supplying our enemies with the means of equipping their fleets.'[6] French
advocates of invading Britain saw the opportunity they had dreamed of for
years. Stripped of its fanciful elements and such bizarre secret agents as
the Chevalier Charles d'Éon, the plan the French and the Spanish government at length approved was simple. Under a unified command the French
and Spanish naval forces would seize control of the Channel and land
troops on the Isle of Wight, at Portsmouth and possibly also Plymouth or
Cornwall. What was to happen next remained a trifle uncertain. Some
argued that Britain, deprived of a major naval base and in the grip of
financial panic, would sue for peace; others maintained that severing
arteries was not enough: only striking at the heart, the capital, would do.
In any event, Britain's enemies had to establish control of the Channel long
enough to put troops ashore.[7]

Vice-Admiral Louis Guillouet, Comte d'Orvilliers, who commanded
the French fleet at the battle off Ushant, sailed from Brest on 4 June to try
his luck again. Not until 23 July did the last elements of the Spanish fleet
rendezvous with his 30 ships, bringing the combined fleet to a total of
56 ships of the line. At most, Britain could scrape together 39 line-of-battle
ships for the defense of the home islands. And as d'Orvilliers made his
rendezvous, the Royal Navy was not only outnumbered at sea but divided
within.

Vice-Admiral Augustus Keppel had arrived home from Ushant
muttering that Vice-Admiral Hugh Palliser, his second-in-command, had
failed adequately to support him. Once Keppel's friend, Palliser was also
Sandwich's friend and protégé, and when in 1775 he had received the
sinecure of the Lieutenant-Generalcy of Marines that Keppel wanted badly
for himself, Keppel quarrelled with Sandwich. Moreover, Keppel did not
allow commanding the Channel fleet to get in the way of his opposing the
American war and the North ministry. These politico-social passions stoked

the debate over who was to blame for the inconclusive outcome at Ushant. When Keppel's complaints about Palliser reached the newspapers, Palliser published his own list of allegations and demanded a court martial for Keppel.

The Admiralty perhaps rather too quickly acceded to Palliser's foolhardy request. Keppel was charged with attacking the enemy before his own line of battle was formed and then with failing to do his utmost, once fighting began, to destroy the French fleet. These capital charges raised the ghost of Admiral John Byng, shot by firing squad on his own quarterdeck, scapegoated for having failed to relieve the British garrison at Minorca. But Keppel enjoyed too much sympathy from fellow officers and too many connections in politics to fear Byng's fate. A court convened at Portsmouth Dockyard acquitted Keppel, a verdict the London mob celebrated by pillaging Palliser's house.

Determined to discredit the whispers that he had skulked while Keppel fought, Palliser asked for his own court martial. Without specific charges on which to rule, the court found his conduct at Ushant not only unblame-worthy but meritorious. Nevertheless, he was ruined. He had no prospect of ever hoisting his flag at sea again.[8] Keppel was not finished. Deliberately provoking the Admiralty into ordering him to haul down his flag, he triggered the resignations of Vice-Admiral Sir Robert Harland, a divisional commander at Ushant, and several of his captains. Having already divided the Navy, the affair decapitated the Channel fleet at a moment of looming peril.

Where did Middleton stand in all this? It is impossible to say. His close working relationship with Sandwich, his high regard for such Admiralty colleagues as Captain Lord Mulgrave, might have inclined him toward Palliser; yet friends such as Adam Duncan and John Laforey championed Keppel; still others, such as Samuel Hood and Richard Kempenfelt, refused to take sides.[9] Either Middleton had no opinion about the Keppel–Palliser affair – which seems unlikely in a man who held such strong opinions about so many things – or else he was careful to keep his views to himself, not only in 1779 but later, for his papers contain not a word of his own about the affair.

In any case, the refusal of Keppel's friends to succeed him prolonged the search for a new commander-in-chief. Finally, Vice-Admiral Sir Charles Hardy offered to exchange the governorship of Greenwich Hospital for command of the Channel fleet. Volunteering a snug berth ashore against the chance of death or disgrace in the Channel was an extraordinary gesture, and a grateful Sandwich accepted. Like Sir John Hawkins in 1588, Hardy hoisted his flag in a *Victory*; like Hawkins, he had not been to sea in 20 years. At 64, however, the amiable Sir Charles was in uncertain health. So Richard Kempenfelt was placed at his elbow as Flag Captain. An exceptional naval thinker as well as a great seaman, Kempenfelt contributed to his profession improvements in matters ranging from signalling, gunnery and tactics to shipboard discipline.[10]

Kempenfelt believed he had been sent aboard the *Victory*, however, chiefly to prop up Sir Charles. Here he may have uncharacteristically given himself more credit than he deserved. 'My situation is extremely disagreeable', he wrote to Middleton on 2 July 1779. 'I would give all the little I am worth to be out of it.'[11] Kempenfelt's disagreeable situation was his friend's extraordinary opportunity. For Middleton's private correspondence with the flag captain gave the Controller a timelier sense of realities in the Channel than Hardy's reports gave Sandwich. Middleton was quick to exploit the opening his superior intelligence from the *Victory* afforded him. Having already ventured to chide Sandwich for not working hard enough, he also hinted that such leisurely habits practically compelled the Controller to mind the First Lord's business as well as his own. 'All I can do at the navy office will avail but little', he wrote, 'if the admiralty continues what it is at present. It is, indeed, so wretchedly bad, that, if I waited for official orders and kept within the mere line of duty, without pressing or proposing what ought to come unasked for, we must inevitably stand still.'[12]

Middleton lost no time crossing the mere line of duty. 'It is going out of my line, my Lord', he conceded to Sandwich on 9 July, 'to say anything of Sir Charles Hardy's fleet; but it occupies so much of my thoughts that I flatter myself you will forgive my saying that I dread the consequences of so much superiority in number as is like to be on the side of the enemy.'[13] Throughout the crisis, he evidently never explained to the First Lord how he managed to keep himself so well informed on the situation in the Channel from his office on Tower Hill. At any rate, Middleton's fear of seeing Hardy outfoxed as well as outgunned also prompted his recommendations to Sandwich. From the *Victory*, Kempenfelt conveyed his deepening anxiety over Sir Charles's inadequacies. 'There is a fund of good nature in the man', his flag captain conceded, 'but not one grain of the commander-in-chief. I hear it often said that the salvation of Britain depends upon this fleet. I never hear the expression but I turn pale and sink. My God, what have your great people done by such an appointment!'[14]

An enterprising commander, Kempenfelt believed, would dog a superior fleet, probing for weaknesses, pouncing on stragglers, keeping it from mischief but avoiding a showdown.[15] Indeed, it is hard to imagine Nelson not finding ways of seizing the initiative from the ponderous, ill-trained and poorly organized Franco-Spanish fleet. And this is precisely what the dashing Lord Mulgrave recommended:

> I own I was much concerned to see any orders for retreating without a battle, under any circumstances [he wrote to Sandwich from the Channel on 2 July] as I think our fleet in its present situation equal to meeting anything, both from the strength of the ships ... and the great superiority of our discipline to that of the Spaniards till they have been a considerable time at sea. The last is an advantage I should be sorry we lost, particularly as it must lessen every day ... I think the fleet we have is sufficient at least to fight any force of the enemy's they may meet. Unless you expect a very considerable reinforcement very early, I see no advantage that can be gained by retreat.[16]

But Hardy was not a man for taking aggressive action, not when committing a blunder might mean losing the war in an afternoon. Middleton, who had never commanded at sea a force larger than three ships, was inclined to be as cautious in the face of the Combined Fleet's numerical superiority as the Western Squadron's commander-in-chief. Moreover, he had under his eye Kempenfelt's letters which, fairly or not, portrayed Hardy as irresolute if not befuddled. So his reading of the situation in the Channel probably helped to speed him to conclusions that his temperament already disposed him to reach. As a way of avoiding a potentially disastrous entanglement, he advised enticing the Combined Fleet up the narrowing Channel, away from waters familiar to French and Spanish navigators, nearer Portsmouth and other ports from which Hardy might expect reinforcements.[17] Such a plan took into account both the Combined Fleet's superior numbers and the British fleet's inferior commander.

Meanwhile, on 16 August the Combined Fleet's 56 line-of-battle ships appeared off Plymouth. Having slipped by Hardy's station near the Scillies undetected, d'Orvilliers momentarily found the Channel lying open before him. He failed to exploit this astounding opportunity, however, and as soon as Hardy learned that the enemy was behind him, he groped his way homeward. By 31 August, aided by darkness and fog, he succeeded in getting between his up-Channel bases and the Combined Fleet once again.

Having re-established his defensive position, Hardy tenaciously avoided action – far more tenaciously, indeed, than Middleton's letters to Sandwich recommended. Drawing the Combined Fleet toward Dover was meant to improve Hardy's chances in the event of a fight; but the commander-in-chief chose to make for Spithead like a rabbit for its hole, dropping anchor there on 3 September. Middleton passed along to Sandwich Kempenfelt's call for more frigates and fireships: frigates, to extend the fleet's intelligence range; fireships, to compensate for being outgunned, should the British get to windward of the enemy.[18] Such advice availed little when not even a visit from the First Lord, who came down to Portsmouth expressly to urge Hardy to put to sea, was enough to dislodge him.[19]

Middleton had enough on his hands at the Navy Office without pausing to advise Sandwich on operational matters. Indeed, he liked to portray himself as a workhorse whose time in harness the First Lord would do well to emulate. 'If I, my lord, who am a professional man', he wrote, 'find myself unequal to the duties of the office I am in, with an application of twelve hours six days in the week, how is it possible that your lordship can manage yours, which is equally extensive, in three or four? Indeed, my lord, it cannot be.'[20] Apparently, Sandwich, who had been a member of the Admiralty Board before the Controller passed his lieutenant's examination, merely shrugged off such remarks.

Some of Middleton's associates were deeply impressed by his industry. 'The Controller', the Navy Office clerk Robert Gregson wrote in 1789, 'is the most indefatigable & able of any in my time. The load of business he goes through at the Board, at the Treasury, Admty, & his own House, is astonishing, & what I am confident no other man will be able to execute.'[21] Still, the numbers Middleton used when enlarging on his slavery to the office do not always add up. For not long after describing himself as a six-days-a-week, 12-hours-a-day man, he informed Sandwich that he was going out of town following the reading of Saturday morning's Navy Office letters and did not intend to be back until 10 on Monday morning.[22] In another letter he prided himself on 'devoting my whole time and attention the other five [days] to the public'. Without time off with his family, he sensibly explained, he could never stand up to the rigors of office.[23] At any rate, if Middleton sometimes exaggerated his exertions, he worked unusually long hours for an eighteenth-century administrator. How habits had changed since Pepys, who thought nothing of taking weekday outings on the Thames and did not bother to carry a watch until he was 32.[24] Yet, even with the Franco-Spanish fleet at large in the Channel, Middleton felt able to get away for a long weekend.

Nevertheless, 'the mainspring of everything naval' showed signs of running down himself. 'The burden [of office] my Lord is too great', Middleton informed Sandwich, 'for the most able sea officer in this kingdom; and a consciousness of my own inferiority in mind and body has frequently made me wish I had never engaged in it.'[25] In moments of fatigue or discouragement Mrs Bouverie's pastures often looked greener to Middleton, but nothing enhanced the charms of retirement like the prospect of not getting his own way. In the midst of the wrangle over dockyard appointments, for instance, he offered to withdraw from the Controllership, a gesture Sandwich ignored. Earlier he had assured Sandwich that he, Middleton, would probably retire himself, whenever his lordship left the Admiralty. But when the First Lord was driven from office in March 1782, the Controller, finding himself indispensable to the evacuation of America, stayed on. He stayed on eight more years, until disappointment over the failure of his scheme for reforming the Navy Office finally got the better of him.

Duty alone would surely not have kept Middleton at his desk for 12 eventful years. Several times – at the end of the American war, for instance – he could have stepped down gracefully (and more than once, when Richard Howe was First Lord, he might have found bitter satisfaction in quitting). His willingness to put up with the humiliations which Howe inflicted on him betrayed how much he loved being Controller of the Navy. He especially enjoyed the challenges of innovation; he was intensely proud of his achievements, to the point of sometimes giving himself more credit for them than he deserved; he liked exercising power and associating with the powerful. The country weekends he so scrupulously observed gave him the rest he needed, but they were also in keeping with the habits of a gentleman. He was not eager to exchange the hustle and bustle of Tower Hill for a quiet corner of Kent in the immediate future.

Keen as he was to give Sandwich the benefit of his opinions on naval operations, Middleton nevertheless recognized that the Combined Fleet's appearance in the Channel was bound to throw his own sphere into confusion. The need to put every available big ship to sea, for instance, disrupted the coppering program. At best the Portsmouth yard had begun coppering eight 74s before Hardy sailed in mid June, but it probably completed fewer. On 19 June, for instance, Portsmouth was directed to forbear from coppering the *Formidable* (90) in order to ready her for sea.[26] Once Sir Charles weighed anchor, the yard's attention shifted to supplying him with reinforcements and making ready to repair battle damage. According to the King's own figures, Admiral Hardy's command included seven coppered ships of the line.[27] The *Victory* had no copper bottom throughout the emergency in the Channel; nor did any other first or second rate.

In the end, though, the crisis worked in favor of the coppering program.

For the circumstances prevailing through much of the summer of 1779 – an outnumbered fleet taking defensive measures predicated on speed and maneuverability to keep itself in being – emphasized the great potential of copper bottoms. No sooner had the *Victory* arrived in Spithead than Kempenfelt wrote to Middleton:

> The fleet that sails fastest has much the advantage, as they can engage or not as they please, and so have it always in their power to choose the favourable opportunity to attack. I think I may safely hazard an opinion that twenty-five sail of the line, coppered, would be sufficient to hazard and tease this great, unwieldy, combined armada, so as to prevent their effecting anything; hanging continually upon them ready to catch at any opportunity of a separation from night, gale or fog; to dart upon the separated, to cut off any convoys of provisions coming to them; and if they attempted an invasion, to oblige their whole fleet to escort the transports, and even then it would be impossible to protect them entirely from so active and nimble a fleet.[28]

Given the skepticism the coppering program met with in some quarters, Middleton could hardly have kept Kempenfelt's authoritative opinion to himself.

Perhaps it was just as well that Middleton always thought of himself as a sea officer first and a land-bound administrator second. For when the Combined Fleet appeared off Plymouth in August 1779 he did not succumb to the panic that seized the local authorities, especially Lt-General Sir David Lindsay, the officer in charge of local defense, and Captain Paul Ourry, the Dockyard Commissioner. Forgetting that d'Orvilliers carried no embarked troops, they convinced themselves that they were shortly to be overrun by the French and Spanish hordes. Swayed by Lindsay's appeals for help, Ourry frantically importuned London for permission to employ hundreds of dockyard workers in stretching a log boom across the mouth of Plymouth harbour, building defense works and shouldering muskets against the invader, if it came to that.

Middleton knew the invader had to get ashore first, and he held out firmly against stripping the dockyard of any of its workforce. For just as it fell to Hardy to keep the Combined Fleet from controlling the Channel long enough to put troops ashore, it fell to the western yards, first and last, to employ every available hand in keeping Hardy's ships at sea. Only in the event that the Combined Fleet failed, Middleton reasoned, would it make any sense for dockyard workers to exchange tools for weapons; in

1. Engraving of the Royal Dockyard at Portsmouth.

2. Engraving of a view of His Majesty's Dockyard at Portsmouth.

3. *A Fleet of East Indiamen at Sea*, Nicholas Pocock.

4. *Deptford Dockyard*, Joseph Farington.

5. *Plymouth Dockyard*, Nicholas Pocock, 1798.

6. *Woolwich Dockyard*, Nicholas Pocock, 1790.

7. *Admiral Charles Middleton* (1726–1813), British School, nineteenth century.

8. *Admiral Richard Howe*, John Singleton Copley.

9. *Commodore Augustus Keppel* (1725–1786), Sir Joshua Reynolds.

10. *John Montagu (1718–1792), 4th Earl of Sandwich at Greenwich,* Thomas Gainsborough.

11. HMS *Bellona*, *c.* 1780.

12. Carronade gun model.

the meantime, they ought to be kept ready to repair battle damage and otherwise assist Hardy. In short, their capacity as skilled workers, not unskilled militiamen, offered the best defense against a landing. Having worked himself into a near panic, Commissioner Ourry was not easily soothed. So Sandwich proposed sending down Edward LeCras, on whom Middleton heavily relied at the Navy Office, to steady Ourry's nerves and impose London's views. Middleton objected that he could more easily spare 'the whole of the pen-and-ink gentlemen', than LeCras, 'unless you should think the quieting of a madman of more importance to His Majesty's service than providing the several yards as well as the whole fleet with stores'.[29] Evidently the First Lord gave priority to holding Ourry's hand, for LeCras made the trip.[30]

Had Ourry known of conditions aboard d'Orvilliers's ships, his fears might not have got the better of him. For sickness ravaged the Combined Fleet – from one mysterious disease the French had 140 sailors die and 2,400 fall sick between 24 July and 16 August alone; shortages of provisions and water especially plagued the French, who had been at sea for far longer than expected.[31] As if d'Orvilliers did not already have his hands full, at the last minute he was advised that a landing would be made in Cornwall instead of Portsmouth and the Isle of Wight. On 3 September, the same day that Hardy anchored at Spithead, the French minister of marine ordered the French commander-in-chief to return to Brest. A week later d'Orvilliers sailed home, where it was felt the fiasco had left plenty of blame to spread around. Unlike Admiral Pierre de Villeneuve a generation later (and Diego Flores de Valdès, naval adviser to the Duke of Medina Sidonia two centuries earlier) d'Orvilliers was not made the scapegoat of a failed attempt to invade England.[32] A fortnight later Kempenfelt predicted, 'If the combined fleet are in port, they'll not appear at sea in a body before the spring.'[33] On 22 October Hardy declared himself ready to sail against an enemy who was no longer there. True, everyone expected the return of seasonable weather to bring the return of the Franco-Spanish fleet, but for 1779 the invasion crisis was over.

Nevertheless, over Middleton's strenuous objections, the Admiralty kept the Channel fleet at sea until late November. Nothing that Hardy might be expected to accomplish, in the Controller's opinion, would compensate for the wear and tear of winter cruising or for disrupting winter refits and repairs. Nothing mattered more, in this season of coppering, than getting the uncoppered ships of the line into the docks.[34] Indeed, despite the cautious tactical advice he pushed on the First Lord, Middleton was altogether opposed to using the Channel fleet in the manner that Sandwich had chosen. Strategic doctrine as it had evolved in the course of the wars with France prescribed for the Channel fleet, or the Western squadron, two main functions. One, the blockade of Brest, open or close, was intended to keep the French from sending naval reinforcements to the West Indies and Asia; to deprive the French Atlantic trade of protection while shielding British trade from the French; to allow the British to engage the French fleet, if it came out, or at least to improve the odds on discovering its whereabouts if it managed to get away. But all this came at the cost of exposing ships and seamen to nearly intolerable stresses and strains and to the risk of fetching up on Ushant or some other lee shore if the wind turned southerly.[35] Even the audacious Edward Hawke had been reluctant to undertake the assignment that ended in his astonishing victory in Quiberon Bay in 1759.[36]

The other function of the Channel fleet was to act as a strategic reserve, a pool from which ships could be drawn, singly or in groups, for service anywhere on the globe. Britain had lost the numerical superiority in heavy ships that such a blockade was thought to require. Freed from having a cat posted at their mousehole, the French came and went as they pleased. But the Bourbon alliance also prevented the First Lord from employing the Western squadron as a true strategic reserve. For the thought of the Combined Fleet being used to cover an invasion of England transfixed Sandwich. In the face of such a threat, the First Lord believed, the Western squadron could not include too many ships of the line. Acting on such a belief, of course, deprived the squadron of the flexibility that a strategic reserve required.[37]

Sandwich's line prevailed in the Cabinet; but in no uncertain terms Middleton warned the First Lord that he was misusing the Channel fleet. In a memorandum drawn up for Sandwich on Christmas Day 1781, the Controller complained, 'The practice that has been pursued for these two summers past of supporting this squadron at the expense of every other important one is so contrary to good policy that I hope it has not escaped the eyes of his Majesty's ministers. The idea of collecting a force to contend with the enemy in this quarter must be destructive in its consequences if any longer adhered to, and, after every effort, prove insufficient in the end.' Instead of the upwards of 30 ships of the line the Admiralty had thrown into the Channel in 1779, 1780 and 1781, Middleton recommended a fleet composed of 15 to 20 of the fastest sailing two-deckers, along with some fireships and frigates, whose task would be to shadow the Combined Fleet when it was at sea, putting in at Torbay – here was Middleton and Kempenfelt's version of the Brest blockade – when the enemy went into port. Robbing every other force to pay the Western squadron made no sense – especially not when the maximum number of heavy ships Britain could gather together would still not come close to matching the Combined Fleet either in numbers or firepower. Three-deckers, the Controller went on, ought to be stationed in the North Sea, where they could protect merchant convoys coming home north about – around Scotland – in order to evade enemy cruisers lying in wait in the western approaches. Middleton could not resist putting in a word on the strategic merits of coppered bottoms. Without them, he assured Sandwich, the Admiralty's foolish policy would have ended in the fleet's 'annihilation'.[38]

Middleton's lurid might-have-beens aside, his main concern was the role the Western squadron ought to be playing – but could not because of the First Lord's obsession with the invasion threat – in Britain's global strategy. 'If the system of starving every other service to make up an insufficient western squadron is still to prevail', he insisted, 'we shall not only lose island after island [in the West Indies] in sight of fleets that are too weak to protect them, but see every possession belonging to Great Britain, and the land forces that are placed in them for their defence, seized by the enemy.' The experience of the West Indian frigate captain and colonial investor shaped the opinions of the Controller. Taught by his own part in shutting off French trade that war was fundamentally an economic enterprise, he expressed his views in the language of orthodox mercantilism. 'The sugar islands are the best and surest markets for our staple commodities', he wrote, 'and the most productive of all our colonies. They are the easiest sources of our revenues.'[39] But they were also indefensible except by sea. None, as he had written from the Leeward Islands station 20 years earlier, was capable of mounting more than a token resistance to an amphibious assault.[40] If sea-power kept the sugar islands British, not enough naval force could be kept on station in wartime to assure their defense. British reinforcements needed to be ready at a moment's notice, and these could best be made up from a strategic reserve already fit for sea. Sandwich had to recognize, Middleton insisted, that saving the West Indies required accepting numerical inferiority in home waters and counting on the Army to repel an invasion.[41] As many three-decked ships as could be got ready in a fortnight, he wrote to the First Lord on Christmas Day 1781, should be sent to join Admiral Sir George Rodney in the Caribbean. 'By giving a superiority in these quarters, you may hope for success but cannot expect it by contending for a western squadron.'[42]

Sandwich was not long for office when Middleton gave him this lecture, nor could he be shaken from his conviction that the best antidote to invasion was a Channel full of British ships of the line. When the North ministry fell in March 1782, Admiral Keppel – the 'professional man' for whom Middleton yearned – replaced Sandwich, whose departure he soon regretted. One of the secretaryships of state went to Lord Shelburne, with whom the Controller, realizing that one could never tell where such an able if unpopular man might wind up (and choosing to ignore that 'the Jesuit of Berkeley Square' despised Scots), had been in correspondence on naval affairs.[43] By July 1782 Shelburne had become Prime Minister, and Middleton returned to the Western squadron theme. 'While ever we attempt to make up a western squadron with a view to cope with the combined fleets', he wrote in a memorandum setting forth his ideas on the campaign of 1782, 'every other service must submit to that ... The making an insufficient western squadron the first object, as was usual under the last administration, has been attended with many inconveniences and might have proved fatal to Gibraltar as well as our Baltic fleets.'[44]

By the summer of 1782, following Rodney's victory over de Grasse in the Battle of the Saints, Gibraltar superseded the West Indies as Middleton's paramount strategic preoccupation. The fortress became a bargaining counter at the end of every war with Spain, for many – including Middleton, Shelburne and the King – doubted its value.[45] But during the American war the besieged garrison had to be supplied, yet another task requiring the assistance of ships of the line. In 1780 an extremely lucky Sir George Rodney not only relieved Gibraltar but also captured a Spanish convoy and its naval escorts before defeating a Spanish battle fleet and taking six of its ships of the line. In 1781, however, the relieving of Gibraltar required the efforts of most of the Channel fleet, a winter operation that disrupted work in the dockyards without matching Rodney's success of the previous year.[46]

On 22 July 1782 Middleton was summoned to see the First Lord (now Admiral Keppel) at the Admiralty and told that Gibraltar would be relieved as soon as the Combined Fleet cleared the Channel. Keppel believed that ten ships of the line would suffice to keep watch on the allies, making ten available for North Sea duty and another ten for relieving Gibraltar. Middleton had been urging just such a dispersal of the Western squadron, but the imminent relief of Gibraltar was news to him, and he doubted whether enough transports had been rounded up for the job. These details come from the office diary the Controller began keeping at midsummer but abandoned, regrettably, scarcely a week later. Well might he have noted, however, the meeting on the Gibraltar question for which he was summoned to the Treasury on 23 July. For presiding at it was the recently appointed Chancellor of the Exchequer, the 23-year-old William Pitt. This was apparently the first encounter between Middleton and the man he served and advised, always at arm's length, until the great Prime Minister died a quarter century later, still in middle age.[47]

Pitt and his colleagues wanted Middleton's opinion on the relief of Gibraltar. The Controller had plenty of opinions on previous relief operations: 'much time has been lost and much hazard run, by not ordering in time proper stores and supplies to be got ready at Spithead, and by not committing the preparation of the whole to one particular board, or rather one man acquainted with sea affairs [did Middleton have himself in mind?], that might expedite the whole and make everything co-operate'.[48] If the Gibraltar relief took Middleton by surprise, he nevertheless had ready answers as to how it might be accomplished. To Pitt and his colleagues he proposed taking supply transports from ships already loaded at Spithead for New York. Since the evacuation of America was under way, New York and Charleston had a surplus of provisions. Any unusual supplies could be loaded at Deptford.[49]

In a manner he found all too familiar, Middleton's superiors failed to give him the support he thought he required. A conversation with Keppel on the 25th revealed that nothing had been done, beyond the steps Middleton had taken himself, to co-ordinate the relief of Gibraltar with other pressing objectives. Middleton blamed Shelburne, who might have been surprised to learn how his once and future correspondent privately sized him up: 'The first minister, as far as I have seen, has not weight enough for his station, nor abilities to conduct it; as a man of business he wants method and application; as a minister, he wants knowledge of the line he has undertaken; and being without weight, can carry no plan into execution.'[50] Middleton's note to himself closed with a lament for the predicament of all civil servants in all times and places: 'In short, I can get no fixed plan from any of the ministers, and therefore can lay none on my part, for preparation. Unhappy country!'[51]

In the end Middleton's unhappy country, in the person of Admiral Lord Howe, relieved Gibraltar for the third time. But the opportunity for the relatively small squadron that Keppel and the Controller advocated was allowed to slip by while the Cabinet considered, and rejected, other projects. Assembling the transports caused further delays – the besetting friction of the American war. Finally Howe sailed – not with the ten ships of the line Middleton recommended – but with 34; in the event the Combined Fleet, at anchor off Algeciras, tried to intervene. Howe, nearly as lucky as Rodney was in 1780, slipped by it, and brought the convoy under the guns of Gibraltar on 16 October. By then, the Spanish had lifted their siege.[52]

Middleton had other aims besides relieving Gibraltar when he proposed making a convoy from ships already available at Spithead. True to the principle of flexibility he urged in all his notes and memoranda on the uses of the fleet, he suggested sending several of Howe's ships of the line on to the East Indies to reinforce the beleagured Admiral Sir Edward Hughes.[53] Instead, eight ships of the Gibraltar fleet sailed to the West Indies, presumably to remind the French of the vulnerability of their sugar islands. In the end, Sir Edward had to make do with the six of the line sent out earlier under Admiral Sir Richard Bickerton. Slightly outnumbering Admiral Pierre de Suffren, Hughes was nevertheless outmanned, owing to sickness in his own fleet, and was bested by the great French admiral in an engagement off the Indian coast. A few days later news arrived that a peace agreement had been signed five months earlier.[54]

Reviewing events of the recent past, Middleton gloomily concluded in August 1782 that 'the past summer has been unprofitably spent; we have undertaken everything and executed nothing; whereas an early disposition and timely communication might have relieved Gibraltar'.[55] If it was true that the Cabinet had let slip an opportunity to succor the British garrison at far less risk and cost than were eventually required, it was also true that the King's ministers made decisions – or failed to make them – under political pressures and distractions that Middleton, from the shelter of administrative office, seldom took into account. Nor was his a voice crying in the wilderness. In its main outlines, if not in the details of execution, Middleton's principles of strategy were ones to which the Admiralty adhered not only in the waning years of the American war but to the end of the maritime struggle with France. In Middleton's scheme, the Channel fleet served as the fulcrum of naval endeavor, from which force might be applied in the East and the West Indies, the North Sea and the Mediterranean, as well as in the Downs, the western approaches, and off Brest. Middleton failed to appreciate the growing importance to Britain of the Mediterranean, in which he had never served; he probably exaggerated the importance of the West Indies, of which he had years of first-hand knowledge. From the outset of the war with revolutionary France, however, the Mediterranean's strategic significance made itself manifest both on land and at sea; until the wars with Napoleon ended the British government continued to pour men and money into the sugar islands at a rate far exceeding their strategic or economic value. Middleton was no original thinker; his views represented a consensus on war at sea that stretched from the

1740s down through Nelson and Collingwood and the end, in 1815, of the long naval encounter with France.

For all his self-confidence, there was something tentative in Middleton's early expression of opinion on matters beyond his 'own line'. As he spoke his mind on operational questions, however, his confidence grew, and by the autumn of 1782 he was writing to Shelburne, a man far less experienced in naval affairs than Sandwich, with great self-assurance. He also had an even more expansive notion of the Controller's duties than he had brought to office with him. He had emphasized to Sandwich the importance of having a seaman on the Admiralty Board. Repeating this theme, he wrote to Shelburne that 'unless the naval force is conducted in the Cabinet by professional knowledge, judgment and method, it cannot prove equal to the many services that will be expected from it'.[56] Middleton changed his tune when Keppel became First Lord. For the professional man he had in mind for a seat on the Admiralty Board turned out to be none other than himself. 'The advantages which a Comptroller from the nature of his office must have in point of naval knowledge is so well known', he explained to Shelburne, 'that every First Lord of the Admiralty whether Sea or Land finds it necessary to consult him on every subject of moment. Should this alteration therefore take place, it will become less material than it has been hitherto, whether the first Lord be of the sea or land, and probably better of the latter kind if a very able one of the former cannot be found.'[57] That Middleton had discovered virtues in having a civilian First Lord might have amused Sandwich. Knowing that Keppel would not welcome awarding the Controller a seat at the Admiralty table, he recommended postponing such a step until after the Admiral no longer sat at its head. But Shelburne remained in office no longer than Keppel had, and the Controller never received the place to which he aspired. He had received one plum, however. On 23 October 1781 he had been made a baronet in recognition of his meritorious service in the American war. Henceforth he was to be known as Sir Charles.

NOTES

1 John Knox Laughton (ed.), *Letters and Papers of Charles, Lord Barham*, 3 vols (London, 1907–11), vol. I, pp. 27–38.
2 Richard Ollard, *Pepys: A Biography* (London, 1974), pp. 79–80.
3 Ibid., p. 80.
4 *Barham Papers*, vol. II, p. 7. He deleted the confession from the draft of a letter he apparently never sent.
5 Ibid., pp. 22–3. Sandwich to Middleton, 24 January 1781. Emphasis added.

6 John Fortescue, (ed.), *The Correspondence of King George III from 1760 to December 1783*, 6 vols (London, 1927–28), vol. IV, No. 2776, pp. 436–42.

7 On the invasion of England schemes, see Georges Lacour-Gayet, *La Marine militaire de la France sous le règne de Louis XV* (Paris, 1902), *passim*; *La Marine militaire de la France sous le règne de Louis XVI* (Paris, 1905), especially pp. 233–6; A. Temple Patterson, *The Other Armada: The Franco-Spanish Attempt to Invade Britain in 1779* (Manchester, 1960), especially pp. 1–78; Admiral Sir Herbert W. Richmond, *The Invasion of Britain* (London, 1941).

8 Peter Kemp (ed.), *The Oxford Companion to Ships and the Sea* (London, 1976), p. 628. Sandwich later came to Palliser's rescue by awarding him the governorship of Greenwich Hospital.

9 In the annotated list of who had chosen sides with whom that Lord Sandwich furnished the King, Captain Laforey was described as 'a professed follower & dependent of Mr Keppell's much given to talking & writing; he is however an excellent officer'. *Correspondence of George III*, vol. IV, No. 2460, p. 225.

10 'Though left in neglect since his fine performance as flag-captain on the East Indian station during the Seven Years War', Corbett wrote of Kempenfelt, 'he was regarded as perhaps the most accomplished and scientific officer on the list.' Julian S. Corbett (ed.), *Signals and Instructions, 1776–1794* (London, 1908), p. 34. Kempenfelt's contemporary Captain Beatson described him in his *Naval and Military Memoirs* (London, 1790) as 'the most experienced in the service with respect to fighting in the line of battle and the manoeuvres of a fleet. His abilities were known and admired by all the naval powers, and he was justly esteemed to be as brave and able a sea officer as this or any other nation ever produced.' Quoted in Corbett, *Signals*, p. 35. James Gardner in his *Recollections* calls Kempenfelt 'the ablest tactician in the navy', and 'a man that has never been surpassed as an able tactician'. R. Vesey Hamilton and John Knox Laughton (eds), *Publications of the Navy Records Society* (London, 1906), vol. XXXI, pp. 16, 24.

11 *Barham Papers*, vol. III, p. 292.

12 *Barham Papers*, vol. II, pp. 3–5. Middleton to Sandwich, [summer] 1779.

13 G. R. Barnes and J. H. Owen, *The Private Papers of John, Earl of Sandwich*, 4 vols (London, 1932–37), vol. III, p. 43.

14 *Barham Papers*, vol. I, p. 293.

15 Ibid., vol. II, p. 292. 27 July 1779.

16 Mulgrave to Sandwich, *Courageux*, at sea, 2 July 1779. *Sandwich Papers*, vol. III, p. 33.

17 *Sandwich Papers*, vol. III, pp. 83–8.

18 *Barham Papers*, vol. I, pp. 296–7. Kempenfelt to Middleton, 5 September 1779.

19 Patterson, *The Other Armada*, pp. 202–4.

20 *Barham Papers*, vol. II, p. 3 [summer] 1779.

21 Quoted in N. A. M. Rodger, *The Insatiable Earl: A Life of John Montagu, Fourth Earl of Sandwich 1718–1792* (New York, 1994), p. 161.

22 *Sandwich Papers*, vol. III, p. 43. Middleton to Sandwich, 9 July 1779.

23 Ibid., vol., III, p. 181. Middleton to Sandwich, 15 September 1779.

24 Ollard, *Pepys*, p. 119.

25 *Sandwich Papers*, vol. III, p. 43. Middleton to Sandwich, 9 July 1779.

26 This estimate is based on NMM, POR/A/29, which records orders to copper ships, not ships actually coppered.

27 These included the 74s *Invincible, Hector, Courageux, Defence, Bedford* and *Shrewsbury*, and the 64-gun *Bienfaisant. Correspondence of George III*, vol. IV, No. 2724, p. 401.

28 Kempenfelt to Middleton, 5 September 1779. *Barham Papers*, vol. I, p. 297.

29 *Sandwich Papers*, vol. III, pp. 69–70.

30 Patterson, *The Other Armada*, pp. 181–93.

31 Jonathan R. Dull, *The French Navy and American Independence: A Study of Arms and Diplomacy, 1774–1787* (Princeton, NJ, 1975), p. 157 and relevant note.
32 Patterson, *The Other Armada*, pp. 227–99; Dull, *French Navy*, pp. 143–58; Geoffrey Parker and Colin Martin, *The Spanish Armada* (New York, 1988), pp. 267–8; Felipe Fernández-Armesto, *The Spanish Armada: The Experience of War in 1588* (New York, 1989), p. 106.
33 *Barham Papers*, vol. I, p. 299, Kempenfelt to Middleton, 19 September 1779.
34 *Sandwich Papers*, vol. III, p. 102, pp. 177–8. Middleton to Sandwich, 15 September 1779.
35 On the Navy's success in coping with some of the difficulties of the Brest blockade, see N. A. M. Rodger, 'The Victualling of the British Navy in the Seven Years War', *Bulletin du centre d'histoire des espaces atlantiques*, nouvelle série no. 2 (1985), pp. 37–53.
36 Ruddock F. Mackay, *Hawke* (Oxford, 1965).
37 Piers Mackesy, 'British Strategy in the War of American Independence', in David L. Jacobson (ed.), *Essays on the American Revolution* (New York, 1970), p. 180; Mackesy, *The War for America*, (Cambridge, MA, 1964), pp. 193–4; Paul M. Kennedy, *The Rise and Fall of British Naval Mastery* (London, 1976), pp. 100–1, 108–9; Ian R. Christie, *Wars and Revolutions: Britain 1760–1815* (London, 1982), pp. 120–1.
38 *Barham Papers*, vol. II, pp. 38–40.
39 Ibid., vol. II, p. 70.
40 Ibid.
41 Mackesy, *War for America*, p. 449.
42 *Barham Papers*, vol. II, pp. 37, 40.
43 'That nation is compos'd of such a sad set of innate, cold-hearted, impudent rogues', he told Richard Price, 'that I sometimes think it a comfort when you and I shall be able to walk together in the next world, which I hope we shall as well as in this, we cannot possibly then have any of them sticking to our skirts.' Quoted in Paul Langford, *A Polite and Commercial People: England, 1727–1783* (Oxford, 1989), p. 328. On Shelburne's baffling personality see John Ehrman, *The Younger Pitt*, vol. I, *The Years of Acclaim* (London, 1969), pp. 85–7.
44 *Barham Papers*, vol. II, pp. 73, 80.
45 Ehrman, *Younger Pitt*, vol. I, p. 94.
46 Mackesy, *War for America*, pp. 322–3, 381–2.
47 All Middleton had to say of their meeting, however, was 'Mr. Pitt presided: two other members and their secretaries present'. *Barham Papers*, vol. II, p. 55.
48 Ibid., pp. 74–5.
49 Ibid., p. 55.
50 Ibid., p. 56.
51 Idem.
52 Mackesy, *War for America*, pp. 479–84.
53 *Barham Papers*, vol. II, p. 57.
54 The best account remains Herbert Richmond, *The Navy in India, 1763–1783* (Cambridge, 1931).
55 *Barham Papers*, vol. II, p. 59.
56 WLC, SP 151, No. 37.
57 WLC, SP 151, No. 39.

6

Laying Up the Fleet

Discredited by its long and unavailing prosecution of the American war, the North ministry fell in March 1782. A government headed by the Marquis of Rockingham and resolved on ending the now unpopular struggle against the rebels came to office. No matter what came of negotiating with the Americans, however, British possessions elsewhere in the hemisphere still needed to be held against the French. With this in mind, the new ministry planned to reinforce the Army in the West Indies with some of the troops removed from North America. Such a move, it was thought, would at least strengthen Britain's defensive position in the sugar islands; at best the British share of these islands might be increased at French expense – if not by armed force, then perhaps at the conference table.[1]

The Rockingham Cabinet made this decision without considering how the regiments destined for the West Indies were to be extracted from their North American garrisons. No sooner did Middleton learn of the Cabinet's intentions than he gave Admiral Augustus Keppel, Lord Sandwich's successor as First Lord, his estimate of the shipping the new policy required. Were the garrisons of New York and Charleston to be evacuated simultaneously, he began, then at least 60,000 tons of shipping would be needed to remove the troops alone; were their ordnance, provisions and stores to be taken away as well, another 25,000 tons would be required. The brute fact was that no more than a third of the 85,000 tons in question was at hand; nor did the Navy Office see any prospect of enough becoming available at any time soon. So Middleton proposed making do with what there was. The New York garrison (larger than Charleston's, but strategically less significant, now that the war's focus had shifted to the Caribbean) should be evacuated first, leaving Charleston for later. This would require between 40,000 and 50,000 tons, which probably could be scraped up by

ordering Charleston, Halifax, St Lucia and Jamaica to send every army
transport and storeship available at each port to New York immediately;
by converting all victuallers to troop transports; and by sending transports
already loaded for Quebec and Halifax on to New York once they had
landed. 'By these means', Middleton declared, 'I am of opinion a proper
quantity of tonnage may be assembled at NY for removal of that garrison
by September.'[2]

If Keppel comprehended the steps in this logistical dance, he did not
prove able to set it in motion. For Middleton's plan could not get round
the military and political obstacles in the way of evacuating America. The
question of the Loyalists, for instance, disrupted every plan for embarking
troops that commanders on the scene tried to make. What was to be done
with these vengeful and embittered people? They could not be abandoned,
not in the aftermath of the Yorktown capitulation, when all but a handful
of them had been left to fend for themselves among the inhospitable
Virginians. But the Loyalists and their belongings made additional demands
on the woefully inadequate pool of shipping – so much so that even
Middleton's estimates fell far short of the tonnage eventually required to
resettle them.[3] Thousands of Loyalists were removed from Charleston; in
New York, David Syrett remarks, 'the evacuation resemble[d] a migration
rather than a military operation'.[4] More than 10,000 chose not to wait for
the Navy to take them off and found their own havens; more than 28,000
were eventually transported to Canada.[5]

Meanwhile, news of Admiral George Rodney's naval victory over the
French in the Caribbean – the Battle of the Saints – reached London in
May 1782, renewing hopes for the conduct of profitable military operations
in the West Indies. The Marquis of Rockingham died in July; the Earl of
Shelburne, with whom Middleton had been in correspondence on strategic
issues, took his place. Nevertheless, the government slumbered on, as if
oblivious to the connection between shipping and the seizing of sugar
islands from the French. Rarely had Middleton been in a better position
to say I told you so, and he did not let the opportunity pass. If the advice
he had given to Keppel in March had been taken, he pointed out in a
memorandum composed for Shelburne in July, then the New York garrison
would have been evacuated in the current year, with Charleston following
in the next. 'But suffering three months to elapse without coming to any
resolution on it', he wrote, 'and permitting the victuallers and transports
to lay unnecessarily at Spithead, and after all to sail for Quebec, Canada,
and the West Indies, without any view to an object of this magnitude that
had been ordered to be carried into execution, is scarcely credible.'

Middleton could not conceal his vexation on discovering that more provisions had been shipped to garrisons already slated for evacuation. Some 12,000 tons of transports had been wasted in such a manner on New York and Charleston, which already had 15 months of rations in store. 'These, my lord, are stubborn facts, and would discredit the cabinet if they were suffered to come before the public.' Even worse were the obstacles the government's own ineptitude put in the way of removing the Loyalists. Indulging his bent for retrospective prophecy, Middleton assured Shelburne that acting on his earlier advice would have spared the Prime Minister 'complaints subsisting of leaving the loyalists to the mercy of an enraged enemy'. Nevertheless, the Controller saw a way out of the situation. By diverting the surplus provisions at New York and Charleston to Halifax, Quebec and Newfoundland, the government could recover the shipping needed to evacuate the main North American garrisons. Any provisions and supplies not required by the northern garrisons could be taken to the West Indies.[6]

Not until early October 1782, however, did the Cabinet order shipping to be made available for the evacuation of New York. The lateness of the season and the size of the task at hand meant that taking the offensive in the West Indies at any time soon was out of the question. As it turned out, the peace preliminaries signed with France and Spain in January 1783 put an end to such thoughts. Only in April did the New York garrison begin packing up, a job made somewhat less complicated when news of the peace arrived.[7] Not until 25 November did the last of the British troops climb aboard the last British transport remaining in New York harbor, and not before some of them had nailed a Union Flag to the top of a greased pole.[8] Why make things easy for Yankee Doodle?

Meanwhile, having recognized that the leisurely evacuation of America precluded a timely offensive in the West Indies, Shelburne turned to diplomacy. At the end of November 1782 preliminary articles of peace were signed between the former rebels and Britain; on 21 January 1783, after convoluted negotiations over imperial holdings in the Caribbean, the Mediterranean, the Gulf of Mexico and the Indian Ocean, news reached England that preliminaries of peace had been concluded with France and Spain.[9]

Despite the frustrations that evacuating America entailed, in the summer of 1782 Middleton found himself in a rare mood of contentment. 'It is a matter of agreeable reflection', the Controller wrote in July, 'that we have at present a force afloat sufficient for every national service.'[10] Scarcely six months after congratulating himself on the state of the Navy's war-making capacity, however, Middleton had to begin dismantling the force he had played such a large role in putting together.[11]

For reasons of shipboard discipline as well as the practical needs of maintenance, ships in commission almost invariably received better care than those in Ordinary, where Pepys once found toadstools as big as a man's hand sprouting from timbers.[12] Middleton was keen to avoid Pepys's unpleasant experience. He was determined, too, to avoid the 'disorder' that had characterized the mobilization against France and Spain. Lack of preparedness, and the frantic effort to make up for lost time, especially when it came to mobilizing ships of the line, accounted for much of the disarray Middleton had found at the Admiralty and Navy Office in 1778. By putting things in better order, the Controller aimed to improve the Navy's readiness as an instrument of war and diplomacy.

With the return of peace, the nearly frantic pace of work in the dockyards and on Tower Hill slackened, giving Middleton time to catch his breath. His Evangelical conscience, however, did not allow him to rest. Free of the war-borne emergencies that engaged so much of his attention, he turned to his long-deferred plans for improving the efficiency of the shore establishment. When he assumed the Controllership in August 1778, he recalled, he had found 'the dockyards without any fixed rules of government'.[13] Such rules existed, however, as Middleton explained in a history lesson he gave the younger Pitt. Dating from 1658, the standing orders of the Navy laid down a common, comprehensive and systematic set of rules and procedures on everything from how to keep rainwater from seeping through gunports to how to build a ship of the line. Over the years, however, so many orders fell into desuetude that each yard virtually went about its business as it saw fit, rarely bothering even to keep London informed of the state of its accounts, stores and work in progress. Buried in five or six folio volumes kept in London, often undated and interleaved among unrelated records, the standing orders were hard to find, let alone follow. The war worsened the confusion, the Controller maintained, leaving 'the dockyards ... without discipline or method, and the board without decision or control'.[14] True, Middleton was a man who exaggerated: had the dockyard conditions been as bad as he sometimes made them seem, or communications between London and the yards as poor as he claimed, he could scarcely have exercised any authority at all.

At any rate, in January 1783 Middleton began assembling the scattered bones of the standing orders into a spinal column of naval administration. 'By employing almost the whole of my leisure time, both in town and in country', he could not resist telling Pitt, 'I have been at last able to abstract and arrange under a few comprehensive heads the whole of these orders to the present month.'[15]

Today any large organization carrying out complicated instructions over long stretches of space and time usually adopts some form of standing orders or procedures. Few eighteenth-century enterprises, however – aside from the state itself – were sufficiently big or complex to warrant having these. It was no accident that the Excise, whose employees worked to a set of detailed and rigorous instructions, was 'one of the most proficient organs of government'.[16] Proficiency is far from the only end that standing orders serve. They are also meant to promote the safety of workers and the public; to keep employees honest and treat them equitably; to enable managers to impose their aims on subordinates; and to provide benchmarks for deciding issues of legal responsibility and political accountability.

Middleton intended the standing orders of the Navy to promote most of these aims. He meant to send sailors to sea in seaworthy ships and to reduce the terrible accidents that befell dockyard workers; to discourage dockyard 'embezzlement' in all its ingenious and costly forms; to minimize the authorities' arbitrary and unfair treatment of dockyard workers as well as the play of favoritism; to communicate the Navy Board's intentions to dockyard officers and to ensure that these officers reported on their doings regularly and in detail; and to ensure that all members of the naval establishment, high and low, were held accountable for their actions.

Standing orders describe what an organization wants, not what it gets. Government agencies prescribe in voluminous detail how aircraft are to be maintained and flown, for instance, but airline personnel still misunderstand or disregard instructions, sometimes with disastrous consequences.[17] Similarly, under London's relentless pressure to hurry ships to sea, dockyard workers must sometimes have found shortcuts through the thicket of warrants on refits and repairs. So the standing orders of the Navy reveal only what the Navy Board wanted done, not what *was* done. They show in outline how Middleton and his colleagues sought to manage the Navy's transition from war to peace.

No sooner had news of the peace reached England than the Board moved to reduce the size of the dockyard labor force. No more artificers, it directed on 24 January 1783, were to be hired without explicit orders from London. In the ensuing weeks the yards were instructed to cease overtime in the ropewalks and sail lofts, to desist from hiring sawyers over 40 years of age, to discharge extra clerks – to cut the payroll, in short, wherever it seemed to invite cutting. It was one thing, however, to lay off scavelmen – unskilled laborers who shovelled the mud from drydocks, swept up after horses and performed sundry odd jobs. It was another thing altogether even to contemplate reducing the number of shipwrights and other skilled workers. For dockyards were complex mechanisms and specialists, to use Middleton's favorite metaphor, were their mainsprings. Devoted to building and maintaining the biggest and most complicated machines of the day, the yards could not let go of shipwrights and black-smiths, caulkers and riggers without running great risks. None could easily be replaced and the best of them would have had little trouble in finding jobs in the higher-paying merchant yards. Better to offer a kind of job security – the one effective lure against higher pay – than to trust, in a crisis, to the vagaries of the labor market.

In March 1782, the high point of the American war, the dockyards carried 9,477 workers on their books. By December 1783, this figure had declined to 9,250, a reduction of only 227, for by the end of the first year of peace the Navy Board was having second thoughts about laying off workers. Replying to the Admiralty's query as to how it planned to save, the Board came up with arguments for not cutting the work force. Owing to the far larger number of apprentices (1,239 as against 777) employed in 1783 than in 1774, the last full year of peace, the yards were actually under strength in terms of shipwrights. The total number of seasoned men available had fallen as the fleet had grown; extensive general repairs were needed to put it on a footing of readiness and to keep the ships in Ordinary from falling into decay. In these circumstances, to reduce the number of shipwrights beyond what could be expected from retirements and other sources of attrition would be a false economy. The same went for black-smiths. So severe had been the loss of anchors and other ironwork in the war that the 380 smiths (including servants) employed in the yards, only 34 more than in 1774, could scarcely keep up with the work of replacing lost equipment, let alone meet current demands. As for caulkers, the number employed in 1774 was not enough even then; the shortage of them had caused vexing wartime delays and making do with fewer than 400 in peacetime would surely slow the pace of postwar repairs. It might be thought that the dockyards could get along with fewer house carpenters, but now was the time to catch up with jobs postponed during the war. Laying up the fleet required more skilled riggers than were needed in wartime. Only the ropewalk workers, the Navy Board conceded, might speedily be reduced in numbers without hampering an orderly transition to peacetime.

The Board chose to see dockyard employment in terms of naval readiness: 'it is our wish with the same inclination towards Economy that their Lordships recommend, to employ the present means to bring forward every part of the Service in such a manner as may prevent that exorbitant imposition on the public and that waste of treasure, that have never failed to be the consequences of leaving the providing the ships & stores, till some unforeseen emergency calls for them'.[18]

By December 1789 the number of dockyard workers had shrunk to 8,260, a decline of 13 per cent since the American war. Throughout the decade, howevever, shipwrights and apprentices held steady at around 3,000. These numbers may have given the dockyards their peacetime reputation as an idler's paradise; but building ships, like building houses and roads, always entails a good deal of standing around. It is not always easy for outsiders to distinguish the rhythms of workers from the strategems of idlers. In any event, Navy Board experts vastly preferred a peacetime surplus of shipwrights to a shortage when war came again.

The one category of naval employment subject to drastic cuts at the end of every war was seamen. Despite the enormous difficulties that manning the eighteenth-century Navy always entailed, no politician wished to be heard advocating any form of long-term service. For the sake of preserving public order as well as of saving money, no paying off of the fleet could come too soon. As early as 30 January 1783, scarcely a week after news of the peace reached London, Navy Board warrants were mentioning the 'great discharge of seamen' already taking place. Withholding seamen's wages invited 'mutinies' – often in the form of sit-down strikes aimed at getting paid rather than at challenging shipboard authority. Since public sympathy lay with men who so obviously deserved to get the money the Navy owed them, the authorities usually winked at the actions of the strikers. On 10 April 1783, for instance, Henry Martin, the Commissioner at Portsmouth, wrote to the Navy Board:

> The riotous and turbulent behaviour of the Seamen, having risen to such a pitch as to render impracticable the carrying on the duty of the Port with the least degree of regularity particularly by their seizing the Lighters & Craft and loading them with such Stores as they please, even of the Ships ordered not to be dismantled, I am of opinion that these disorders can be no otherwise remedied than by using the utmost Dispatch in paying off the Ships now in Harbour, for which some thousands of Pounds in addition to what is already here, will be requisite. I could therefore wish you would be pleased to apply to their Lordships for the necessary Orders to pay them off.[19]

The Board immediately forwarded Martin's letter to the Admiralty and, notwithstanding the 'riotous and turbulent behaviour of the Seamen', recommended that their Lordships should comply.[20] From a wartime high of 90,000 in 1782 the officers and men of the Navy plummeted to 20,000 in 1784, before subsiding to roughly 18,000 for most of the rest of the decade. Such a low level of recruitment guaranteed a shortage of seamen when war was renewed. Everyone recognized the danger; no one, Middleton included, came up with a practicable remedy.[21]

The transition from war to peace also marked a shift in the responsibilities of the major dockyards. In wartime the King's yards concentrated on repairs and refits; shipbuilding was farmed out to merchant yards. The return of peace, however, enabled the King's yards to resume the building of ships, which naval opinion held they did better than merchants working on contract (whether Middleton and like-minded friends were right or merely ill disposed toward merchant builders is another question). In wartime ships were often patched together and hastily put to sea again. Peace gave the yards time and space to make good on temporary repairs. Such ships as could most quickly and cheaply be made ready for sea (they were more likely to be put in Ordinary than actually placed in service) were to receive first priority.

No sooner were ships paid off than shipwrights surveyed them, so that the Admiralty and Navy Board could decide which to keep at sea, which to put in Ordinary, and which to convert to sheer hulks and other dockyard uses, which to repair, which to sell, and which to break up. Finding somewhere to put this greatly expanded fleet was not an easy matter. Should the patrons of lending libraries all suddenly return the books they had borrowed, few libraries would have enough shelving to accommodate them. The same went for ships returning to Britain from duty stations around the globe. There were not enough moorings to go around. Permanent moorings were expensive, but a ship inadequately moored was a standing danger to everything near. Something needed to be done to relieve the overcrowding at all the naval ports. Chatham, Portsmouth and Plymouth each had at least 50 ships to contend with (Portsmouth had more than 70) within months of the war's end. Almost plaintively, in the early weeks of the peace, the Navy Board asked the dockyards to keep London informed as to what space might be available near them.[22] In mid-November 1783 the Board told the Admiralty that 'We are under the greatest difficulty of finding room for the Line of Battle Ships of the largest Class and excepting the River Medway we have not the means of laying down a new mooring and then only at Ochamness, where the Officers inform us that seven pair may be fixed'.[23]

At length, Middleton and his colleagues hit upon the expedient of double moorings. Their masts removed, ships were to be lashed alongside each other by means of lines passed through the second or third gunports both fore and aft. Every seven ships at each port were to be formed into divisions and placed under the watchful eye of a 'superintending master' living aboard the center ship of his division. This was a new wrinkle. Formerly, ships in Ordinary had been in the care of boatswains, who divided their time between looking after the maintenance and security of their own vessels and assisting the Master Attendant.[24] Expert seamen, as stressing the first word in their title implies, Masters Attendant had overall responsibility for everything afloat, including the handling of ships in crowded harbors, rigging them and making them ready for sea.[25] So it made sense to give them assistants with similar qualifications and experience (which, with respect to shiphandling and piloting, at least, boatswains did not have). Like Masters Attendant, Superintending Masters were to be drawn from the ranks of the most senior masters, usually those of first and second rates. As heads of seven-ship divisions, they would oversee the boatswains who, relieved of the duty of assisting the Masters Attendant, could devote more time to their own ships.[26]

Fewer hands, of course, meant fewer ships at sea. Swelled by the demands of the American war, the Navy shrank to meet the expectations of rate-payers. To the Navy Office fell the task of adjusting the number of ships kept on service to the number of men Parliament was willing to pay for. Against the need for economy, Middleton and his Board balanced the requirements of naval readiness. So it was not simply a matter of cutting back the fleet helter-skelter, as had happened in the aftermath of previous wars, but of working according to an overall plan. By November 1783 the Navy Board had a plan in hand. The cheapest, most easily accomplished and most strategically-urgent tasks were to come first. The 'peace establishment' – a fixed number of frigates and cutters designated to cruise home waters as well as guardships assigned to each major dockyard and river – was to be completed as quickly as possible. Next the western dockyards (Plymouth and Portsmouth) were to turn to repairing the most serviceable ships of the line, fitting in such frigates as they had time and space for. Meanwhile, starting with the big ships and working their way down, they were to begin replacing iron fastenings with copper-alloy bolts (about which more will be said later). Sheerness and the river yards of Deptford and Woolwich, whose facilities were cramped and waters shallow, were to concentrate on repairing frigates, mooring them at Plymouth and Portsmouth when they were finished. 'Upon the whole and after the most attentive consideration of the subject in its several parts', the Commissioners concluded, 'we recommend this Plan to their Lordships as the most eligible in point of Oeconomy as well as Policy, as the best calculated to answer the important purposes of establishing and preserving a powerful Fleet, and of being able to bring it into immediate Service.'[27]

By 1786 work on the tasks that followed from these recommendations was well along. Middleton took it upon himself to summarize what had been done in a memorandum written with an eye to his plans for Navy Office reform.[28] Ninety ships of the line had been put in good condition – meaning that they could be readied for sea in a matter of weeks – more than two and a half times the number available when Middleton took office in 1778. In 1786 11 ships (ten of the line and one 50-gun frigate) were being built. Twelve were undergoing large repairs. Seventy more – 29 ships of the line and 41 frigates – remained to be repaired if the dockyards had the time and Parliament voted the money.[29]

Despite his penchant for mechanical metaphors, Middleton was no watchmaker Controller, setting things in motion and leaving the tinkering to subordinates. The war had already seen abundant proof of that. His preoccupation with tidying up the standing orders of the Navy, like his approach to hiring transports, his absorption in the coppering program and his offering of strategic advice when none had been asked for, betrayed an almost obsessive – and possibly excessive – regard for detail. Yet there is little evidence that being disposed toward 'micro-management', to resort to the language of our own day, ever caused Middleton to lose sight of the main goals of administrative policy. Details had little intrinsic interest; like pieces of a jigsaw puzzle, they were of value only for what they contributed to the large pictures he always kept in mind.

Take, for instance, Middleton's scheme for leaving new ships on the stocks instead of launching them. The smaller point at issue was diminishing the prospect of rapid decay from dry rot – one notorious consequence, in the hasty and haphazard mobilizations of previous wars, of rushing ships built of green timber to sea.[30] The larger issue was naval readiness, a main focus of the Controller's peacetime preoccupations. The Navy's numerical inferiority in ships of the line in the war against France and Spain had been a harrowing yet instructive experience, he wrote to Admiral Keppel in March 1783. The odds had been worsened at the outset by the Franco-Spanish lead in readying ships for sea. Middleton's proposal for keeping ships on the stocks partly aimed at closing this gap. Once a ship was launched, the expenses of upkeep multiplied. Such a ship had to be assigned a place in the Ordinary, found a mooring, kept painted and ventilated and have her bottom scraped and sheathed. Meanwhile, her timbers would be decaying – at great speed, if they had not been properly seasoned – and might have to be shifted, at considerable additional cost, before she could safely put to sea. In short, a new ship in the water was a much greater drain on the shore establishment's resources than the same ship on the stocks, and a distraction from maintaining older vessels. Far better, Middleton went on, to launch as few ships as possible in peacetime. By leaving them on the stocks and roofing them over to preserve them from the elements, a practice followed by the Venetians, Russians and Swedes, they could still be brought forward to the point where they could be made ready for service within six weeks of launching.

As was his habit, the Controller promised that a multitude of benefits would accrue from adopting his proposal: the yards could concentrate on keeping ships already afloat in sea repair; giving older ships priority over new ones would permit large savings to be made in timber and labor costs; room for mooring new ships at the already overcrowded ports would not have to be found nor would the expense of new moorings – at between £2,000 and £3,000 a ship – be incurred; a supply of seasoned timber would always be on hand should it prove necessary to build new ships in wartime; ships on the stocks would prove more durable for having been seasoned properly (Middleton claimed that such ships would probably last an entire war without needing major repairs); leaving them to season instead of providing them with even skeleton crews would help alleviate peacetime manning problems.[31]

His scheme did not work out quite as the Controller had hoped. The Admiralty under Lord Keppel approved the recommendations the Navy Board made under Middleton's aegis, but on New Year's Eve 1783 Admiral Lord Howe succeeded Keppel as First Lord (he had served in the post a little more than two months at the beginning of the year), bringing to office his close relationship with the King and his reputation as a great seaman. Here was the professional man Middleton had asked for, but hardly the one he wanted. The Controller's experience with Howe the sea officer left him regretting his relationship with Sandwich the civilian, whom he had once been so ready to scold and disparage. Middleton blamed Howe for scuttling the proposal to leave new ships seasoning on the stocks. That this was only one item in a steadily lengthening list of grievances each man came to hold against the other suggests that their professional differences were merely outcroppings from a bedrock of personal antipathy.[32] Unfortunately, in the case of leaving ships to season, the Controller's side of the story is the only one available. No sooner had Howe taken office than the Admiralty

Board resumed the dockyard visitations Sandwich had discontinued during the war. Not bothering to inform the Navy Board of its plans was affront enough, in Middleton's book. But then Howe and his colleagues compounded the slight by dismantling certain of the dockyard innovations that the Controller and his associates had put together. Following the visitation, three ships out of four that were to have been left on the stocks and roofed over were ordered to be launched. Only the *Leviathan*, a 74 barely begun at Chatham, escaped. Nevertheless, Middleton expected vindication – 'how far the Navy Board were right in proposing the measure' – from this ship and the King's yacht, which had also been roofed over several years.[33]

Thwarted by Howe – at least in his own eyes – from keeping new ships out of the water until they were needed, Middleton had better luck with his scheme for setting aside naval stores. Britain relied on home supplies of oak timber and certain kinds of ironwork, but most naval stores – planks, masts, pitch, tar, hemp and other commodities – came from abroad.[34] Except for a brief period during the American war, when the Dutch appeared to be in a position to intercept the Baltic trade (the eastern littoral of the Baltic being the chief source of supply), Middleton and other naval officials worried less about acquiring these items, for which Britain had long been willing to pay premium prices, than about making good use of them once they were in hand. At the outset of a naval mobilization the demand for stores suddenly ballooned. Shortages were especially acute when Middleton assumed office in late summer 1778 and worsened under the need to repair the damage Keppel sustained in his encounter with d'Orvilliers in August. Demand drove prices skyward, the Controller recalled and, by increasing the Navy's debt, weakened its credit. For stores were paid for by means of Navy bills – promises to pay issued 'in course', or in strict chronological sequence from the date of their registration at the Navy Office. A larger debt stretched out the course. Stretching out the course lengthened the period of maturity and deepened the discount the holder of a bill had to accept if he decided to cash it in on the market.[35] Bill holders needing cash faced discounts of 22 per cent in the year following French entry into the war (by no means an unprecedented figure: in 1711, during Queen Anne's reign, Navy bills were being discounted at 33 per cent).[36] The discount rate fell off sharply toward the war's close, when the Navy had an ample supply of stores on hand, but the confusion in which they were kept worsened. In their eagerness to be paid off, it will be recalled, 'riotous and turbulent' seamen had unloaded stores and dumped them ashore as fast as they could. Sorting out the mess the sailors had created in striking for wages must have occupied the workers at Portsmouth yard for months. A Navy Board survey revealed that no two dockyards were keeping stores in the same way. None paid much attention to an order requiring them to keep enough stores on hand to provision ships for eight months' sea service. Storehouses contained too many items that were no longer used and too few of those currently in demand. Everywhere disorder reigned.

In the surplus of stores on hand or promised for delivery, Middleton saw an opportunity to restore order at little additional expense. Essentially, he proposed creating from the existing inventory of naval stores a huge spare-parts warehouse. Each ship was to have its own supply of stores set aside in a designated berth in a storehouse of the dockyard of its home port. For instance, the *Bellona*, in Ordinary at Portsmouth, would draw on the stores put aside for her there. In principle, boatswains and carpenters should be able to find in these berths nearly all the essential items they required to make their ships ready for an eight-months' cruise. New store-houses building at Portsmouth, Plymouth and Chatham could be arranged along these lines from the outset; the river yards would need to await the expansion of their facilities.[37] Once again, Middleton's two themes of economy and readiness neatly came together. Having a plentiful and well-ordered supply of naval stores on hand at the outset of a war would ensure a rapid and orderly mobilization. Having control of such a supply would discourage panic-buying and ensure the Navy Office of favorable credit terms when it came time to negotiate with merchants. When he made these confident predictions, of course, Middleton had no idea that Britain would soon need to find the naval stores required to support for many years a fleet of more than 900 ships.[38]

Simple as setting aside stores seems in principle, it did not go as smoothly as Middleton predicted. For one thing, hundreds of items, from sailmakers' needles to the yardarms of three-deckers, fell under the new classificatory scheme. And getting the dockyards to comply with orders from London on any but routine matters invariably required a fair amount of tugging and hauling. In 1787, more than three years after the plan for setting aside stores went into effect, the Navy Board admonished the yard officers that it had yet to receive their reports on stores issued in 1784 and 1785, 'at which we are much disples'd'.[39]

The new storehouses at the bigger dockyards were part of the major expansion of shore facilities that took place in the 1780s, and these facilities were another source of the grievances accumulating in Middleton's head against Lord Howe. Woolwich was adding a new mastpond, masthouses, boathouses and wharves to the tune of at least £100,000; at Chatham a new rigging house and ropewalk had gone up, as well as the new storehouses built since 1781; Sheerness, in a decrepit state at the outset of the American war, had essentially been rebuilt at a cost of upwards of £60,000; Portsmouth had undergone an extensive plan of both new building (the storehouses) and the renovation of docks, mastponds, boathouses and wharves; Plymouth had experienced a similarly ambitious renewal. Since the peace between £50,000 and £80,000 had been spent annually on all this work, and Middleton expected that it would take another four or five years to bring it to completion.[40] If the Controller took satisfaction in overcoming some of the longstanding inadequacies in dockyard facilities, he was profoundly dissatisfied over the way in which these construction projects had been managed. For want of know-how, he asserted, some of the work had been poorly done and almost immediately required expensive repairs; some had cost far more than they should have; still other projects, for lack of adequate supervision and audits (to say nothing of yard officers possibly looking the other way), had allowed contractors to fleece the public. The plain fact was that shipwrights, a frequent target of Middleton's wrath, were ignorant of civil architecture. Building a ship of the line was one thing; building a storehouse or a wharf was another. Besides, shipwrights had enough work on their hands building ships; carpentry required different skills. Renovating dockyard facilities, the Controller insisted, called for the talents of a proper civil surveyor of architecture, or what in our day would be a combination of architect, civil engineer and general contractor.

Middleton thought he had found just the right person in John Marquand, who supervised the building of the marine barracks at Chatham early in the Controller's tenure in office. But the shipwrights undermined Marquand. They 'endeavoured by every means in their power to lessen his consequence, and to make his situation unpleasant'. The Admiralty – 'Lord Howe's Admty', as Middleton put it – sided with the shipwrights and Marquand was dismissed. How unhappy Marquand made the yard officers and the building contractors was proof enough, by the Controller's lights, of how good he was at his job. Claiming that the renovation of the dockyards could not be successfully completed without him, Middleton urged Marquand's reappointment as soon as possible.[41] The marine barracks at Chatham are still standing (along with a fair portion of the dockyard's other eighteenth-century buildings); perhaps their solidity is evidence for the solidity of Middleton's claims. But it is also hard not to detect in his strictures against the dockyard officers an air of jurisdictional disappointment, a whiff of another lost struggle. Marquand was the Navy Board's appointee; the Admiralty had overruled the Navy Board and aligned itself with Marquand's enemies, who happened also to be Navy Board employees. Were the shipwrights, by definition skilled woodworkers all, really as ill suited to house carpentry as the Controller professed to believe? Or were his attacks on them really shafts aimed at the interfering Lord Howe?

Eager to claim credit for wartime achievements, the Navy Board was equally determined that the coppering program should not be seen as merely a wartime expedient. 'Every Alteration, Improvement & Experiment concerning Copper', the Commissioners informed their Lordships, 'has originated at this Board, not altogether from Our Own Opinions, but from the Variety of the preparations and Experiments that have been laid before Us in the progress of it & which has forced us to press it forward with such confidence.'[42] Because copper sheathing remained experimental, putting at risk the seaworthiness of the Navy's ships, the Board kept a close watch on the program from the beginning.[43] The dockyards were told to report on the state of the bottom of every coppered ship taken into dock.[44] Plates wore away more rapidly than expected, the yards reported. London instructed them to apply thicker ones – 32 ounces to the square foot, instead of 24 – especially at the bows. Anchor flukes ripped off sheathing as ships weighed anchor; the Navy Board recommended thicker sheets below the catheads and greater care on the part of boatswains.

Early reports appeared to confirm Middleton's optimistic claims for the watertight seal. On 18 January 1782, for example, the Portsmouth yard reported that 'the planks and seams of ships coppered on prepared paper are found as fresh and dry after several years use as when first applied'.[45] Nevertheless, doubts about the seal soon began to creep in. Disquieting news arrived from fleets at sea. Following the Battle of the Chesapeake, in September 1781, the copper-bottomed *Terrible* (74), had to be scuttled after the firing of several broadsides nearly shook her timbers apart, rendering her unseaworthy. The captain of the *Resolution*, in Rear-Admiral Sir Samuel Hood's squadron, wrote 'that copper-bottomed ships, when they once begin to show their defects, drop all at once, which is the case of the *Invincible*, who is now in as bad a state as the *Terrible* was, and several others, which they are afraid even to trust home'.[46] On 29 August 1782 came the foundering of the *Royal George* at the naval anchorage at Spithead, taking to the bottom hundreds of crewmen, wives, other women and children, and Middleton's old friend and shipmate, Rear-Admiral Richard Kempenfelt. Exactly why the 100-gun first rate capsized remains unknown. Heeled for repairs below the waterline, she may have been heeled too far, allowing water to rush in the bottom tier of gunports; or rotted timbers held by rusted bolts and concealed beneath her coppered bottom may have given way, flooding the ship.[47]

Meanwhile, the dockyards were making their own discoveries. Take the case of the *Edgar* (74), sheathed in the prescribed manner before her launching at Woolwich in June 1779.[48] In August 1781 the Portsmouth yard found her iron bolts in good condition,[49] but three months later her captain reported that several of her copper plates had come off.[50] By April 1783 the Navy Board evidently had reason to be concerned about the state of the *Edgar*'s bottom, for it ordered the Portsmouth yard to drive a dozen bolts from her and each of two other 74s (*Fortitude* and *Alexander*) and send them up to London 'with labels describing where they were driven from and let us know in what condition the seams appear to be in under such of the Plates as you take off and the State of the Paper'.[51] Examining the bolts did nothing to reassure the Navy Board, for on 14 April it directed the yard officers to 'have some of the most intelligent and best Carpenters of the Ships at your Port join with the Shipwright officers in inspection of *Edgar*'.[52]

Middleton claimed that such inspections were intended merely to help the Navy Board decide whether all ships should henceforth be sheathed in copper.[53] But the Controller was not a man who readily admitted mistakes, and the sequence of events following the April 1783 inspection of the *Edgar* suggests an alternative explanation. For in May the Board received from Liverpool the disquieting news that corroded iron fastenings had been found in merchant ships sheathed in the same way as the Navy's. 'From which, and having lost more ships lately than heretofore', the Liverpool correspondent went on, 'the merchants are at present [so] very much alarmed, that they have stripp'd off the Copper from several Ships' bottoms sooner than the time allow'd [three voyages' worth], adding Copper fastenings of Bolts … where it was judg'd necessary in addition to their former Iron Fastenings.'[54] Iron bolts drawn from the *Edgar* and several other ships of the line told the same story: copper, iron and sea water made a bad combination.[55] This was the same lesson shipwrights had learned in 1768 from the voyage of the *Dolphin*.[56]

Presented with the evidence from the *Edgar*, the Navy Board in early July 1783 ordered the yards to forebear coppering any but copper-alloy-fastened ships – of which the Navy had only a few.[57] Meanwhile, with a view to laying up copper-bottomed ships in Ordinary, a task the dockyards had never faced, Middleton had sent all master shipwrights a questionnaire. The yard officers' replies all agreed that there was no going back on copper sheathing. Against the ravages of the teredo, copper was far more effective than fir; its durability was a godsend to dockyards hard-pressed to meet the demands of the American war. Even in peacetime, the frequent dockings required to keep a much bigger fleet sheathed in fir would delay other maintenance work.[58]

No yard, however, had confidence in the seal devised to keep copper sheets from making contact with iron fastenings. 'Where the ship strains', Portsmouth bluntly noted, 'it will be impossible to prevent all access to the sea water.'[59] Only Woolwich saw no difference in the effect on iron bolts of fir and copper-sheathed bottoms. Chatham reported, 'The corrosion of bolts drawn from coppered ships is treble of those from ships sheathed with wood, of which the *Robust* is an example.'[60] Woolwich warned that no iron-fastened ship sheathed for more than three or four years could safely put to sea on any service.[61] On the paramount issue, yard officers were unanimous: copper-alloy bolts should replace iron fastenings on all copper-sheathed ships. 'If metal bolts be used', Portsmouth said, 'copper sheathing may be adopted with additional propriety.' 'Our experience', Sheerness declared, 'suggests it to be most advantageous to have copper bolts under water; but no iron bolts may be left where the others are used, that they may not be affected by them.' If some iron fastenings were to be replaced, all should be replaced. Essentially, the dockyard officers confirmed the conclusions that the *Dolphin*'s inspectors had reached 15 years earlier: copper-sheathed ships required copper fastenings.

Despite having solicited the master shipwrights' advice himself, Middleton was still not willing to concede that the seal did *not*, as he once put it, 'effectually preserve … the fastenings of the ships from the corrosion of the copper sheathing'.[62] Putting his own gloss on the dockyards' findings, he assured the Admiralty that the returned questionnaires vindicated the coppering procedures in force at his urging. 'If copper was the only enemy we had to contend with', Middleton insisted, 'we should not have a doubt of the propriety of continuing the use of Iron Bolts.' Accidents afloat, sloppy work ashore and green ship timbers were more to blame than copper for corroding iron. The worst enemy of iron bolts, he suggested, was bilge water, against which no safeguard existed.[63]

For the dockyard officers, recommending against fastening copper-bottomed ships with iron was simply a professional judgement. For Middleton the stakes were higher. He had championed the seal against skeptics; he had hailed it as a long-term solution to a difficult and expensive problem; he had hectored the dockyards into following his instructions to the letter; he had overridden fears for the seaworthiness of coppered vessels; he had been only too willing to take credit for the seal's apparent success. Nevertheless, he grudgingly deferred to the contrary opinion of men he often scorned. For the sake of retaining the benefits of copper sheathing and 'in order to remove the ill-grounded apprehensions of superficial observers' (unnamed but presumably numerous and possibly influential), the Navy Board recommended that the Admiralty 'extend the use of compound metal [i.e., copper alloy] bolts to every Class of Ships under the water line, and to replace every defective iron one, in the old Ships now afloat, as they come under examination and repair'.[64] Being thus confounded evidently affected Middleton's memory, for in later years he never remembered the coppering of the fleet as anything but an unqualified success; he never acknowledged that the watertight seal might have been a mistake.

On 1 July 1783 the Navy Board warned Portsmouth that 'a scheme of fastening with metal bolts all ships of the line as well as frigates under the load draft of water is in agitation and likely to be soon adopted for general use'.[65] On 13 August orders went out to use metal bolts on ships of 44 guns and fewer.[66] The yards were to abandon the methods that had enabled them to copper so many ships in such a short time in favor of the procedure the Deptford officers recommended in 1768.

The Navy Board had already studied the financial impact of switching from iron to copper fastenings. A first rate's 18 tons of iron bolts cost £630; the same quantity of copper alloy bolts was worth £2,520 – a difference of £1,890, or an increase of 400 per cent.[67] The difference in price between the iron and the alloy bolts in a 74-gun ship of the line was estimated at £1,312, in a 32-gun frigate at £393, and so on,[68] estimates which turned out to be remarkably accurate. Middleton tried to lessen the impact of these figures on the Admiralty Board by emphasizing just how much value their Lordships would be getting for the money: an alloy bolt, he claimed, would last a century! Less extravagant were his claims that converting to alloy bolts would reduce the demands on yard blacksmiths, lessen dependence on foreign supplies of iron, and increase the durability of ships.[69]

The Navy Board contracted with copper merchants and smiths for huge quantities of bolts. Owing, perhaps, to improvements in manufacturing techniques, as well as to competition among suppliers and the large orders the Navy placed after 1783, the Board benefitted from a decline in costs. From a price of nearly £133 per ton in 1776, copper bolts fell to £95 13s 4d in September 1784.[70] In the course of 1784 contractors made deliveries to the yards in lots varying from 50 to 150 tons,[71] of which a good share were sent on to merchant yards. By supplying private shipbuilders from government stores the Navy Board not only aimed to ensure that all contract-built ships were put together with copper fastenings; it also sought to exert control over the quality of the hardware that went into the King's ships. The bolts for a 64-gun ship refastened in November 1784, for instance, cost £1,178, or £117 less than the Navy's estimate.[72] Nevertheless, the aggregate costs of rebolting were so large that in 1787 the Surveyor of the Navy felt obliged to explain to Parliament why the Extraordinary Estimate, under which repairs and shipbuilding fell, was much greater 'than usually granted in the last or any former Peace'. Copper bolts cost three times more than iron ones, 'and the general introduction of Copper for Ships Bottoms adds considerably to the expence'.[73] Of course, the expense of converting from iron to copper fastenings far exceeded the cost of materials. The labor required to replace the iron bolts and the time that rebolting took from other work also drove up the bill.

So it made sense to combine rebolting with routine repairs and, as autumn 1783 approached, the work went into full swing. Ships of the line and frigates requiring the fewest repairs were taken in hand first.[74] For the most part, the yards did the work in the course of dockings for other repairs.[75] The *Bellona* (74), for instance, whose model Sandwich and Middleton had shown the King, was originally coppered in March 1780. Her sheathing underwent three repairs – in June 1781, January 1782 and June 1783 – before all her copper was removed in October 1785. It is a safe guess that her iron bolts were replaced with copper ones before she underwent resheathing in April 1786. Over the next 15 years, the *Bellona* was coppered four more times, for a total of six copperings in 21 years. Each new skin lasted an average of three-and-a-half years – less than Middleton had hoped, but far longer, and presumably to far greater effect against the worm, than the fir sheathing it replaced. Some sheathing jobs lasted far longer than others and at this distance in time it is impossible to say why. The age and the size of the ship in question, the quality of the workmanship that went into coppering, the duty stations on which the ship was employed (cruising in the East or the West Indies was sure to invite the attention of the teredo) would all have entered in. The *Indefatigable* (64), for instance, fastened with copper when she was launched at Buckler's Hard in July 1784, went ten years before requiring resheathing. The *Jupiter* (50), which Middleton nominally commanded when he was named Controller of the Navy (remember that in his enthusiasm for copper sheathing he had offered to pay from his own pocket the cost of coppering a frigate), was sheathed in June 1778, the month following her launching, and recoppered in April 1782. The sheathing applied in November 1784, however, lasted nearly a decade. It could be that the 1784 sheathings of the *Indefatigable* and the *Jupiter* lasted so long precisely because both ships were fastened with copper alloy bolts. The *Bellona*'s experience, however, appears far more typical.[76]

Partly because of the high stakes involved, partly because of the novelty of the procedures in question, partly because here was a clear case (at least in the Controller's mind) of London leading and the dockyards following, Middleton had always made the coppering program a test of the state of communications between the Navy Office and its outlying dependencies. As a way of keeping track of which ships had been refastened with copper bolts, for instance, the dockyards were ordered on 14 April 1785 to 'mark [them] with a tick in red ink' in the weekly Progresses forwarded to London.[77] This simple method apparently did not allay confusion, however, for 18 months later (October 1786) the Navy Board asked the dockyards to report which ships' bottoms were iron-fastened and which were fastened with copper.[78] Finally, the Board concluded that it had got its records straight, for at the end of September 1787 it noted, 'The use of copper fastenings are [*sic*] become general.'[79] This was not quite correct. In early October the Portsmouth yard was told to examine the bottoms of the *Victory* (100) and three other ships recently mobilized in a crisis over the prospect of French intervention in Holland. The end of the crisis seemed to afford a good opportunity to refasten Thomas Slade's great ship, still held together with iron bolts after more than 20 years in service. After informing the Admiralty of its plans, the Navy Board changed its mind and then reversed itself again, telling Portsmouth on 5 November to 'redock *Victory*, drive out the iron fastenings and refasten with copper'.[80]

The refastening of the *Victory*, one of the Navy's largest and best-known ships, marks the end of a period that began in 1761, when the Board ordered the experimental coppering of the 32-gun *Alarm*. A quarter century of trial and error at length produced a set of techniques for coppering bottoms to which the Navy adhered until the end of the sailing-ship era.

Coppering may have had another far-reaching, unanticipated effect. The frequent dockings that older methods of sheathing required had entailed a fair amount of shore leave for ships' companies, which were left with little to do while the dockyard workers swarmed over their ships. Sailors could look forward to leave especially in the three weeks a vessel was actually in the dock. Dispensing with frequent dockings meant the loss of cherished time ashore. Coppered ships could spend years 'off the ground', as the time between dockings was called. Urged on by Middleton and others, naval policy-makers were quick to exploit this capability, especially in wartime, with its urgent and incessant demands for keeping at sea as many ships as could be found. By reducing maintenance, coppering made it easier to think of wooden ships as machines than as the largely vegetable contrivances they were. They were driven as hard as could be. The endless, brutally monotonous, dangerous blockades of Brest and Toulon wore out ships, but they wore out men too, officers and lower deck alike, keeping them away from home for months and years on end. The Admiralty's ignoring that men were not machines may have contributed to the Great Mutiny at the Nore in 1797. For among other things the 'mutiny' was a strike, a withholding of labor in protest against a leave policy perceived as capricious, parsimonious and unfair.[81] In that respect the troubles at the Nore resembled the French Army mutiny of 1917.[82]

The refastening of the *Victory* represented both the culmination of Middleton's overall policy – coppering the fleet as a new imperative of naval warfare – and an implicit recognition of his policy's potentially ruinous flaw. For without the pressures the war for America exerted on the Navy, both afloat and ashore, the fleet would never have been coppered so quickly. And without Middleton's watertight seal, coppering could not have been so quickly and cheaply carried out. But if it was a short-run success, the seal was a long-run failure, and had to be abandoned in favor of the procedure shipwrights had recommended near the outset of the coppering experiments. In the *Victory* two strands of naval history came to be fortuitously entwined. Coppered under Middleton's aegis as Controller of the Navy, Nelson's flagship sailed toward Trafalgar under Barham's (Middleton's) orders as First Lord of the Admiralty.

In retrospect, it is hard to see how Middleton could have believed that the watertight seal would work. The constant 'working' of the wooden hull of a ship at sea, the inadequacy of available vegetable and mineral sealants, the lack of machine tools capable of establishing narrow tolerances in metalwork and the uneven quality of dockyard workmanship all contributed to failure. Sea water seeped in, conducting between the copper sheets and the iron fastenings the weak but pernicious electrical current that sapped the integrity of a ship's hull.

It is hard to understand Middleton's confidence – and easy to be condescending about the eighteenth century's scientific ignorance – until one remembers the *Challenger* accident of 1986. The designers and builders of the space shuttle, regarded as a marvel of late twentieth-century technology, had every confidence in the O-rings, which sealed the joints in the rocket-engine housings. Perhaps it is not too far-fetched to see in the history of the watertight seal similarities with the history of the seal whose failure blew up the *Challenger* and its crew.[83] In both cases, bureaucracies short of time and money and under great external and internal pressures to produce results took risks they might not otherwise have taken. In the absence of the great war emergency, the Navy Board might have rebolted the ships of the line; in the absence of its commitment to an ambitious schedule, NASA might at the least have cancelled a cold-weather shuttle launch.

Naval administrators must incessantly weigh time against money. War usually tips the balance in favor of time, to gain which no expense – or shortcut – seems too great. Given the circumstances England faced in 1778, it is hard to gainsay Middleton's decision, carried out with a view to making war at sea, to copper the fleet expeditiously. But it was also a decision that cost the navy dearly when peace returned, bringing with it the leisure to undo the mistake.

NOTES

1 David Syrett, *Shipping and the American War* (London, 1971), pp. 232–3.
2 NMM, MID/2/26. Middleton to Keppel, March 1782.
3 David Syrett, *The Royal Navy in American Waters 1775–1783* (Aldershot, 1989), p. 223.
4 Syrett, *Shipping and the American War*, p. 238.
5 Ibid.
6 John Knox Laughton (ed.), *Letters and Papers of Charles, Lord Barham*, 3 vols (London, 1907–11), vol. II, pp. 76–9; NMM, MID/10/1, Papers relating to the American War; MID/7/1, A State of the Transports under the Direction of the Navy Board on the 23d of July 1782.
7 Syrett, *Shipping and the American War*, pp. 238–41. On the transports ordered to New York from Halifax alone, see the letterbook of Henry Duncan, the Halifax Dockyard Commissioner. Should bad weather keep him from loading masts during the winter, Duncan wrote to James Frazier, master of the *Peggy*, on 13 December 1783, 'You are to make your ships as useful for the reception and lodging of the Loyalists as possible, treating them with all manner of civility'. NMM, HAL/F/1.
8 *New York Times*, 23 November 1985.
9 Piers Mackesy, *The War for America* (Cambridge, MA, 1964), pp. 489, 505–10; Hamish M. Scott, *British Foreign Policy in the Age of the American Revolution* (Oxford, 1990), pp. 310–38.
10 NMM, MID/2/37, Supply of Gibraltar.
11 *Barham Papers*, vol. II, p. 226.
12 John Ehrman, *The Navy in the War of William III, 1689–97* (Cambridge, 1953), p. 202.
13 *Barham Papers*, vol. II, p. 225. Middleton to William Pitt, 18 September 1786.
14 Ibid., p. 226.
15 Ibid., p. 228. A copy of the abstract of the standing orders is to be found in PRO, 30/8/111, Chatham Papers, Middleton to Pitt, 23 September 1786.
16 John Brewer, *The Sinews of Power: War, Money and the English State, 1688–1783* (New York, 1989), pp. 102, 108–9.
17 Consider, for instance, the crash of American Airlines Flight 965 near the airport at Cali, Colombia in December 1995, when the flight crew entered an incorrect sequence of navigational data into the flight-management computer, *New York Times*, 12 September 1996; or the crash of Valujet Flight 592 in the Florida Everglades in May

1996, blamed by investigators on a fire caused by expended oxygen canisters loaded on to the airliner in contravention of Federal Aviation Administration regulations, *New York Times*, 24 May, 5 June 1996. A National Transportation Safety Board report also blamed the accident on supervisory failures of the airline and the FAA, *New York Times*, 20 August 1997.

18 NMM, ADM BP/3, Navy Board to Admiralty, 8 December 1783.

19 NMM, ADM /BP/3, Commissioner Martin to Navy Board, 10 April 1783.

20 'Rec'd and ordered', Secretary Stephens noted in the margin. NMM, ADM BP/3, 11 April 1783.

21 The best study of this intractable problem is Stephen Gradish, *The Manning of the British Navy during the Seven Years War* (London, 1980).

22 See, for instance, NMM, POR/A/31, Navy Board to Portsmouth Dockyard Officers, 3 November 1783.

23 NMM, ADM BP/3, Navy Board to Admiralty, 19 November 1783.

24 According to Charles Proby, the Commissioner at Chatham, boatswains serving in the Ordinary were busy men indeed: 'The half of them when the Ships in Ordinary are numerous attend the Muster in the morning when they are charged with the different Detachments of the Ordinary men to perform the following Duties of the Port. Transporting, docking, undocking, masting, unmasting, cleaning, pumping, attending in launches Ships coming up and down the River whether in Commission or not and also in conducting them to and from other Ports. Removing fitted Rigging into Store & into the Ships, examining the Moorings, repairing and fitting the Bridles and other occasional works many of which require at least two Officers.' NMM, ADM BP/3, Commissioner Proby to Navy Board, 7 March 1783.

25 Daniel A. Baugh, *British Naval Administration in the Age of Walpole* (Princeton, NJ, 1965), p. 297.

26 PRO, ADM 106/2905, 30 April 1789.

27 NMM, ADM BP/3, Navy Board to Admiralty, 5 November 1783. A rough draft of this document, with corrections in Middleton's hand, is in NMM, MID 2/54.

28 See Ch. 7.

29 NMM, MID/6/4, Observations on the Estimates, given into Parliament by the Navy Board 21 March 1786, on the calculation that a permanent Peace establishment would take place towards the end of the year 1790.

30 Robert G. Albion, *Forests and Sea Power: The Timber Problem of the Royal Navy, 1652–1862* (Cambridge, MA, 1926), pp. 11–14, 82, 101, 392–7; Baugh, *Naval Administration*, pp. 242–4.

31 NMM, MID/2/26, March 1783, To Lord Keppel on the importance of bringing forward the fleet in peace.

32 See Ch. 7.

33 NMM, MID/6/4, Observations on the Estimates given into Parliament by the Navy Board 21st March 1786.

34 Baugh, *Naval Administration*, p. 276.

35 See Baugh's excellent discussion of naval credit in *Naval Administration*, especially pp. 470–1.

36 Ibid., p. 486.

37 NMM, MID/2/54, rough draft in Middleton's hand of Navy Board letter to Admiralty, 'A scheme for managing ships' stores in peacetime'. Probably written in late 1783.

38 Ibid.

39 PRO, ADM 106/2509, 14 March 1787. Establishment of stores sent and directions to be observed.

40 NMM, MID/6/4, Observations on the Estimates given into Parliament by the Navy Board 21 March 1786.

41 Ibid.

42 PRO, ADM 106/2210, Navy Board to Secretary of the Admiralty, February 1783.

43 Standing orders on coppering are collected in PRO, ADM 7/409. Abstract of standing orders as to Shipbuilding, etc.(1805) 4, Copper & Copper Sheathing.

44 NMM, ADM/B/198, 3 February 1779.

45 NMM, POR/A/30.

46 Historical Manuscripts Commission, No. 24, *Rutland Manuscripts*, 4 vols (London, 1888–1905), vol. III, Captain Lord Robert Manners to Rutland, 10 March 1782, p. 50. Quoted in Rodger, *Insatiable Earl*, p. 297.

47 R. J. B. Knight, 'The Introduction of Copper Sheathing into the Royal Navy, 1779–1786', *Mariner's Mirror*, 59 (1973), pp. 304–5.

48 NMM, ADM/B/198, 20 February 1779; PRO, ADM 106/1253, 2 June 1779.

49 PRO, ADM 2/571, 25 May 1781; NMM, POR/A/30, 1 August 1781.

50 PRO, ADM 2/573, 12 November 1781.

51 NMM, POR/A/31, 3 April 1783.

52 Ibid., 14 April 1783. The fate of the *Ramillies* (74) may have given the Navy Board additional grounds for worry. First coppered in February 1780, she had to be coppered again in May of the same year, whether owing to sloppy dockyard work or to an accident befalling her hull the records do not say. On her passage home from the West Indies in September 1782 she sailed into a hurricane off the Newfoundland Banks and 'became very leaky, so that Adm. Graves was obliged to quit her and cause her to be destroyed'. PRO, ADM 180/7, Abstract of Progresses: Coppering. Whether corroded iron bolts had contributed to the *Ramillies*'s leakiness was a question the answer to which she took to the bottom with her.

53 NMM, MID/9/1. Three drafts of the report appear in this file: Middleton's rough draft, a copy bearing his emendations, and a fair copy.

54 Ibid. 'Observations on the Practice of Coppering Ships Bottoms, and of the Effects in consequence thereof at Liverpool.' A merchant named Baker, the report said, was having a new 600-ton ship fastened with copper bolts in order 'to prevent the Ill Effects they apprehend to Iron alone from Coppering the Bottom'.

55 NMM, POR/A/31, 21 May 1783.

56 See Ch. 3.

57 Ibid.

58 NMM, MID/9/1, 'Yard Reports Concerning Copper Sheathing'.

59 Ibid.

60 Ibid.

61 Ibid.

62 G. R. Barnes and J. H. Owen (eds), *The Private Papers of John, Earl of Sandwich, First Lord of the Admiralty, 1771–1782*, 4 vols (London, 1932–37), vol. IV, p. 285.

63 Ibid.

64 Navy Board to Philip Stephens, Secretary of the Admiralty, 5 November 1783. Printed in John B. Hattendorf, *et al.* (eds), *British Naval Documents, 1204–1960* (Aldershot, 1993), No. 293, p. 501.

65 NMM, POR/A/31, 27 June 1783.

66 Ibid.

67 NMM, MID/9/1, Navy Office, 2 July 1783. An Account of the Quantity and Value of Iron, & Metal Fastenings, under the Load Draught of Water, to a Ship of each Class, with the Difference of Expence, between Iron and Metal Bolts.

68 Ibid.; John Fincham, *History of Naval Architecture* (London, 1851), p. 97, gives a somewhat higher set of figures. The estimated increased expense of replacing a first rate's iron fastenings with copper alloy bolts was £2,272; for a 74-gun ship, £1,559; and so on down to a brig, for which the additional cost was estimated at £138.

69 NMM, MID/9/1, Navy Office, November 1784.

70 NMM, ADM/BP/8, 4 February 1788.

71 NMM, POR/A/31.

72 PRO, ADM7/656, Lists and Descriptions of Ships. A 74 coppered in 1796 had fastenings worth £1,900, only £150 more than the estimate of 1783, despite the intervening inflationary effects of the war of the French Revolution. Copper plates and bolts together came to roughly £3,700, or about one-ninth of the cost of the hull. PRO, ADM 95/7, estimates for Building Ships.

73 PRO, ADM 95/5, Ships Built & Repaired.

74 NMM, POR/A/31, 3 September 1783.

75 NMM, ADM/BP/6b, Navy Board to Admiralty, 13 July 1786. 'By copper fastening all ships as they come under a course of repair, and covering their bottoms with copper, they may under the Precautions and inspections now used in the execution thereof ...'

76 This assertion rests on an examination of the records for 22 ships of the line listed in PRO, ADM 180/7. Abstract of Progresses, 1st to 6th Rates, 1770–1803.

77 NMM, POR/A/32, 14 April 1785.

78 NMM, POR/A/33, 23 October 1786.

79 Ibid.

80 Ibid., 4 October, 2 November, 5 November 1787.

81 Rodger advances this line of speculation in *Insatiable Earl*, pp. 298–9.

82 On the French case see Guy Pedroncini, *Les mutineries de 1917*, 2nd edn (Paris, 1983); Leonard V. Smith, *Between Mutiny and Obedience: The Case of the Fifth French Infantry Division during World War I* (Princeton, NJ, 1994).

83 *Report to the President by the Presidential Commission on the Space Shuttle Challenger Accident* (Washington, DC, 1986), pp. 40, 82, 104, 148, 176–7, 198–9. Diane Vaughn, *The Challenger Launch Decision: Risky Technology, Culture, and Deviance at NASA* (Chicago, IL, 1996).

7

Reforming the Navy Office

'From the extensive superintendance of my Office', Middleton wrote to Lord Shelburne in early September 1782, 'and acquainted with the several particulars in the naval department, I flatter my self, I shall be able to contribute largely to any plan of reformation that may be resolved on.'[1] Here Middleton showed his disagreeable side as a political intriguer, writing behind the back of August Keppel, the First Lord of the Admiralty, to another Cabinet member of long acquaintance.[2] Ever eager, the Controller aimed to turn Shelburne's ambitious plans for political and administrative reform to the Navy's (and his own) particular advantage. The early 1780s were as propitious a time for putting such measures into effect as the eighteenth century ever afforded. The American war had administered a powerful jolt to English public life. Alienating proponents of conciliation, disappointing advocates of coercion, driving taxes and the national debt to unheard-of heights and ending in the seemingly calamitous loss of the American colonies, the war exposed grave shortcomings in the machinery of politics, administration and public finance, whose workings had remained essentially unaltered since the days of the Tudors, and in some respects, of the Plantagenets. Reformers had been agitating for change since before the war, and suppressing the American rebellion had first diverted attention from their agenda. When victory proved elusive, however, blame came to be laid on deficiencies in the instruments of policy as well as on the errors of policy-makers. Losing the war drew additional adherents and gave new salience to the cause of reform.

Two tendencies, related yet distinct, animated the reform movement. Dressing political objectives in the guise of saving money, the adherents of 'Economical Reform' aimed at reducing the influence of the Crown – all those means of enticement, coercion, blandishment and reward that enabled the state to get what it wanted, especially as such influence was exercised through Parliament. Backers of the other tendency aimed at cutting costs and increasing administrative efficiency.[3] Merchants and bankers, for instance, feared that the loss of American territory would also entail the loss of American markets, crippling the British economy for decades. Such fears proved entirely unfounded, but the experience of a ruinously expensive war made administrative reform seem essential.

Middleton had been speaking the idiom of this second tendency all along, so as the war wound down and reformers came to power, the Controller was quick to offer his own list of proposals.

If Shelburne was averse to Scots, the Scottish Middleton harbored private misgivings about Shelburne. On 25 July 1782 Middleton confided to an office diary, 'The first minister, as far as I have seen, has not weight enough for his station, nor abilities to conduct it; as a man of business, he wants method and application; as a minister, he wants knowledge of the line he has undertaken; and being without weight, can carry no plan into execution.'[4] Still, only one reforming first minister could hold office at a time, lightweight or not, so the Controller swallowed his reservations about Shelburne and urged on him his ideas for reform.

Not long after taking office, Shelburne had evidently solicited Middleton's views on the shore establishment, and the Controller never failed to take advantage of such an opening. Snatching moments from the crises over the relief of Gibraltar and the evacuation of America, Middleton drafted a response. Writing in haste ('neither my Engagements nor my line of application allow me time to study the Arrangement of words', a busy man let it be known),[5] the Controller covered topics ranging from remedies against the ancient abuse of 'Chips',[6] to the duties and responsibilities of the First Lord of the Admiralty. Like any high official who ever asked for Middleton's advice, Shelburne got more than he bargained for: Middleton even threw in some advice on negotiating a peace settlement, a subject entirely beyond the range of his official duties. Ill organized as the Controller's proposals were, however, many of them survived as the guiding principles of the Navy Office reforms he relentlessly pushed over the next eight years. Recommendations made to Shelburne in 1782 became the basis of proposals offered to William Pitt after he was made Prime Minister in 1784, urged on the Committee of Inquiry on Fees in the Public Offices in 1786, and presented to Chatham, the First Lord of the Admiralty, in 1788. With respect to reforming the Navy Office, Middleton became a master of repeating himself.

To many reformers, reducing the influence of the Crown essentially meant attenuating the impact of patronage on politics and policy – at least in so far as handing out jobs and favors was under the control of the government and its supporters. One obvious way of doing this was by diminishing the number of sinecures available for distribution by the Crown. Posts whose duties (when there had been any) had lapsed without interrupting the salaries they paid were not conspicuous at the Navy Office itself.[7] But, Middleton, who invariably assumed that he had a broad mandate when it came to giving advice, did not have to look very far in the military realm to find sinecures. 'There is one establishment', the Controller asserted, 'that has not even the shadow of a professed purpose.'[8] He had in mind the Marine Staff, composed of a general, a lieutenant-general and three colonels of marines, none of whom performed any duties in exchange for salary.[9] Other notable examples of grand titles empty of great responsibilities were those of Vice-Admiral of England, Rear-Admiral of England and Vice-Admiral of Scotland. Such posts should either have duties restored to them and go to the most able men available, or else they should be abolished. 'It has too generally been the case', Middleton insisted, 'that places have been created for men, not Men sought out for places, and that men and families of interest have been allowed to accumulate offices without any view to public interest or the claims of merit or service.'[10] Holding up the Marine Staff as an instance of the evils of patronage has a certain piquancy, for surely Middleton had not forgotten that he had once unsuccessfully petitioned Lord Sandwich's help in getting an (unreformed) colonelcy of Marines for himself.

Time and again Middleton had asserted that selection and promotion by merit should run up and down the naval establishment on both its civil and its military side. After all, he had good reason to think that he had benefited handsomely from the workings of this principle himself. Indeed, he may have exaggerated in his own mind the degree to which his head for business, his energy and forthrightness and his years of demonstrated competence at sea had got him ahead; he may have chosen to ignore, for instance, the extent to which his faithful support for government candidates in East India Company elections had gained him the notice of Lord Sandwich (or, in the manner of the self-made rich, he may have seen his Company holdings simply as further proof of merit). Nor did he recognize that more than once he had found it expedient to set aside the claims of merit in favor of other considerations, such as the demands of family loyalty. How many posts, whether sinecures or real jobs, did Middleton doggedly pursue on behalf of his ne'er-do-well brother George? How many favors, in terms of employment, did he seek for his in-laws the Gambiers? Did he, as enemies charged, tend to find greater merit in his co-religionists'

117

applications for naval employment than in those of ordinary sinners? Perhaps he did.

Meritocratic criteria for selecting and promoting civil (and military) servants have long been in place throughout the West. In its actual workings, however, the machinery of meritocracy is subject to a great deal of slippage and faltering; outcomes are not all as benign as its champions once believed;[11] and in recent years its fairness as a reward system has been called into question. In any event, Middleton was far from being the last public official to espouse, on the grounds of both efficiency and fairness, giving a job to the best-qualified person (whatever that problematical phrase might be held to mean), and then to seek ways, on behalf of a relative, friend or political ally, of getting around the principle he had embraced. Nor was he the last to fail to see the inconsistencies in his behavior.

Now that choosing and promoting civil servants on the grounds of merit has been so widely embraced, it might be tempting to see Middleton as a man ahead of his times, as a far-sighted precursor of the great Victorian reformers. Such a view is probably without merit. With an eye to strengthening national security by enhancing the Navy's power at sea, Middleton was bent on improving the efficiency of the naval shore establishment. He did not couch his advocacy of meritocratic principles in terms of fairness or justice. If he opposed giving aristocrats sinecures or jobs they were unqualified to perform, he did not challenge the existing social and political order. Indeed, his Evangelicalism disposed him to see it as God's handiwork. It could be tidied up, but it ought not to be rearranged. By commending merit as a tool for promoting efficiency, Middleton sought to bring ashore principles usually at work at sea, where there was little room for supernumeraries and no forgiveness for incompetence. In short, Middleton was profoundly conservative. Conserving the existing order required him to look beyond his own nose, but not into the nineteenth century.

Middleton's war experience, in fact, had more to do with shaping his recommendations on Navy Office reform than any abstract ideas on promoting administrative efficiency. His suggestions for improvement also expressed the frustrations and anxieties he had so often felt in his capacity as wartime Controller. Not surprisingly, the profile of the ideal Controller he sketched for Shelburne looks like a Middleton self-portrait:

> As the whole conduct of the Board must naturally depend on his exertion, he in his professional line should have a comprehensive knowledge, and

extensive Abilities. In his principles, he should be conscientious and upright. In his conduct impartial, firm and decisive. In the expenditure of public money strict and frugal, in advancing the public service provident and liberal, in receiving information open, and in giving a fair trial to whatever promises Improvement, Candid and patient. In short, as in the Management of his department the serviceable state of the whole Navy and the Expenditure of the public money required in it depends, his knowledge and his care must extend to everything connected with it, and therefore to his professional skill he must join great application and method and a general knowledge of business and accounts.[12]

Even a man who had all these qualities, as Middleton apparently believed he did, could not exercise them to the Navy's best advantage. For the Controller had neither the rank nor the authority commensurate with the responsibilities of his office. In an age of far-flung empire and distant warfare, the Navy Board could not afford to do business as it had done under Henry VIII. For Middleton, being *primus inter pares* was no longer enough. This was a theme he returned to again and again throughout the 1780s. In the memorandum to Shelburne he was content to suggest that his successor should be drawn from the admirals' list, so as to avoid the awkwardness of a mere post-captain like himself issuing quasi-orders to sea officers who outranked him. The Controller's formal military rank mattered less to Middleton, however, than his real authority and influence, which nothing less than membership of the Admiralty Board could secure. The head of the civil side of the Navy, he pointed out, had to be in nearly constant touch with his colleagues on the operational side; he needed to know the intentions of the Cabinet, where the First Lord sat with respect to naval policy (Middleton remembered being kept in the dark on the evacuation of America); he had to be able to confer with the First Lord on secret matters; and he needed to have a hand in appointing senior sea officers. By sitting among their Lordships, Middleton argued, a Controller could more effectively perform such duties. That the head of the shore establishment should play a formal role in selecting commanders-in-chief at sea was the most audacious item in Middleton's list of bold (and self-aggrandizing) recommendations. It was also the one that senior admirals would have had the hardest time swallowing, and it disappeared from later versions of his demand for the Controller to have a place at the Admiralty table.

The key to Middleton's thinking on all this was his conviction that 'the

Comptroller is next in consequence though not in rank to the First Lord'.[13] If he were next in consequence, the inference ran, then he ought to be next in rank. The Controller ought to be nothing less than a deputy First Lord. Middleton never put it this way, but the grievances and resentments he expressed against the successive First Lords with whom he served suggest that he came close to thinking it. If he was certain that the wartime Controllership, for all its limitations, had at least been filled by an exceedingly able man, one of undoubted probity and tact, he was far less certain that the same could be said of the head of the Admiralty. He did not mention Sandwich by name, but it would have taken a far duller man than Shelburne to wonder whom he meant. The patronage within the purview of the First Lord, Middleton warned, put him second only to the First Lord of the Treasury (at the moment none other than Shelburne himself) in terms of the influence he could wield on behalf of the government. Subordinating his power of appointment to party interests rather than using it to reward merit, the Controller darkly suggested, might go so far as to jeopardize national security. He stopped short of saying this was what Sandwich had done. Nevertheless, he did lay some serious charges at the feet of the former First Lord:

> The present State of the Fleet, its want of discipline, the little Subordination existing amongst the Officers, the Service of particular ships, made to submit to the Parliamentary attendance of Commanders, the shameful corruption that meets the Eye in the several departments of the Dock Yards, are all materially proofs of the prostitution of it. If we add to this, that the equipment and application of our Naval force in time of War, is in a manner wholly submitted to his judgments, and that in the promotion of Officers he has no cheque, but his own sense of what the King's service requires, and which but so often has availed little against his desire of strengthening himself by yielding to private Solicitations, and had loaded the public with hundreds of undeserving half-pay Officers, it is evident that the choice of men to fill this office requires the utmost care and circumspection, in order to prevent the abuse of a power that cannot well be limited by the best contrived regulations.

As an indictment of his former colleague it is hard to see what Middleton's breathless and hurrying sentences leave out. Always inclined to look down his nose at the civilians holding seats on both the Admiralty and the Navy Board, he insisted that if a landsman had to be named First

Lord, he should at least be someone 'of general Application' (he had constantly, and without much justification, accused Sandwich of being lazy), 'a lover of Sea Affairs' (which Sandwich had amply demonstrated he was), and he should be surrounded by admirals, 'that his want of professional knowledge may not affect the Service'.[14] Once Middleton found himself trying to work with the very sea officers he claimed to prefer as First Lords, however, he changed his mind, and yearned for landlubbers instead.

Shelburne must have found Middleton's opinion on whether the Controller of the Navy should have a seat on the Admiralty Board (like his views on negotiating a peace settlement) rather beside the point. Such a step would have done little to advance Economical Reform. The collection of fees in public offices, however, went to the heart of Shelburne's concerns. Of all the targets of reformers, none was more entrenched, pervasive or cherished by the recipients than these gratuities. The Navy Office was no exception. A newly minted lieutenant, for instance, paid a small fee to the clerk who drew up his Passing Certificate. And so on for the countless routine transactions requiring Navy Office paperwork. Fees made up an important part of a clerk's earnings, for salaries were low; they were slow to be adjusted upward – far slower than they might have been had the custom of fees not existed (but more quickly than the pay of sailors, which did not rise between the end of the seventeenth century and the mutiny at the Nore in 1797). In many cases clerks earned a good deal more from collecting fees than from wages. The Chief Clerk of the Navy Office, for instance, was paid a salary of £250 a year; he took in at least another £2,500 in gratuities.[15] Clerks were avid for war, for the more numerous the transactions they performed, the higher their earnings. They also felt, moreover, that there was something demeaning about salaries, something about accepting the King's money that made them dependent in a way that receiving payment for doing the public's business did not. Yet some fees shaded off into bribes, especially in the dockyards, where opportunities to make things happen were greater. A merchant supplier might like to see his ship unloaded more quickly, for instance, and a small sum placed in the right hands was likely to help in getting this done, just as failing to make such a gesture might well produce delays.[16]

Middleton was not so much opposed to the clerks' collecting fees as he was to their pocketing them. In his view, such fees should go into a fund for defraying miscellaneous office expenses, a suggestion not likely to have endeared him to those subordinates who used them to make ends meet.[17] The question of fees was not paramount among Middleton's concerns, yet it proved to be the lever by which he sought to prise up resistance to reform of the Navy Office.

Despite the urgent tone of Middleton's memorandum to Shelburne, the Controller must have realized that not only did the First Minister have far more pressing issues than naval reform to contend with – the negotiations ending the American war, for one – but also that the Shelburne ministry was extremely unstable. Narrowly based and internally divided, it was incapable of acting as a sturdy engine of reform.[18] Disliked, distrusted and under fire from many quarters for the peace settlement he had made, on 24 February 1783 Shelburne resigned.

The turbulence that had set in at the fall of Lord North continued unabated. 'Something of a political nightmare', John Ehrman calls the period 1782–84.[19] The cause of the trouble was the inability of King and Parliament to agree on a ministry. Each camp accused the other of acting unconstitutionally to get its way. George III nearly abdicated before swallowing a coalition government headed by Lord North, whom he had turned against, and Charles James Fox, whom he could not abide. He retaliated by persuading the House of Lords to vote down the ministry's India Bill and then ignoring the Commons majority's demand to reinstate the Fox–North Coalition. The King finally prevailed. Having already made Pitt his first minister, in April 1784 he dissolved Parliament. Portraying the election in terms of a contest between an embattled monarch and a selfish and reckless aristocratic Opposition, the Crown's supporters ran a clever and ultimately successful campaign. For the newly elected House of Commons produced a majority that in general supported the King's prerogative against the claims of party. For the Foxites, the election was an even greater calamity than it seemed at first glance. Pitt remained head of the government for the next 17 years at a stretch.[20]

Among the freshly minted Members of Parliament was none other than Charles Middleton, whose term in Parliament was at least one aspect of his public career of which a proud man was evidently not especially proud. His papers reveal almost nothing of his membership of the Commons. If he was interested in politics, he had never before evinced any political ambitions. He appears to have run in 1784 as a favor to or as a means of ingratiating himself with Pitt, to whom he later confessed his uneasiness about Navy officials holding 'navy seats'.[21] He stood as a member for the Navy borough of Rochester, which included the Chatham dockyard. As it turned out, Middleton made little impact on debates in the Commons. The consummate backbencher, he was content to support Pitt's ministry, and to speak out, when the time came, on behalf of the abolition of the slave trade.

Middleton was less helpful to Pitt as an MP whose vote he could count on than as a naval *éminence grise* whose advice he could trust. Old enough to be the Prime Minister's father (true, in Pitt's early years in power, many officials were old enough to be his father – for a time he was a decade younger than any of his Cabinet colleagues), Middleton was not a member of his innermost circle.[22] He did have ties with insiders such as his cousin Henry Dundas and the vivacious William Wilberforce, Pitt's soulmate for a time. On at least one occasion he entertained the Prime Minister at Teston and was flattered by Pitt's interest in his accomplishments as an improving farmer. But the two were not close. Pitt's chilliness, his reserve toward all but a handful of men and women rivalled Middleton's. They respected each other; they were well enough acquainted to enable them to work together easily. They had the kind of relationship that promotes the conduct of official business. There is no evidence that Middleton, ambitious as he was, ever presumed on his friendship with the Prime Minister. Unlike many politicians, Pitt was deeply interested in administration. He liked to associate with experts. In his early years in office especially he had more affinities with officials such as Middleton than with members of his far from cohesive Cabinet.[23]

Middleton found in Pitt a first minister with a greater interest in reforming the shore establishment than Shelburne had evinced, and a firmer grip on office than 'the Jesuit' had ever enjoyed. Once the election of 1784 went his way, Pitt surveyed a political landscape still dominated by the gigantic shadow of the American war. The most worrisome consequence of that unsuccessful struggle had been the enormous increase in the national debt. Seventy-five million pounds in 1756, when the Seven Years War broke out, the debt had ballooned to £134 million by 1764. Nevertheless, the outpouring of money produced a great victory, and by 1774, the debt had been reduced to £128 million. A decade later, however, it had soared to £243 million, with nothing but a humiliating defeat to show for it. The interest alone on such a sum seemed an unbearable burden. Merchants and investors feared national bankruptcy and gloomily predicted the ruination of Britain's trade and commerce.

Driven by anxiety over the national debt, the impulse to reform that had animated the erratic Shelburne also dominated Pitt's early years in office. Like his predecessor, Pitt strove to make government cheaper and more efficient. To find ways of achieving this elusive goal he established in 1785 the Commission on Fees in the Public Offices, whose mandate ran far wider than its title. For in addition to looking into the question of fees, the Commission was charged with, among other responsibilities, establishing the general principles the government bureaucracy should observe with respect to ranks and salaries, hours of work, retirements and pensions, and oaths and securities against misconduct.[24]

In such principles Middleton discerned a means of advancing his own particular ideas. For Pitt believed in the exceptionally durable idea that men successful in private life know how to save the government money, and in two of the commissioners he appointed, Middleton found malleable allies. Francis Baring, a fabulously wealthy London merchant, a founder of the eponymous investment bank, a director and soon-to-be chairman of the East India Company, was growing deaf when he accepted appointment; his merchant colleague John Dick was nearly blind.[25] Middleton was more than willing to serve as their ears and eyes as they examined the office under his purview, and the recommendations they eventually issued might be said to have revealed his talent for ventriloquy. The commissioners would most benefit from his assistance, the Controller admonished Baring, if Middleton were to remain in the background, confining his communications to themselves and Pitt, supplying information officially only when absolutely necessary.[26] From Sir Francis he received just the reply he must have hoped for:

> I am very happy to assure you that the material part of the System which you have recommended appears to be satisfactory to my Brethren as well as myself … After the zealous, cordial and candid manner in which you have promoted the objects of our Commission, by facilitating our enquiries by every means in your power, it would be unjust to yourself, [and] to the publick, if the Commissioners came to any resolution contrary to your opinion, upon any point of real importance, without having had a full and free discussion with you previous to their determination.[27]

The material part of Middleton's system appeared at its most polished and complete in a document called 'Observations on the Navy Board Department'[28] produced in a fair copy sometime in early 1787 and incorporating most of the recommendations he had made to the Commission on Fees in 'Observations on the 1786 Naval Estimates'[29] (and earlier to Shelburne, Pitt and possibly anyone else who could be made to listen).

They must represent his mature views on the subject, for they did not change in any important respect for the rest of his time in office.

The benchmark for Middleton's observations remained the American war. Once again he unfurled his tableau of the embattled Controller, surrounded by inattentive, inconstant and incompetent colleagues and beset by froward underlings. The only power he had had during the late war, he asserted, arose from his personal influence. He had prevailed, he assured Baring, only by 'obstinate perseverance in the teeth of the irregularity, ignorance, and negligence of the Yard officers, which were provoking beyond description'.[30] Seldom had Middleton or anyone who knew him, for that matter, made such an insightful remark into his character. Years earlier, one of Lord Sandwich's anonymous informants had written of the Controller as 'naturally industrious & persevering'.[31] Obstinate perseverance accounted for many of his successes and some of his failures. Yet although fitting him to a T, it was not a trait that could be expected or even desired of every incumbent in the office of Controller. Middleton's use of the phrase betrayed his tendency to identify his own temperament with the requirements of executive office.

There was more to Middleton's 'Observations' than the self-aggrandizing, self-referential portrait of the Controller he had in any case already painted many times over. His chief impression – and vexation – when he joined the Navy Board was that of 'a number of Men … herding together … where all deliberate and all examine (if so it may be named) without distinction and without Arrangement'.[32] The remedy for this indiscriminate herding, he emphasized, was the mainspring of his plan for reform: 'I come now to submit the expediency of arranging the board into general classes or committees, as the chief circumstance, on which the force and facility of this vast complicated machine will in a great measure ultimately depend.'[33]

Sorted into categories, the diverse business of the Navy Board was to be assigned to three great committees: one for Correspondence, one for Accounts, one for Stores. In Middleton's view a committee system would avoid overwhelming one person with too many responsibilities. Members would benefit from the advice of colleagues; free from the distractions of unrelated business, they could more speedily dispatch their own. Acting as checks on each other, they would also serve to strengthen the chain of command running from the dockyards to the Navy Board. By such a system Middleton meant also to restore sea officers to the dominant role they had formerly played, he contended, in the affairs of the shore establishment. Naval stores, for instance, had been allowed to drift into the realm of the

Surveyor, the civilian naval architect responsible for building and repairing ships. As the *sine qua non* of operations at sea, however, stores properly belonged under the supervision of sea officers, who knew from experience the full weight of the notation 'to be stored for six months', or 'stored for Channel service', next to the names of ships ordered to be readied for sea. Indeed, stores had come under the purview of a sea commissioner during the American war, but they had reverted to the Surveyor soon after the peace.[34]

Middleton's taxonomy of a reformed Navy Office gives off a roseate glow:

> The Committee of *Correspondence* would not then be distracted with *Accounts* and *Stores*, nor the committees for these be hindered by a Correspondence which had no particular relation to them. By such an arrangement the correspondence (as surely it requires) would be kept up in just order and punctuality, the accounts would not be hurried over, nor referred to incompetent or improper hands, but be nicely and thoroughly examined; and the Contracts for stores duly considered and fairly executed ... Our expenses would more perfectly accord with the grants of Parliament, superfluities would be retrenched, improper fees prevented, and the attendance on duty, in general too remiss, would be rendered necessarily punctual and constant.[35]

The Controller was too tough-minded, too experienced in the ways of the Navy, to believe his own assurances that the reorganization he proposed would make all well. Nor did he minimize the likelihood of resistance. 'Persons unacquainted with the office', he conceded, 'may possibly be alarmed at the idea of innovation, and those who do know it, because they are in it and have no great share in the load of the business, may be concerned at the approach of any increasing weight.' But anyone as well-informed as he was, he had no doubt, would see things his way: 'I must own it as my deepest conviction, that there appears to me an absolute necessity for change.'[36]

Early 1787 was as propitious a time for change as any since Middleton had assumed office nine years earlier. Recovery from the American war was well under way. The Sinking Fund, Pitt's arrangement for reducing the national debt and sustaining the government's credit, had been put in place in 1786; the Prime Minister remained avid for change; the Controller of the Navy still had his ear. It was not only Pitt's ear he required, however, but also that of the First Lord of the Admiralty. Working together, the two high officials could make a formidable team.[37] But an uncongenial First Lord could thwart a Controller's ambitions, and Middleton had faced such a First Lord since 1783, when Admiral Lord Howe took office. Middleton's reforms were not the only ambition Howe was in a position to thwart. In 1787 the Controller also became eligible for an admiral's flag, the prize coveted above nearly all things by every ambitious post-captain.

Once they made post, captains rose further up the ladder of naval rank strictly by seniority. Even for promotion within the flag ranks, the date of making captain mattered, not the date of promotion to rear-admiral. True, not all the captains who arrived at the zone of eligibility were selected for promotion as active-duty rear-admirals. As a means of dealing with a super-abundance of captains the Admiralty had hit upon a method of super-annuation. Passed-over captains were named Rear-Admirals in General Terms without any distinction of Colours, and quickly known within the service as 'yellow admirals' (each admiral's rank was divided internally into red, white and blue squadrons, red being the most senior and blue the least).[38]

Middleton had been named a post captain as of 22 May 1758. Of the ensuing 29 years he had served 17 on active duty, barely five of them at sea. He wanted his flag and he wanted to remain Controller of the Navy too. Howe insisted that a rear-admiral's flag must be hoisted at sea, not at Somerset House.

What was wrong between Middleton and Howe? Exactly Middleton's age, Howe had shown himself to be one of the great sea commanders of the day. While Middleton had been snapping up privateers in the Caribbean, in 1759 in a rising gale off a lee shore Howe had led the line-of-battle ships of Hawke's fleet in pursuit of the French among the rocks of Quiberon Bay. He had been a resourceful and energetic leader in the American war; he was further to distinguish himself in the coming War of the French Revolution. Horatio Nelson, who to be sure could be extravagant with praise, later called him 'the first and greatest sea officer the world has ever produced'.[39] A member of an aristocratic family closely tied to the Hanoverian dynasty, Howe was a particular friend and naval favorite of King George III. He may have felt some of the aristocrat's disdain for a striving commoner like Middleton as well as the sea officer's disregard for the pen-and-ink gentlemen with whom the Controller disliked being identified.[40] In Howe's distinction and condescension Middleton may have found much to resent.

He certainly resented what he regarded as Howe's unfriendly actions toward the Navy Office since he had become First Lord. Middleton wanted

John Marquand, who built the marine barracks at Chatham, retained as a general contractor for all dockyard renovations. Howe opposed the appointment. Middleton wanted all ships on the stocks in the King's and merchant yards roofed over against the weather. Howe canceled these arrangements and ordered the ships to be launched instead. Middleton wanted Captains Edward LeCras and Samuel Wallis, appointed extra sea commissioners during the American war, to be retained during the peace. Howe let them go. Middleton occasionally gave vent to his frustration over Howe's high-handedness, which he was quicker to detect in the First Lord than in himself. 'Unhappily, I must think it, for the public, as well as unpleasant to myself', he wrote to Baring. 'I have been rather thwarted than supported for these last five years in my endeavours of oeconomy and improvement.'[41] Either Middleton was loose with his dates or he meant to indict Keppel along with Howe. Yet it would have been obvious to Baring that he had Howe in mind when he complained that the Controller 'has no opportunity of explaining his views to and consulting the approbation of the present First Lord as he did with his predecessors'.[42]

No hint of the chilliness of the relationship between the First Lord and his naval colleague emerges from the account Middleton provided for Pitt of his only meeting with Howe over the question of his flag. Summoned to the First Lord's office on 23 September 1787, Middleton wrote, he was informed that a promotion to flag rank was to take place immediately, and several captains junior to him on the list would be included in it. In short, Middleton was to be passed over. In a maneuver known to administrative chiefs from his day to ours, Howe assured Middleton that, if it were up to him alone, he would attach a flag to the controllership, but opinion in the service would never stand for it, and he must bow to opinion. Middleton did not confide to Pitt whether he believed this for a moment. 'It was impossible for me to hesitate one moment on the choice', he went on, 'as declining the flag would have been sacrificing the object of 40 years' service.'[43] Always a ready man with a precedent, he cited Savage Mostyn, Charles Saunders and Hugh Palliser as captains who had achieved flag rank after serving as Controllers of the Navy. But Middleton's precedent actually supported Howe's position. Each of the three had resigned the controllership to hoist his flag, precisely the step Middleton did not want to take.

He obviously meant to enlist the Prime Minister's help in his struggle with Howe. 'It appears to me that Lord Howe, from what he said', he went on, 'would have acquiesced in such an arrangement if the measure was to originate with his Majesty and the cabinet, and in such case no captain would have ventured to find fault with it.'[44] A far duller man than Pitt would have taken the hint. But it is doubtful whether the Prime Minister would have allowed himself to be drawn into this affair had he not also been discontented with the First Lord. For Howe had kept aloof from the Cabinet; he was not on good terms with the Duke of Richmond, the Master General of the Ordnance, whose authority over artillery at sea as well as by land made him an official the Navy always had to reckon with; nor did he get on with Henry Dundas, the Home Secretary (and Middleton's cousin); and he had a distant relationship with Pitt himself. As John Ehrman suggests, although the screen across the front of the Admiralty building in Whitehall had been constructed to bar seamen clamoring for back pay, Howe's associates might have been excused for thinking it was intended to shield him from them.[45] So Middleton's maneuvering to get his flag by circumventing Howe opportunely served Pitt's desire to rid the Cabinet of an uncollegial colleague. Unwilling to swallow the challenge to his judgement that the Prime Minister's intervention represented, Howe resigned in July 1788.

Admirals who had the makings of a good First Lord seemed for the moment to be thin on the ground. Heeding the advice of his close friend William Wilberforce, Pitt turned to a civilian, naming to the post his older brother John, the second Earl Chatham. Pitt was slightly uneasy about choosing a close relative for such an important post. But he wanted in the job someone he could trust, someone he knew would co-operate. If the appointment embarrassed some of Pitt's close associates, Chatham was nevertheless an able man.[46] True, he was also a lazy, unpunctual one – 'the late Lord Chatham' some people called him while he remained very much alive. Skeptics were assured that the new First Lord could lean on the old Controller, Rear-Admiral Sir Charles Middleton, who continued in office. Once he had prevailed over Howe, the mechanism of seniority continued to ratchet him upward. Named a vice-admiral on 1 February 1793, he became an admiral on 1 June 1795 (the first anniversary of Howe's celebrated tactical victory over the French fleet), ending up an Admiral of the Red in the so-called 'Trafalgar promotion' of 9 November 1805.

With Howe out of the way and the agreeable Chatham installed in his place, in midsummer 1788 the time for putting Middleton's plans for reforming the Navy Office into place appeared finally to have arrived.

In 1781 Middleton enlarged the Evangelical circle at Teston by obtaining for his old friend the Revd James Ramsay appointment to the vicarage. Before taking orders and serving many years as a parson in the West Indies,

Ramsay had been surgeon's mate aboard the *Arundel* (24), which Middleton commanded in 1759–60. The duties of his ecclesiastical living at Teston left him time to act as Middleton's private secretary; drafts of many of the Controller's papers for the 1780s are written in the clergyman's angular hand. In 1784 Ramsay published his *Essay on the Treatment and Conversion of African Slaves in the British Sugar Colonies*, which argued, among other things, for the abolition of the slave trade. By many accounts Ramsay's pamphlet ignited the movement to abolish the trade in African slaves. According to one version of the story, Ramsay's revelations shocked Margaret Middleton (presumably Charles Middleton, who had served many years in the West Indies and had been left ashore during a naval mutiny in Sierra Leone, a major source of slaves, was *not* shocked). She urged her husband, a backbench MP, to enlist more influential Members in the cause of outlawing the trade. Middleton sought out Pitt's intimate friend William Wilberforce, just undergoing his conversion to Evangelicalism. And so the trail led back to Ramsay. The Middletons invited Wilberforce to Teston, where he was introduced (or reintroduced) to the Evangelical pamphleteer.

This is a plausible story, but it is too simple and too narrow to be the whole story. Indeed, the movement to abolish the slave trade is a complicated tale, made even more complicated in recent years by disagreements over how it unfolded and what it meant. Earlier historians saw it as confined in its origins and course to a narrow, elitist stream.[47] More recently writers have characterized the movement as a popular flood on which the mass petitioners of the industrializing North exerted far more influence than any coterie of London co-religionists.[48]

In any case, Middleton's participation in the movement to abolish the slave trade was confined to the London coterie. His kind of participation is hard to assess. His papers breathe not a word of the subject. Such evidence as does exist consists mainly of a string of Ramsay-like anecdotes. Yet these are telling anecdotes, for they convey the doings and qualities of a person who today might be called a facilitator. Except for one speech in Parliament in which he attested, as a sort of expert witness, that a sailor in the British Navy slung his hammock in a space 14 inches wide, more than was allowed any African chained aboard a slaver, Middleton remained in the background. As a facilitator, he did what many rich and influential people devoted to a cause have done. He attended dinners, introduced the like-minded to each other, and made Teston available for meetings of abolitionist strategists. Such activities do not leave much trace except as anecdotes (perhaps Middleton contributed money to the campaign, but no record of a donation survives). In one Middleton dined among the high and mighty at a party arranged in Wilberforce's honor by Bennet Langton, a leading London host, and including among the guests Joshua Reynolds, James Boswell and William Windham.[49] Wilberforce wrote to friends and in his diary of breakfasts at Sir Charles Middleton's, dinners there with Ramsay and others, and long talks over the fire.[50] The blue-stocking Hannah More, rising playwright, budding Evangelical, friend of both Middletons and Mrs Bouverie, breathlessly assured her sisters that 'Teston will be the Runnymede of the Negroes'.[51]

More's prediction missed the mark. For one thing, the predicament of millions of black Africans was inexpressibly more dire than that of a handful of King John's barons. For more than a century before the sudden emergence of abolitionist sentiment, slave labor had been the prime mover of the Atlantic economy, that lucrative trade in people and goods between England, Africa and the West Indian plantations Middleton defended in his sea-going years. No nation had been more successful than Britain in establishing slave-labor colonies overseas.[52] The abolitionists, anti-abolitionists charged, threatened British prosperity. Not only economics, they claimed, but also history and geography were against them.[53] Yet although the anti-abolitionists were loud and clever and the planters well represented in Parliament, the slave traders were not. In 1787–88 a reforming spirit still animated the Pitt administration, and Pitt's dear friend Wilberforce was the chief parliamentary advocate of abolishing the trade in slaves. Moreover, the first minister found the issue easier to embrace than, say, reforming the House of Commons or freeing Catholics of their civil disabilities.[54]

Yet events were moving against the campaign to abolish the slave trade. The abolitionists who gathered at Middleton's and elsewhere laid plans to introduce major legislation in the Parliamentary session of 1788–89. In October 1788, before Parliament convened, the King fell suddenly and calamitously ill. He was said to have become a lunatic. It now seems that George III was suffering from a rare hereditary metabolic disorder called acute intermittent porphyria, which in some ways mimics madness, but this is a twentieth-century diagnosis of eighteenth-century symptoms.[55] Whatever it was, the King's malady threw Cabinet and Parliament into turmoil. The Regency crisis ensued, as unedifying a spectacle as struggles over power can be. Pitt put aside all but the most urgent questions of government to deal with it.[56]

The second blow delivered against the prospects for an early abolition of the slave trade was the outbreak and early course of the French

Revolution. The well-meant but patronizing emblem of the abolitionist movement showed a kneeling African in chains bearing the motto 'Am I not a man and a brother?'. In the West Indies in 1790 black slaves answered by rising against their French masters. British reformers wondered what was to keep the contagion from spreading to the *British* West Indies, where Ramsay had hoped that abolishing the trade in slaves would produce a more docile work force. At home, the Revolution divided the ranks of the abolitionists. Anglicans such as Middleton shrank away from radical Dissenters, whom they suspected of plotting against the established order to which they themselves were deeply attached. Soon the words and deeds of British admirers of the French revolutionaries made virulent anti-Jacobins of middle-class reformers such as Wilberforce.[57] Fear of revolution cast its long, dark, undiscriminating shadow over calls for reform.

The same events that told against the abolition of the slave trade also foiled Middleton's plans for reforming the Navy Office. On 28 May 1787 Pitt told the House of Commons that no one familiar with the Navy Office 'would wish that its examination and reform should be delayed a single hour'.[58] He emerged triumphant from the Regency crisis in the spring of 1789, but he never returned to administrative reform with the whole-heartedness he had evinced in the years following the election of 1784. When all looked well for the Controller's plans, Chatham's indolence scarcely seemed to matter; it might even have encouraged Middleton to think that he was all the less likely to be crossed. But as the King's illness came to distract the Prime Minister from nearly all other business, a less-than-energetic First Lord proved a hindrance to reform.

Middleton was too keen an observer not to notice how sharply the wind had shifted:

> Should your Lordship and Mr. Pitt [he wrote on 7 June 1789] seem inclined to postpone the consideration of the Committees [the heart of his reform plan] to a future opportunity, I will not urge it any farther at present, but must hope that the subject will have a fair discussion hereafter, as I verily believe there can not be a better method proposed for chequing abuses, providing against insufficient appointments, and saving large sums on the Wear and Tear and Accounts than doing business by Committees.[59]

Three weeks later Middleton wrote to Chatham about a modification he pointedly hoped the First Lord would bring to the attention of Pitt and

William Grenville, currently Paymaster of the armed forces, the Prime Minister's cousin, confidant and a like-minded reformer. He was prepared to lighten ship in the interest of keeping reform afloat. Essential as he believed his committee system to be, the Controller said, he would not object to creating a system of departments assigned the same functions (correspondence, stores and accounts) that his plan called for. Stripped of the committees' consultative powers, such a contrivance would be less effective but perhaps more easily brought about.[60]

Middleton's more modest proposals went nowhere. Supposing that he would reach the Prime Minister's ear through his older brother's proved mistaken. By late 1789 he had grown discouraged enough or frustrated enough to hint at resigning. It is impossible to say whether discouragement or frustration played the greater role. Perhaps Middleton meant to wash his hands of affairs, come what may; perhaps he hoped to get his way by threatening to quit. This is always risky, for such bluffs are often called and resignations accepted. In an undated letter to Chatham – its context suggests late December 1789 or early January 1790 – Middleton conceded even more ground. 'As I understand it to be the wish of government to make as little alteration as possible in the present constitution of the Navy Board', he began, going on to recommend at least the adding of an assistant Controller, a secretary and a surveyor of civil architecture. Compared with the ambitious scheme he had drawn up for Shelburne and then for Baring and his colleagues, this was a skimpy recommendation indeed. Middleton emphasized that he stuck by his longstanding proposals:

> I must ... request to be understood, that, by this concurrence with a more prevailing opinion, I have not in the least degree given up my own sense upon this matter, which has been formed, not upon theoretical arguments & speculations, but upon an intimate and practical investigation constantly and laboriously exercised for these twelve years; and I must here take the liberty to declare, that I have not yet heard a single objection made to the chief regulations proposed by the Commissioners of Enquiry, which has not confirmed me, on the one hand, in my opinion of their rectitude, and convinced me, on the other, that the Objections either have not or could not have bestowed on the subject a due examination.

Stiff-necked as ever, Middleton insisted that he was right and his opponents were wrong. When he listened to himself speaking through the Commission on Fees, he agreed with everything he heard. He went on to hint that perhaps his usefulness to government had come to an end.[61] He had come dangerously close to painting himself into a corner.

Perhaps he did not mind. By 1790, as he pointed out, he had been in office continuously for 12 years, almost five of them during a great naval emergency. Even allowing for the relatively leisurely administrative pace of the eighteenth century (a relativity he could not have been aware of) and for his obvious energy and enthusiasm for work, the wear and tear on Middleton, as on the ships he oversaw, must have been enormous. He was 63 – old by eighteenth-century standards, more than twice the age of the Prime Minister, who was to die at 46. Perhaps the more time he spent at Somerset House in London, the better Teston looked.

Learning in February 1790 that no action on the reports of the Commission on Fees was to be taken at any time soon, he could not conceal his disappointment and disgust. In a letter to Pitt he poured out his anger and resentment. He could have managed well enough at the Navy Office, he asserted, had the prospect of reform never been raised. But once it was, and once he was known within the office to be the arch-reformer, then all the masters of subterfuge, obfuscation and delay, all those fearful for their jobs and perquisites, had coalesced against him. The Office, he claimed with customary hyperbole, was on the verge of falling apart. 'This consideration of the evils resulting from a lost enquiry is and must be peculiarly mortifying to me', he complained, going on to enumerate the grounds of his mortification in perhaps the longest sentence he ever wrote. 'I have no way left to extricate myself', he concluded, 'but to resign [the office]; and this I would not do from disgust or personal disappointment, but, candidly and sincerely, from a deep sense of my own insufficiency to render the public in this respect any further service.'[62]

What Pitt made of this venting of spleen is not known. If he read it carefully he would have noticed that Middleton caught himself at the end, softened the tone of his letter as if suddenly aware that he might have overdone it. Pressed by worries on other fronts, the Prime Minister evidently did not try to dissuade the Controller from resigning. Middleton submitted his formal letter of resignation on 15 March 1790; by then he had recovered his composure. 'I am so firmly persuaded (however erroneous my judgement may be)', he wrote to Pitt, 'that the present situation of the navy office could afford me no means of continuing any longer useful, that I flatter myself with yours and Lord Chatham's candour in admitting the propriety of my resignation.'[63]

Among Middleton's papers is a draft in a clerk's hand endorsed 'Reasons for resigning the office'. Referring to himself in the third person, he recited his version of the history of reform and the leading role he had played in it. He thought it only fair to state

> that, at the time of Sir Charles Middleton's resignation, the fleet is left in the best possible state; the number of serviceable ships, the greatest ever known in this country; the stores, appropriated to them, arranged in the most perfect order; the arsenals filled with every kind of proper stores, to the value of two millions sterling; three of the foreign yards completed since the peace ... The home yards are also in the greatest possible progress and even now ready for the most complete exertions. The use of copper has been established in all the branches to which it could be applied. In short, the remoter objects of the department are now in so fair a state, that nothing is wanting to perfect our naval economy, but the internal arrangement of the office itself respecting persons and their particular duties, in order to carry on business with life and despatch.[64]

It was not, then, the best of all possible worlds, but in terms of the state of the Navy in 1790 Middleton exaggerated only a little.

The internal rearrangement of the Office was longer in coming than Middleton expected when he wrote to Francis Baring in 1786, yet nearer than he probably assumed when he resigned in discouragement four years later. The Admiralty endorsed his plan for reorganizing the Navy Board into committees under the direction of the Controller in May 1796, and forwarded it to the Privy Council, which established Middleton's long-sought system the same year.[65]

As loudly as Middleton declaimed against the intolerable position in which he found himself in 1790, when he left he was careful to close the door softly behind him. Indeed, he left it ajar, continuing to communicate his views on naval affairs to Pitt and Chatham, who evidently maintained their regard for their difficult, erstwhile colleague. In 1790, for instance, a confrontation with Spain over Britain's right to trade in Nootka Sound (Vancouver) provoked the mobilization of 40 British ships of the line. Middleton not only offered Pitt his advice on how best to carry out this so-called 'Spanish Armament' but volunteered to return to sea duty![66] Sail-and-cutlass rattling were enough to induce the Spanish to back down, and Middleton apparently had no counsel for Pitt in 1791 as he blundered through a murky crisis, and a smaller naval mobilization, over efforts to settle a Russo-Turkish war.[67]

Despite a momentary turbulence stirred by events on the far sides of the world, the British economy continued to boom in early 1792, recovery from the American war was virtually complete. In February Pitt delivered a famous budget speech surveying economic progress since the end of the last war, congratulating himself and the country on the financial reforms his administration had carried out, and making optimistic predictions about the year to come. 'Never fear', he had told a fretting Edmund Burke the previous September, 'depend on it we shall go on as we are, until the day of judgement.'[68] The year 1792 turned out to be the last one of peace for a long time to come, and Pitt's speech became famously ironic.

Of all the issues that might have led to war with revolutionary France, the one that most certainly provoked intervention in 1793 had drawn Britain into continental warfare before and would do so twice again. In November 1792 the French army occupied the Low Countries (Belgium) and seemed to be threatening the Dutch Republic. A great power controlling Belgium and Holland dominated not only the economic, political and maritime life of north-western Europe but also the Channel ports through which an invasion of Britain could be mounted. No British government since Queen Elizabeth I had been prepared to see this happen uncontested. The French revolutionary government had no intention of giving up its territorial gains and by February 1793 Lord Grenville, the Foreign Secretary, maneuvered it into accepting the onus of declaring war.[69]

Scarcely more than a year later Middleton was back in government. This time he did not serve long. Brought back as a Lord of Admiralty in May 1794, he resigned again in October 1795. Under Chatham, who continued as First Lord, he became senior naval adviser, a position later known as First Sea Lord. Chatham himself was not long for office. He did not carry much weight in the Cabinet, despite being the Prime Minister's brother. Easy-going to a fault, fond of the bottle, he could not keep up with the accelerated tempo of a department at war. In November 1794 Pitt required Chatham to exchange places with George, second Earl Spencer, the Lord Privy Seal. Spencer took over the Admiralty. A newcomer to the Cabinet, an especially well-connected aristocrat, a prodigious bibliophile, he was 35, a still young man whom his opponents underestimated.[70] On Middleton his impact was unexpected and profound.

The old sea lord greeted the new First Lord in his customary bustling, self-confident, advice-giving manner: 'When I first came to the Admiralty Board', he declared, 'I found no regular time fixed for beginning business nor any plan formed for carrying it into execution – the office extremely defective in attendance and no dependance whatever in anything being carried into execution. As Lord Chatham's ministerial concerns did not allow of a regular attendance in office hours, the whole of the business very soon fell into my hands.'[71]

Whatever Middleton hoped or expected, the whole of the business did not remain in his hands; he did not continue on as a *de facto* acting First Lord. Spencer was determined to act on his own behalf. As the senior sea officer on the Admiralty Board, Middleton's responsibilities ran far and wide, but no sooner had he written to Spencer than he complained to Dundas of feeling constrained. 'It is really impossible to get the King's ships to sea in any given time', he wrote, 'and unless such measures are used as no unprofessional man will see the necessity of [a dig at the landsman Spencer?], I see no prospect whatever of carrying on the service ... It never fell to my share before to carry on business in this fettered way.'[72]

As Controller Middleton had endured plenty of frustration over getting the King's ships to sea, a task at which he excelled. The fetters that truly chafed, and in the end proved unendurable, belonged to operational issues. Middleton had always itched to have a hand in directing operations at sea; he had freely given advice on such matters to the imperturbable Sandwich, even though he recognized that once a ship weighed anchor its movements and disposition were beyond the Navy Board's reach. Now that he was one of their Lordships himself, operations were properly his business. His views on the operational realm were as strong and decided as his views on everything else, and they soon brought him foul of Lord Spencer.

Middleton's membership on the Admiralty Board came to grief over a military expedition to the West Indies. Never before had Britain attempted such a large operation overseas (Dundas informed the Transport Board that the Army would require shipping for from 25,000 to 30,000 men). Why such a huge and risky undertaking against a group of islands no bigger, for the most part, than the Isle of Wight or Martha's Vineyard? Think of Saul Steinberg's famous *New Yorker* drawing of Manhattan, in which that island looms larger than the entire United States beyond the Hudson River. The West Indies loomed similarly in the minds of eighteenth-century policy-makers, British and French alike. In this case, however, reality matched perception. The Caribbean islands remained the hinge of the Atlantic economy. In the late 1780s the foreign trade of the French Saint Domingue (now Haiti) exceeded that of the entire United States. In the same decade, only Britain's trade with northern Europe surpassed in official valuation its trade with the West Indies.[73]

The islands were as vulnerable as they were rich – thinly settled, poorly garrisoned, utterly dependent on their sea lines of communication with Europe. In time of war it had long been the policy of each of the antagonistic powers to swoop down on the West Indian trade of the other. In his youth, of course, Middleton had profited handsomely from his role as wolf in the sheepfold.[74] Seizing control of the more important French islands, it was thought, might cripple France's ability to make war. The war with revolutionary France had already seen the failure, in more favorable circumstances, of a British expedition against the French West Indies. In 1793–94 Britain had continental allies – that crucial ingredient to success against France present in the Seven Years War and absent from the American war. But in the event, the West Indian expedition foundered; France improved its position in the Caribbean at British expense; a royalist landing on the French mainland failed; and the continental allies appeared to be on the verge of dropping out of the war.

Worsened prospects for success seemed to make a West Indian expedition all the more imperative. Middleton had misgivings about heeding this siren call. Britain, he feared, did not have the ships to meet such dubious commitments. The sea lord drew a simile from the estate manager:

> It is this system of unlimited conquest [he wrote to Spencer] that cripples us everywhere, and diverts the fleet from its natural use. It is like a farmer wishing to occupy a larger farm without money to manage it. The consequence is, that he begins a beggar and ends a ruined man. Our situation is truly similar: once behindhand and always behindhand.[75]

More powerful voices within the Pitt government thought otherwise. Henry Dundas, now Secretary for War, was adamant on the need for another West Indian expedition. It was, he insisted, the only course of action open to Britain under the conditions prevailing in 1795. Middleton's misgivings about the naval requirements of an expedition the size Dundas contemplated were waved aside. In mid August the Cabinet committed itself. Newspapers announced that Major-General Ralph Abercromby, another Dundas kinsman, had been named to command the land forces; command of the accompanying naval squadron had gone to Rear-Admiral Hugh Christian. Here, in so far as Middleton was concerned, is where the trouble truly began.

For Christian was a very junior flag officer. He had made rear-admiral only in the promotion of June 1795 (the same in which Middleton had risen from vice-admiral to admiral), largely in recognition of his services as head of the Transport Board, where he displayed the kind of expertise and initiative also valuable in a naval commander of combined or amphibious operations.[76] Dundas apparently assumed that Christian would be sent out to replace Vice-Admiral Sir John Laforey as commander-in-chief, Leeward Islands station. But Spencer could not bring himself to recall Laforey. At the same time, he recognized that there was not room for two admirals at one station. Taking account of Christian's lack of seniority, the First Lord nominally made him second in command of the Leeward Islands station. This expedient involved putting Laforey where he would be less likely to interfere with Christian's amphibious operation. The senior admiral was to be shifted to Jamaica as commander-in-chief, Caribbean, and room made for him there by putting Rear-Admiral William Parker in command of naval forces off Santo Domingo. The instructions for performing this dance were drawn up while Middleton was out of the office recovering from an attack of gout.

When he returned he informed the First Lord that shuffling senior admirals such as Laforey and Parker to and fro was a breach of naval etiquette, an affront to everyone in the higher reaches of the service. Laforey and Middleton were old friends; they had served together in the West Indies; Laforey belonged to the Huguenot circles in which Middleton had moved since marrying Margaret Gambier. Even among those privy to this affair it would have been hard to disentangle the claims of friendship from the requirements of principle and the tug of service loyalty; it is virtually impossible today. In Middleton all three were probably at work. The inexperienced Spencer deferred to Middleton. Admiral Laforey, he decided, would stay put on the Leeward Islands station.

Spencer neglected to tell Dundas or Abercromby about Middleton's arrangement, however; they learned of it only on the eve of the scheduled departure of the West Indian expedition. Dundas was shocked. On 12 October he wrote to Spencer, 'I confess myself truly alarmed by what you tell me relative to Sir John Laforey. That he is very unpopular in the West Indies is apparent from every letter one has the occasion to see.' Conceding that the First Lord had to take feelings in the Navy into account, he nevertheless insisted that 'the ground on which I am alarmed goes much deeper'. He feared Abercromby would see in Spencer's arrangement an invitation to a divided naval command; not wanting to be dragged into disputes within the Navy, he might decline to serve, and Dundas had no other general officer on whom he could rely.[77]

The First Lord himself was not especially happy with Laforey's performance as commander-in-chief. In July he had written to complain of his languid conduct of affairs on the Leeward Islands station. 'The inactivity of our very numerous fleet now there', he told Laforey, 'gives so much dissatisfaction, I cannot avoid writing a few lines ... to repeat and enforce what I am fully persuaded you are very much aware of, the great necessity of a better disposition of the naval force.'[78] Nevertheless, for the moment he stuck by his man. Replying to Dundas's strenuous objections to keeping Laforey in the Leeward Islands with Middleton's equally strenuous defense of naval etiquette, he insisted that so senior an admiral could not be removed from command without having some charge to bring against him. All would be well, he assured Dundas, if Laforey were merely instructed not to interfere with plans Abercromby and Christian had made together and Christian were admonished to be kind to his senior naval officer, for 'The truth is that Adm Christian is too young an admiral for the command of so extensive an expedition. [Laforey] who, though old and therefore perhaps a little less active than one could wish, is however perfectly acquainted with that station [and] would be unprecedentedly and unjustly degraded in the eyes of the whole service.'[79]

Dundas was not to be mollified. He went to see Pitt about Spencer's and Middleton's expedient. The Prime Minister, he informed the First Lord, 'was much alarmed about it ... His feeling is that the [naval] service still remains in danger from collision.'[80] If the alarm of Dundas and Pitt were not enough to tip the balance against Spencer's arrangement, the Secretary for War tossed in the alarm of Abercromby, enclosing for the First Lord's perusal a copy of a letter he had just received from the general. Writing from Southampton, where he was embarking his troops, Abercromby insisted that 'an undertaking of so much importance to the nation, must not stand on a basis, so insecure, as the collision of the interests and passions of individuals'. Piling up his objections to Spencer's expedient in a series of rhetorical questions, Abercromby ended by asking, 'Is not the whole unity of design and execution destroyed by this divided command?'.[81] Abercromby was a man of strong convictions and great strength of will. He had sat out the American war rather than serve against a cause with which he sympathized, thereby undoubtedly slowing his own advancement.[82] Dundas had good reason to believe that the ablest soldier he could find to command the expedition to the West Indies might wrench himself from his grasp. Indeed, on 18 October Abercromby wrote to William Huskisson, the Under-Secretary for War. What, he wondered, were Laforey's friends (Middleton included) up to? Were they trying to cut him in on the prize money that might arise from the expedition? Abercromby was unsure he could accept a command under the terms of Spencer's expedient.[83] Abercromby entertained no illusions as to the benignity of military or naval ambition. As Michael Duffy has put it, in the General's opinion 'Soldiers and sailors ... were not generous, disinterested people. They would willingly cut each other's throats for fame or profit.'[84]

Spencer was caught between three tough and intimidating Scots. Dundas and Abercromby pulled him in one direction, Middleton in another. Dundas happened to be related to both his countrymen, but in this affair the claims of consanguinity were as nothing compared with the competing demands of principle, tradition, sound military practice and interdepartmental and interservice rivalry. Struggling in the web, Spencer tried to evade responsibility for sorting things out. Abercromby misunderstood the situation, he informed Dundas; all along Christian had understood that he was to be nominally under Laforey's orders; a divided command was not at issue; and as to a possible injury done Laforey in advising him to stand aside in the matter of the West Indian expedition, 'his friend C.M. is convinced he will not consider it as such'. Less certain of his ground than he no doubt wanted to appear, Spencer ended by insisting that the Cabinet needed to decide the question of command.[85]

Perhaps Abercromby had exaggerated the danger of a divided command, Dundas replied, but the General's apprehensions had already been expressed by Mr Pitt. Then he turned the screws on Spencer. Assuring him that the matter of the naval command rested entirely with his Lordship did not keep Dundas from laying out alternative courses of action: Spencer could allow his expedient to stand; he could leave Laforey in an undivided command; he could recall Laforey; he could replace both Laforey and Christian with another senior admiral – 'in short, settle it any way you please and I shall *order* Abercrombie [*sic*] to go'.[86] Here was the clincher. Dundas was putting squarely on Spencer's shoulders the responsibility, should it come to that, for sending out the largest overseas expedition in British history under an apprehensive, resentful and disgruntled Army commander. Reminding Spencer for the umpteenth time of Pitt's uneasiness about the command arrangement as it stood, he assured him that the Prime Minister also agreed that it was not a matter to lay before the Cabinet.[87]

Spencer caved in. Unable to persuade his colleagues to help to make his choice any the less lonely, he decided to recall Laforey. It is hard to see how he could have done otherwise and remained within the government. Dundas's unrelenting pressure, his own misgivings about the elderly commander-in-chief of the Leewards and the specter of an Abercromby dragged out to the Caribbean against his will, were enough to persuade the First Lord to abandon the expedient his senior naval adviser had urged on him. Read against the string of irate letters Middleton had fired off to one official or another in the course of his career, his note on Laforey's recall seems muted:

> Having very freely and candidly delivered my opinion of Sir John Laforey's professional abilities and the unprecedented measure of recalling him [he wrote Spencer], I can only lament its being carried into execution ... I have put your Lordship's letter into Mr. Nepean's [the First Secretary's] hands, who will carry the contents into execution, but your Lordship will make allowance for my feelings, when I say that my reputation is too much concerned to take an active share in the business ...[88]

Middleton apparently believed that he could dissent from the order telling his old friend to haul down his flag and still keep his seat on the Admiralty Board, but Spencer was not having it, not after the buffeting he had taken from Dundas, Abercromby and Pitt. 'In every measure determined upon and officially proposed to the Board by the First Lord', he firmly instructed Middleton, 'every member of the Board is considered as ready to take an active part by the signature, and though the responsibility unquestionably rests on the First Lord, the other members are always understood to concur in his measures.' He went on to insist that Middleton sign the order recalling Laforey.[89] Middleton gave an Evangelical twist to his refusal: 'No consideration will induce me to concur in what I think an unjust measure, however recommended, because I know myself amenable to a much higher tribunal than any on earth. As your lordship seems to insinuate a removal from office, I can only say that my seat is at your lordship's service.'[90]

In Middleton's last letter to Spencer a tone of wounded, autumnal regret overtook the chilly hauteur of his letter of resignation. Whatever naval prerogatives he believed he had defended against the War Office in the struggle over the West Indian expedition, he plainly identified in generational terms with Laforey:

> Considering my time of life, and I hope I may be allowed to say without vanity my laborious and faithfull services, I could not but think that my signature would not have been so peremptorily required, ... if it had not been meant to convey to me that I took too much upon myself, and that my general behaviour in my situation was not such as ought to be patiently submitted to. I certainly never could nor would consider myself at the Board of Admiralty as much absolutely ministerial in things to which I

was required to sign my name as a young man who might more reasonably be expected to defer to greater experience and authority.[91]

Could the young man he had in mind have been Spencer? In any event, as Middleton neared the end of his letter the coals of resentment glowed more brightly. He was not one to ask himself whether the advice he gave was invariably sound or to blame himself for outcomes that could be laid to someone else. 'On the whole', he assured the First Lord, 'I shall certainly quit [the seat at the Board] with more pleasure than I had come into it. At the same time, my personal feelings would never have forced me to the step I have taken, if your Lordship's language had not rendered it indispensable.'[92]

What contemporaries saw in such tangled episodes as this depended on where they stood, and this is no less true of historians. Naval historians such as Julian Corbett, for instance, regarded the run-up to the West Indian expedition of 1795–96 as a case of Army encroachment on Navy preroga- tives.[93] Dundas, pushing for more than was rightly his to demand, is made the villain of such pieces. Even for Army historians such as Sir John Fortescue, Dundas is a villain.[94] From this distance, however, Dundas looks less like a man seeking to expand the influence of the War Office than one who feared making the West Indian expedition any more unwieldy and precarious. For all his talents, Abercromby had no experience in combined operations. In this respect he was as much the novice as Christian, who, for all the brand-newness of his flag, was nevertheless skilled in the art of packing landsmen into transports, expertise an amphibious expedition could not do without. Once they began working together the two officers discovered that they got along well, and Christian was no more eager than Abercromby to subject their relationship to the prospect of interference from a senior sea officer on the Leeward Islands station. From Southamp- ton he expressed his concerns about Spencer's expedient. 'I am not a little anxious', he wrote to Huskisson, the Under-Secretary of War, 'upon the great point of arrangements. The more I reflect upon it the more am I surprized at such persevering obstinacy on the part of Sir CM.'[95]

Christian attributed to Middleton the very trait the sea lord saw in him- self.[96] In the course of his long career ashore, obstinate perseverance had served him well: in coppering the fleet, in supplying America, in developing the carronade, in reorganizing the standing orders of the Navy, in improving peacetime readiness and leading a huge shipbuilding program, in reform- ing the Navy Office, and in countless lesser attempts to overcome the inertia natural to a large and complex enterprise such as the naval shore establishment. But obstinate perseverance may also have a tiresome, provoking and unproductive quality. Having taken his cousin's measure long ago, Henry Dundas had found it advisable to warn the new First Lord that

> It will be proper for me to have a very confidential conversation with you on the subject of Sir Charles Middleton. He has very great official talents and merit, but he is a little difficult to act with from an anxiety, I had almost said an irritability of temper, and he requires to have a great deal of his own way of doing business in order to do it well.

Certain of Middleton's letters, Dundas went on, left him 'entertaining doubts how far under all circumstances it would be right to urge him to remain, and at the same time I cannot help feeling that his retiring from the Admiralty at this time would be an irreparable loss'.[97]

Within less than a year Spencer found circumstances that kept him from urging the sea lord to remain. Middleton left defeated and by no means expecting ever to return.[98] In his last letter to Spencer he thanked the First Lord for not asking him to continue at the Board until his successor had been named, 'as I am anxious to get a little country air and exercise before the winter sets in'.[99]

NOTES

1 William L. Clemens Library (hereafter WCL), Ann Arbor, Michigan. SP 151, Middleton to Shelburne, 9 September 1782.

2 N. A. M. Rodger, *The Insatiable Earl: A Life of John Montagu, Fourth Earl of Sandwich 1718–1792* (New York, 1994), p. 165.

3 John Brewer, *The Sinews of Power: War, Money and the English State, 1688–1783* (New York, 1989), pp. 85–6. John Ehrman, *The Younger Pitt*, 3 vols (London, 1969–96), vol. I, p. 60.

4 John Knox Laughton (ed.), *Letters and Papers of Charles, Lord Barham*, 3 vols (London, 1907–11), vol. II, p. 56.

5 WCL, SP 151, Middleton to Shelburne, 9 September 1782.

6 The dockyard privilege of taking home small scraps of timber for use as firewood had over the years become the habit, winked at by warders and sentries, of carrying away pieces big enough to serve the purposes of a house carpenter. From such 'scraps' much of Portsmouth was said to have been built. On 'Chips' see Daniel A. Baugh, *British Naval Administration in the Age of Walpole* (Princeton, NJ, 1965), pp. 321–2.

7 One exception was the Treasurership of the Navy, which by Middleton's time made few demands on its incumbent, who for some years was the Controller's enormously influential cousin Henry Dundas.

8 WCL, SP 151, Middleton to Shelburne, 9 September 1782.

9 In a story set in 1813 Jack Aubrey, Patrick O'Brian's fictional naval hero, explains to

his wife, 'Have I never told you about the Marines, sweetheart? It is a plum they give you when you have done well. They cannot promote you – there is no such thing as promotion out of turn once you are a post-captain, and even the King could not make you an admiral over the heads of the captains above you on the list – if he did, half his senior officers would resign. So since they cannot promote you, and since you cannot eat a baronetcy or the naval medal, they make you a colonel of the Royal Marines instead, and you draw a colonel's pay, without doing anything for it.' *The Surgeon's Mate* (London, 1981), p. 146.

10 WCL, SP 151, Middleton to Shelburne, 9 September 1782.
11 Michael Young, *The Rise of the Meritocracy, 1870–2033: An Essay on Education and Equality* (London, 1958).
12 WCL, SP 151, Middleton to Shelburne, 9 September 1782.
13 Ibid.
14 Ibid.
15 Ehrman, *Pitt*, vol. I, p. 176.
16 Baugh, *British Naval Administration*, p. 305.
17 PRO, 30/8/111, Chatham Papers, Middleton to Pitt, 16 September 1784.
18 John Norris, *Shelburne and Reform* (London, 1963), pp. 118, 200–1, 271, 293.
19 Ehrman, *Pitt*, vol. I, p. 77.
20 Frank O'Gorman, *The Emergence of the British Two-Party System, 1760–1832* (London, 1982), pp. 14–18; Paul Langford, *A Polite and Commercial People: England, 1727–1783* (Oxford, 1989), pp. 559–64.
21 PRO, 30/8/111, Chatham Papers.
22 Richard Pares, 'The Younger Pitt', in *The Historian's Business and Other Essays* (Oxford, 1961), p. 125.
23 Ehrman, *Pitt*, vol. I, p. 167.
24 John Torrance, 'Social Class and Bureaucratic Innovation: The Commissioners for Examining the Public Accounts, 1780–1787', *Past and Present*, 78 (February 1978), pp. 56–81; John E. Breihan, 'William Pitt and the Commission on Fees, 1785–1801', *Historical Journal*, 27, 1 (1984), pp. 59–82.
25 Ibid., p. 63.
26 NMM, MID/2/1, Middleton to Baring, 2 December 1786.
27 Ibid., Baring to Middleton, 3 December 1786.
28 NMM, MID/14/6.
29 NMM, MID/6/4.
30 NMM, MID/2/1, Middleton to Baring, 2 December 1786.
31 Quoted in Rodger, *Insatiable Earl*, p. 162. 'This gentleman', the informant went on, 'adopts no plan without persuing his object with unremitting assiduity & indefatigable labour, his natural disposition being in this respect assisted by the pertinacity derived from certain religious opinions.'
32 NMM, MID/14/6, Observations on the Navy Board Department.
33 Ibid.
34 On the need for competent sea officers on the Navy Board, see Middleton's letter to the Admiralty Board, NMM, MID/2/54, 8 December 1783.
35 NMM, MID/14/6.
36 Ibid.
37 Ehrman, *Pitt*, vol. I, p. 314.
38 Baugh, *Naval Administration*, pp. 130–8. Baugh's discussion of the mid-eighteenth century holds for the later decades as well. See also N. A. M. Rodger, *The Wooden World: An Anatomy of the Georgian Navy* (London, 1986), p. 299. *The Yellow Admiral* (New York, 1996) is the title of Patrick O'Brian's eighteenth in his sequence of novels on the British Navy in the age of Napoleon.

39 Quoted in Julian S. Corbett (ed.), *Fighting Instructions, 1530–1816* (London, 1905), p. 257.
40 The standard biography remains Sir John Barrow, *The Life of Earl Howe* (London, 1838).
41 NMM, MID/2/1, Middleton to Baring, 2 December 1786.
42 Ibid.
43 *Barham Papers*, vol. II, p. 259.
44 Ibid.
45 Ehrman, *Pitt*, vol. II, p. 315.
46 Ibid., p. 315n.
47 Coupland's *Wilberforce* takes this view, as does the book of the Quaker abolitionist leader Thomas Clarkson, *History of the Rise, Progress, and Abolition of the African Slave Trade by the British Parliament* (London, 1839).
48 The leader of this tendency is Seymour Drescher. Among his many publications is 'Whose Abolition: Popular Pressure and the Ending of the British Slave Trade', *Past and Present*, No. 143 (May 1994), pp. 136–66. A recent contribution is J. R. Oldfield, *Popular Politics and British Anti-Slavery: The Mobilisation of Public Opinion against the Slave Trade* (Manchester, 1995).
49 David Brion Davis, *The Problem of Slavery in the Age of Revolution, 1770–1823* (Ithaca, NY, 1975), p. 220.
50 Coupland, *Wilberforce*, pp. 92–3, 100.
51 Quoted in M. G. Jones, *Hannah More* (Cambridge, 1952), p. 85.
52 Ehrman, *The Younger Pitt*, vol. I, p. 387; David Eltis, *Economic Growth and the Ending of the Transatlantic Slave Trade* (Oxford, 1987), p. 4; A. L. Stinchcombe, *Sugar Island Slavery in the Age of Enlightenment: The Political Economy of the Caribbean World* (Princeton, NJ, 1995).
53 Seymour Drescher, 'People and Parliament: The Rhetoric of the British Slave Trade', *Journal of Interdisciplinary History*, 20, 4 (Spring 1990), p. 574.
54 Robin Blackburn, *The Overthrow of Colonial Slavery, 1776–1848* (London, 1988), p. 151.
55 Porphyria as an explanation for the King's illness was proposed by the physicians Ida Macalpine and her son Richard Hunter, notably in *Porphyria: A Royal Malady, Articles Published in or Commissioned by the British Medical Journal* (London, 1968) and *George III and the Mad Business* (New York, 1969). A recent article is M. J. Warren, *et al.*, 'The Maddening Business of King George III and Porphyria', *Trends in Biochemical Sciences*, 21, 6 (June 1996), pp. 229–34. This famous episode is also the theme of Alan Bennett's play *The Madness of George III* (1992), the film version of which was renamed *The Madness of King George* (1995).
56 The best account of the crisis is Ehrman, *Pitt*, vol. I, pp. 644–66.
57 Leonore Davidoff and Catherine Hall, *Family Fortunes: Men and Women of the English Middle Class, 1780–1850* (London, 1987), p. 149; Davis, *Problem of Slavery*, p. 380; Blackburn, *Colonial Slavery*, pp. 146–7.
58 Quoted in Ehrman, *Pitt*, vol. I, p. 316.
59 NMM, MID/2/39, Middleton to Chatham.
60 Ibid., Middleton to Chatham, 27 June 1789.
61 Ibid., Middleton to Chatham, undated.
62 *Barham Papers*, vol. II, pp. 337–45. Middleton to Pitt, 8 February 1790.
63 Ibid., pp. 346–7.
64 Ibid., pp. 347–50.
65 J. R. Breihan, 'William Pitt and the Commission on Fees', *Historical Journal*, 24 (1984), p. 74.
66 *Barham Papers*, vol. II, pp. 351–3; Paul M. Kennedy, *The Rise and Fall of British Naval*

Mastery (London, 1976), p. 122.

67 On the 'Ochakov Affair', which foreshadowed the Eastern Question, that hardy perennial of nineteenth-century great-power diplomacy, see Ehrman, *Pitt*, vol. II, pp. 3–41.

68 Quoted in Ehrman, *Pitt*, vol. II, p. 88. On the budget speech see Ehrman, *Pitt*, vol. I, pp. 273–81.

69 Among the many treatments of these issues a succinct account is Michael Duffy, 'British Diplomacy and the French Wars', in H. T. Dickinson (ed.), *Britain and the French Revolution, 1789–1815* (London, 1989), pp. 127–46.

70 This paragraph relies on Ehrman, *Pitt*, vol. II, pp. 379, 417, 463.

71 British Library (hereafter BL), Althorp Papers, G175, Middleton to Spencer, 19 December 1794. He went on to recommend for the post of First Secretary of the Admiralty a Mr Grant, a director of the East India Company and a fellow Evangelical known to Pitt, Dundas, Wilberforce and Lord Cornwallis. To Middleton's effusion Spencer's only reply was the chilly secretarial endorsement 'Lord Spencer to Sir Chas. Middleton: will not disturb present arrangements by appointing Mr. Grant Sec'y to Admiralty'.

72 Ibid., Middleton to Dundas, 20 December 1794.

73 This and the following paragraphs rely heavily on Michael Duffy, *Soldiers, Sugar, and Seapower: The British Expeditions to the West Indies and the War against Revolutionary France* (Oxford, 1987), pp. 6, 10.

74 See Ch. 1.

75 Julian S. Corbett (ed.), *Private Papers of George, Second Earl Spencer, First Lord of the Admiralty, 1794–1801*, 3 vols (London 1913) I, p. 151. Middleton to Spencer, 25 August 1795. In a letter of 11 June Middleton warned that a consequence of setting afoot another expedition to the West Indies would be that 'Our arrangements of cruizing squadrons in the Bay [of Biscay] are broken up – and if not repaired by a preparation of Line of battle ships & frigates, we may give the enemy an opening for recovering that important station'. BL, Althorp Papers, G176. Middleton to Spencer, 11 June 1795.

76 On the use of these terms see Richard Harding, *Amphibious Warfare in the Eighteenth Century: The British Expedition to the West Indies, 1740–1742* (Woodbridge, Suffolk, 1991), especially pp. 1–15.

77 BL, Althorp Papers, G179, Dundas to Spencer, 12 October 1795.

78 Ibid., G178, Spencer to Laforey, 8 July 1795.

79 Ibid., G179, Spencer to Dundas, 12 October 1795.

80 Ibid., Dundas to Spencer, 18 October 1795.

81 Ibid., G176, Abercromby to Dundas, 16 October 1795.

82 *Dictionary of National Biography*, vol. I, pp. 43–6.

83 BL, Althorp Papers, G176, Abercromby to Huskisson, 18 October 1795. Naval commanders-in-chief received a share of all prizes taken on their stations, a practice often deeply resented in the Navy by those beneath them in the hierarchy.

84 Duffy, *Soldiers*, p. 167.

85 BL, Althorp Papers, G179, Spencer to Dundas, 19 October 1795.

86 Ibid., Dundas to Spencer, 20 October 1795. Dundas's emphasis and spelling.

87 Ibid.

88 Ibid., G176, Middleton to Spencer, 23 October 1795; also in *Spencer Papers*, vol. I, pp. 182–3. A somewhat different version appears in *Barham Papers*, vol. II, pp. 420–1.

89 BL, Althorp Papers, G176, Spencer to Middleton, 25 October 1795. A slightly different version appears in *Barham Papers*, vol. II, pp. 421–2.

90 *Spencer Papers*, vol. I, p. 183.

91 BL, Althorp Papers, G176, Middleton to Spencer, 27 October 1795.

92 Ibid.
93 See Corbett's remarks in *Spencer Papers*, vol. I, pp. 133–4.
94 Duffy, *Soldiers*, pp. 153–4.
95 PRO, Coloniai Office 318/18, Christian to Huskisson, 23 October 1795.
96 See above, p. 125.
97 *Spencer Papers*, vol. I, pp. 6–7, Dundas to Spencer, 14 December 1794.
98 He did tell Dundas, however, that 'I cannot take my leave, both of you and public business, without assuring you that, upon any crisis which may seem to demand my services as an officer, in any respect, I shall think it my duty cheerfully to stand forth and sacrifice my ease and other personal considerations to the honour and advantage of my country'. *Barham Papers*, vol. II, p. 421.
99 BL, Althorp Papers, G176, Middleton to Spencer, 27 October 1795.

Afterword

A Man of Ripe Experience

Few biographers of Nelson can resist recounting the story of how the stupendous news of their hero's victory at Trafalgar reached London. Toward midnight on 5 November 1805, according to Carola Oman's version, two sea officers hurrying by different roads from the West Country, one on horseback, the other by carriage, clattered into the courtyard of the Admiralty at virtually the same moment. The day had been one of the foggiest in memory, so thick that few pedestrians had ventured out for fear of being run down by an errant wagon. The two exhausted officers asked to see the Secretary of the Admiralty, for whom they bore identical dispatches from Vice-Admiral Collingwood.[1] The Secretary, William Marsden, left his own account of what happened next. Mindful of the need to inform the First Lord at once, he had no time to savor being the first person in England to learn of Trafalgar. But finding his superior at such an hour did not prove easy: 'The First Lord had retired to rest, as had his domestics, and it was not till after some research that I could discover the room in which he slept. Drawing aside his curtain, with a candle in my hand, I awoke the old peer ... from a sound slumber; and to the credit of his nerves, be it mentioned, that he showed no symptom of alarm or surprise, but calmly asked "What news, Mr. M?"'[2]

The old peer in question had, until the previous April, been Sir Charles Middleton. Elevated to the peerage as Lord Barham, a plum he had characteristically insisted on extracting from the King, much to the monarch's annoyance, he had been named First Lord of the Admiralty chiefly as a means of rescuing Pitt from political embarrassment. For Lord Melville (formerly Henry Dundas, Charles Middleton's kinsman and the Prime Minister's longstanding political ally) had been driven from office. A parliamentary inquiry disclosed that Alexander Trotter, Paymaster of the Navy, an appointee and henchman of Melville's, had played the stock market with Navy funds. Trotter actually paid back what he had lent to himself, so no public money was lost. Melville evidently neither knew about nor profited from the Paymaster's venture. He had himself taken steps to keep office-holders from an old habit of treating public funds as private purses. Practices once tolerated were now coming to be seen as financial irregularities. Melville had undoubtedly been not only easygoing but notably incurious about the doings of his subordinates. The Parliamentary Opposition was after big game, and in Melville, Pitt's lieutenant for more than 20 years, they found it. On 9 April, following days of angry debate, he resigned.[3]

Melville's resignation came at yet another moment of crisis in the long series of naval wars with France. The Peace of Amiens, signed in 1801, broke down in 1803, and among the schemes Napoleon (who proclaimed himself Emperor in 1804) set in motion as war resumed was one for the invasion of England. Amassing at Boulogne every serviceable boat his agents could find and building additional landing craft to order, he planned to seize control of the Channel for long enough (12 hours might do it, he thought) to put troops ashore on the other side. By means of land warfare, the element of his mastery, he would put out of business the sea power lying athwart his imperial ambitions.[4] Not even Napoleon, for all his well-known ignorance of war at sea, could have believed that such a feat would be as easy as he sometimes made it sound. Never mind the hazards of ferrying, in small craft, thousands of potentially seasick men and horses across 20 miles of notoriously unpredictable waters. Command of these waters had to be wrested, if only temporarily, from a government which for more than 200 years had pursued the cardinal policy, in time of war, of controlling them itself.

In pursuit of this policy, it will be recalled, British squadrons established, depending on circumstances, the close or distant blockade of enemy (and unfriendly) ports in the Mediterranean, the Atlantic and the North Sea; they patrolled the western approaches to the Channel and the Downs (the narrows off the Kentish coast). On those occasions when Spain joined France in maritime war against Britain, British watchfulness extended past Vigo down to Cádiz. This system put an enormous strain on ships and men. The vagaries of wind and weather, as well as chronic shortages of resources, often left gaping holes. During the Seven Years War, and at times during the War of the American Revolution, scurvy and other diseases interfered with the blockaders' ability to keep the sea.[5] By the close of the eighteenth century, however, an increase in the size of the Navy, improvements in shipboard diet, innovations in under-way replenishment and years of unremitting experience brought strategic blockade to a peak of efficiency

150

that seldom fell far short of the limits of endurance of the ships and sailors involved.

The whole object of the system, in the end, was to keep Napoleon from doing what he had in mind. No enemy must be allowed control of the Channel long enough to throw an invasion force across it. So the collapse of the Peace of Amiens once again set the British cats prowling outside the French mouse holes, ready to pounce should the French attempt to escape. By the time Barham succeeded Melville as First Lord, British commanders from the Texel in the North Sea to Toulon in the Mediterranean had been watching for more than two years every move the French made; Spain, hoping to improve its imperial holdings at British expense, had entered the war. In January 1805 Admiral Pierre Charles de Villeneuve, commander of the French squadron at Toulon, profited from northerly gales to give Nelson the slip. Disappearing into the Atlantic, Villeneuve set in motion Napoleon's scheme for denuding the Channel by luring the British into a wild-goose chase.

The invasion crisis hardly seemed the time to make an old man First Lord of the Admiralty. Pitt looked elsewhere before settling on his erstwhile naval adviser. He sounded out Robert Jenkinson, Lord Hawkesbury, the Home Secretary, but that able man preferred to remain leader of the House of Lords. No other politician seemed suitable. The eligible active-duty sailors carried political or professional liabilities. Admiral Lord Gardner was thought not to have the requisite administrative talents for the post; Admiral Lord Keith (George Elphinstone) was too junior to both Gardner and to Admiral William Cornwallis, flying their flags at sea, to be named First Lord without gravely offending the senior leadership of the Navy. So he turned to Middleton, who took office on 30 April and became Baron Barham of Teston on 1 May.[6] Seventy-nine at the time of his appointment, Barham had not held public office for 15 years, save for his brief and unhappy stint on the Admiralty Board in 1794–95. Evangelical politics and estate management kept him busy, and daily horseback rides kept him fit. Yet naming a well-connected (if not universally admired) elderly gentleman as First Lord of the Admiralty seemed better suited to peacetime politics than to a wartime emergency. For no politician can ever have too many good connections; in terms of allaying the jealousies of office-seeking allies, the older the gentleman the better. Surely Pitt, sick and distracted as he was by 1805, would not have given domestic political considerations primacy over the defense of the realm. It seems far more likely that Middleton was named First Lord of the Admiralty and created Lord Barham because Pitt's judgement prefigured that of Julian Corbett a century later. Barham was 'the man who, for ripe experience in the direction of naval war in all its breadth and detail, had not a rival in the service or in Europe'.[7]

If Barham's experience was unrivalled anywhere, he had not been at the center of naval affairs for some years. As First Lord he was at least a generation older than most of the principal commanders at sea. For instance, he was named a post captain in 1758, the year Nelson was born. He had not been to sea in more than 40 years. He was at best barely acquainted with any of the seagoing officers in whom he had to place his confidence. All this must have lent some weight to the Whig Member of Parliament Thomas Creevey's sneer that in Barham, Pitt had come up with a 'superannuated Methodist'.[8] The brevity of Barham's tenure as First Lord – he left office when Pitt died, in February 1806, having served only eight months – the focus of contemporaries and historians alike on the drama of events unfolding at sea, the presumption that old age is synonymous with decrepitude, and possibly even Creevey's remark all contributed to a longstanding impression that Barham must have been content to serve as a figurehead, dozing at the Admiralty table while his colleagues, subordinates and the squadron commanders did all the work. Even Sir John Laughton, the editor of Barham's published papers, helped reinforce this impression. A leading late Victorian naval historian, Laughton wrote most of the entries on naval officers that appear in the first edition of the *Dictionary of National Biography*. Laughton's Middleton is an undistinguished sea officer and an able, energetic and accomplished Controller of the Navy and naval reformer. But as First Lord, Laughton asserts, Barham mostly kept to his own rooms, leaving the strategy and policy of the Trafalgar campaign to others.[9]

Laughton's assessment was unencumbered by familiarity with Barham's voluminous papers. Once he had edited a three-volume selection of them for publication by the Navy Records Society he came to regret his piece for the *Dictionary of National Biography*. For almost the whole of the third volume is given over to the Trafalgar campaign, and in the introduction Laughton completely reverses his earlier judgement: 'the First Lord of the Admiralty ... was in reality – as is more certainly shown in these pages – the master mind and director of the whole campaign'.[10] Admiralty Board minutes, which I have perused for the period of Barham's tenure, reveal a First Lord as immersed in the details of strategy and tactics as he had been caught up in the particulars of coppering a ship of the line a quarter of a century earlier. His hurried scrawl is everywhere, making dispositions, demanding to be informed, admonishing the dilatory, scolding colleagues and subordinates alike, exhorting commanders at sea.[11] Once again, as during his time at the Navy Office, he acted on his conviction that the success of broad schemes lay in the mastery of detail.

The story of the Trafalgar campaign has been told many times.[12] If Barham's short but eventful term in office represented, in style and approach, a reprise of his career at the Navy Office it was less in the day-to-day management of affairs than in the making of decisions that he left his mark. Napoleon had already amassed his invasion force at Boulogne and Villeneuve's squadron had made good its escape from Toulon when Barham took over. His task was to make sense of a puzzle, to extract, from the shape of the manifold and disparate pieces on the board and the relations they bore to each other, clues to the overall strategic picture, and once he had this picture in hand, to strike at the enemy as quickly and forcefully as he could.

One key piece of the puzzle – Villeneuve's whereabouts and intentions – fell into place with a dispatch Nelson sent to the Admiralty via the brig *Curieux*. Weighing the scraps of intelligence that came his way, Nelson concluded that Villeneuve, who had added five Spanish ships of the line to his own squadron, had headed for the Caribbean. Perhaps he was up to the old mission of raiding the British sugar islands. Nelson followed him, in the hope of forcing an encounter. But the French admiral, demoralized by rumors that the ferocious conqueror of the Nile and Copenhagen was at his heels, decided to return home. Nelson sent the *Curieux* ahead with his hunch that the enemy was making for either Cádiz or Toulon; he intended, he said, to hunt him down. On the dash to London the *Curieux* spotted Villeneuve's fleet, homeward bound, in mid-ocean. This news reached the Admiralty in the early morning hours of 9 July.

Barham reacted immediately. Seizing the chance to ensnare Villeneuve before he could join up with the French fleet at Brest, thereby establishing the long-sought superiority over the British in the Channel, he ordered Admiral Cornwallis to uncover Brest in favor of cruising the Bay of Biscay; part of Cornwallis's fleet, under Admiral Robert Calder, was to patrol the waters off the north-west edge of Spain. With the ships of the line so disposed and frigates stretched far and wide watching for enemy sail, Barham's scheme was meant to catch the combined fleet in a net of superior British force. It nearly did so. On 22 July Calder ran into Villeneuve, steering for Ferrol, off Cape Finisterre. Partly owing to Calder's tactical timidity, partly to Villeneuve's unexpected aggressiveness, partly to vagaries of the wind, two days of fighting proved inconclusive. Breaking off the encounter, Villeneuve made it into Ferrol and Calder rejoined Collingwood.[13]

Calder's failure to inflict any more than a glancing blow on Villeneuve did no lasting damage to Barham's design. Tightening the noose on the combined fleet evidently required a more skillful and deadly hand. Nelson, some historians have suggested, would not have let slip the opportunity that presented itself to Calder. But Nelson was still available. Having chased Villeneuve back and forth across the Atlantic, leaving the Mediterranean, which was his chief responsibility, largely free from hostile ships, he returned to England for a much needed rest. He had been continuously at sea more than two years.

Meanwhile, the invasion threat evaporated. In August word came to Napoleon of a Russian–Austrian coalition forming against him. Turning his back on the Channel and the scheme on which he had expended so much time, money and ingenuity, he moved to meet this far greater challenge to his position in Europe than any Britain could mount. Abandoning at Boulogne all the preparations he had made, he faced his army toward the Rhine and the opportunities for some decisive action in central Europe. For the opportunities lost at sea, he forever heaped blame on his admirals, especially the hapless Villeneuve. Like the Duke of Medina-Sidonia, commander of the Spanish Armada, Villeneuve became the scapegoat for the failings of a ruler ignorant of the exigencies of sea warfare. Nevertheless, the French commander made a decision that remains inexplicable, unless it can be attributed to a failure of nerve. After repairing the damage suffered in the July encounter with Calder off Finisterre, Villeneuve put to sea from Ferrol. Instead of sailing north and rendezvousing with Vice-Admiral Honoré Ganteaume, the French squadron commander at Brest, Villeneuve went south. He thereby failed to establish the numerical superiority that had been his aim since escaping from Toulon. Convincing himself that the British would outnumber him in the western approaches no matter what he did, in mid August he made for Cádiz. There he remained, under the watchful eye of Collingwood, until emerging in October for what became the Battle of Trafalgar.

It scarcely mattered to the unfolding of Barham's strategy whether Napoleon's invasion scheme was still on. For the essential requirement of policy was maintaining supremacy at sea, not preparing to repel an invader. Indeed, as far as the naval authorities were concerned, such preparations as drilling militia and strengthening shore defenses were distractions from the vital task. Barham must still have had vivid memories of the steps he had taken in 1779 to quell the panic provoked ashore by the Combined Fleet's appearance in the Channel. Then he had had his hands full keeping dockyard workers at their tools instead of shouldering muskets against the improbable descent of French and Spanish infantry. It was British superiority at sea that kept such troops seasick aboard their transports or dying of boredom in barracks across the Channel. Such superiority could never be too great or too decisive; no opportunity to enhance it at the expense of an enemy could be allowed to slip by.

On 13 September Barham summoned Nelson to the Admiralty. Alerted to the combined fleet's presence in Cádiz and aware that the shelving of the invasion plan freed it to cover the Grand Army's Mediterranean flank as it advanced toward central Europe, the Admiralty made plans to keep Villeneuve's command from lending Napoleon any such assistance. Villeneuve having fled from the Mediterranean, the British aimed to keep him out. In a memorandum of 4 September to Pitt, Barham sketched out his ideas:

> What I would propose is this: To extend Lord Nelson's command to Cape St Vincent including Cadiz and Gibraltar. To send him out immediately in the *Victory* and such line of battle ships as can be spared, to take the command of the ships at this time off Cadiz. To leave as many line of battle ships off that port under vice-Admiral Collingwood as will effectually secure a blockade of the port and of the combined fleets now assembled there.

Having assured himself of the security of Gibraltar, he was 'to visit the other parts of his command and form such a squadron as will embrace every duty belonging to it'.[14] Barham's draft instructions to Nelson, composed on 5 September, essentially recapitulated his memorandum for the Prime Minister. 'You are', the instructions read in the Admiralty's ancient formula, 'hereby required and directed to proceed with the *Victory* and the ships named in the margin [not mentioned in the draft], whose captains have orders to place themselves under your orders, to the Bay of Cádiz, where you may expect to find Vice-Admiral Collingwood and Vice-Admiral Sir Robert Calder, and the squadron of HM ships under his command ... And whereas, from the opinion we entertain of your conduct and abilities', the instructions concluded, 'we have thought fit to extend your command to Cape St Vincent, you will proceed to form the best system for the management of so extensive a command that circumstances may admit of at the time.'[15] If Barham did not grant Nelson *carte blanche*, he nevertheless gave him a freedom consistent with his responsibilities. What the two men said to each other in their interview of 15 September is unknown, but they would not have needed to say much. Together they represented more than three-quarters of a century of experience in naval affairs. Handed the tools by the First Lord, it was up to the sea commander to do the job.

Two days following his audience with Barham, Nelson went on board the *Victory* and sailed from Portsmouth for the last time in his career. On the voyage south he explained to his captains, assembled on board his flagship, his famous plans for the decisive engagement he fully expected to take place should Villeneuve venture from Cádiz. What he envisaged, Nelson emphasized, was nothing less than the 'annihilation' of the combined Franco-Spanish fleet. This was an unusual word for a commander to utter in the age of sail, when sea battles were far more likely to end as inconclusive draws, in the manner of 22 July, than with one side devastating the other. But Nelson was an unusual commander, and at the Nile in 1798, when he had caught the French fleet at anchor, he had already shown himself a master of annihilation. On 19 October Villeneuve brought the Combined Fleet out of Cádiz, shadowed by the British frigate *Curieux*.

Shortly before noon on the 21st the two squadrons under Collingwood and Nelson came crashing down, roughly as planned and almost simultaneously, on the Franco-Spanish line of battle. In the event, Trafalgar fell short of the annihilation Nelson aimed for; the terrible gale that sprang up in the aftermath of the battle destroyed more of the Combined Fleet's ships than British gunners had. Nevertheless, in terms of the loss of life, Trafalgar was a 'massacre', as John Keegan has called it. If it fell short of the butchery of contemporary land warfare, the total of 8,500 killed and wounded, of some 50,000 present, was unprecedented in war at sea.[16] And however much Napoleon tried to minimize its significance, Trafalgar blunted the challenge that France, jointly with various maritime allies, had mounted to British naval mastery. The threat was far from ended, the war against the French empire still had nearly ten years to run, but never again did a combined fleet attempt to turn the strategic balance in the course of a day's fight.

Foremost among the Trafalgar dead, of course, was Nelson himself. A French sniper in the mizzen-top of the *Redoutable* shot him down as he walked the quarterdeck of the *Victory*, resplendent and unmistakable in his bemedalled uniform. Already a great popular hero, he became, by virtue of his victory at Trafalgar, the apotheosis of the fighting admiral. Borne home aboard his flagship, in January 1806 his body was laid to rest, following an enormous state funeral, in St Paul's Cathedral. There is no evidence that Barham attended, either as First Lord of the Admiralty or as one among scores of admirals, both active duty and retired. A month later, when Pitt collapsed, the First Lord left the office he had occupied for a brief but crowded nine months and returned to Teston, where in 1813 he died, just another obscure country gentleman.

For all their differences in age, temperament, skill, experience and public acclaim, Horatio Nelson and Charles Middleton shared a knowledge of sea warfare and of sailing ships. The *Victory* expressed these ties. Her keel laid down in 1756, two years before Middleton made post captain and Nelson was born, she was Admiral Charles Hardy's flagship in the Channel in 1779, when Middleton was Controller of the Navy. Coppered in 1782, as part of Middleton's vast program, she was rebolted and recoppered in 1787, bringing the great experiment of the American war to a successful if belated close. So if Barham as First Lord put the ship in Nelson's hands, as Middleton the Controller he had supervised far more closely than any naval policy maker before or since, all the elements that went into keeping such ships at sea. The *Victory* remains at Portsmouth, a monument not only to Nelson and all the men who sailed in her, but also to the dockyard workers who built her and those who kept her in service, Middleton included.

Middleton's greatness as a naval administrator lay not in presiding over a triumph but in fending off disaster. True, the American war ended in a British defeat, but without the Controller's exertions at the Navy Office, things could have been worse. He was in some respects the ideal man for an emergency: taking risks, casting precedents aside, abiding by his own counsel, he pushed through, at the height of a great war, technical innovations scarcely imaginable in peacetime. By unsnarling the supply line to the expeditionary force, he succeeded in keeping starvation at bay. Once Cornwallis was defeated and 'the world turned upside down', he ensured the evacuation of America in a reasonably orderly fashion. In peacetime he turned with scarcely a pause to making the most of the harrowing lessons of a lost war. The Royal Navy's performance in the wars of the French Revolution and Napoleon suggests how well these lessons were learned.

NOTES

1 Carola Oman, *Nelson* (London, 1946), p. 639. The best of the recent contributions to a huge literature is Tom Pocock, *Horatio Nelson* (London, 1987). An able biography that pays less attention to events at sea is Christopher Hibbert, *Nelson: A Personal History* (London, 1994).

2 William Marsden, *A Brief Memoir of the Life and Writings of the Late William Marsden, Written By Himself* (London, 1838), p. 116.

3 The best recent account of this tangled episode is John Ehrman, *The Younger Pitt*, 3 vols (London, 1969–96), vol. III, pp. 752–65.

4 John Keegan, *The Price of Admiralty: The Evolution of Naval Warfare* (New York: Viking, 1989), p. 12. The classic account is Julian Corbett, *The Campaign of Trafalgar*, 2 vols (London, 1910).
5 N. A. M. Rodger, 'The Victualling of the British Navy in the Seven Years War', *Bulletin du centre d'histoire des espaces atlantiques*, new series, 2 (1985), pp. 37–53.
6 Ehrman, *Younger Pitt*, vol. III, p. 765.
7 Corbett, *Campaign of Trafalgar*, vol. I, p. 80.
8 John Gore (ed.), *The Creevey Papers* (London, 1963), p. 33.
9 *Dictionary of National Biography* (London, 1894), vol. XIII, p. 341.
10 John Knox Laughton (ed.), *Letters and Papers of Charles, Lord Barham*, 3 vols (London, 1911), vol. III, pp. xiv–xv.
11 PRO, ADM 3, Admiralty Board Minutes.
12 The fullest account remains Corbett, *The Campaign of Trafalgar*. See also Geoffrey Bennett, *Nelson the Commander* (London, 1972); Edouard Desbrière, *The Naval Campaign of 1805: Trafalgar* (trans. Constance Eastwick), 2 vols (Oxford, 1933); David Howarth, *Trafalgar* (London, 1969); Oman, *Nelson*; Alan Schom, *Trafalgar: Countdown to Battle* (London, 1990); and Oliver Warner, *Trafalgar* (London, 1959).
13 My account relies on the accessible Keegan, *Price of Admiralty*, pp. 25–9.
14 *Barham Papers*, vol. III, p. 313.
15 Ibid., p. 315.
16 Keegan, *Price of Admiralty*, p. 90.

Select Bibliography

MANUSCRIPTS

Manuscript sources on which this book relies include the Middleton papers and Navy Board and Admiralty records at the National Maritime Museum in Greenwich; Admiralty, Colonial Office, Treasury Board documents, and the Chatham papers, all at the Public Record Office, Kew; the Liverpool and Althorp papers at the British Library; the Howe papers at the Huntington Library, San Marino, California; and the Mahan papers in the Naval War College Archives in Newport, Rhode Island.

PRINTED SOURCES

The principal books and articles on which I relied are included.

Albion, Robert, *Forests and Sea Power: The Timber Problem of the Royal Navy 1652–1862*, Cambridge, MA, 1926.

Barnes, G.R. and J.H. Owen, *The Private Papers of John, Earl of Sandwich*, 4 vols, London, 1932–36.

Barrow, John, *The Life of Earl Howe*, London, 1838.

Baugh, Daniel A., *British Naval Administration in the Age of Walpole*, Princeton, NJ, 1965.

— 'Great Britain's "Blue-Water" Policy, 1689–1815', *International History Review*, 10, 1 (February 1988), pp. 33–58.

Beaglehole, J.C., *The Life of Captain James Cook*, Stanford, CA, 1974.

Black, Jeremy, *Pitt the Elder*, London, 1992.

Black, Jeremy and Philip Woodfine (eds), *The British Navy and the Use of Naval Power in the Eighteenth Century*, Leicester, 1988.

Blackburn, Robin, *The Overthrow of Colonial Slavery, 1776–1848*, London, 1988.

Bowler, R. Arthur, *Logistics and the Failure of the British Army in America, 1775–1783*, Princeton, NJ, 1975.

Breihan, John R., 'William Pitt and the Commission on Fees, 1785–1801', *Historical Journal*, 27, 1 (1984), pp. 59–82.

Brewer, John, *The Sinews of Power: War, Money and the English State, 1688–1783*, New York, 1989.

Bryant, Arthur, *Samuel Pepys*, vol. I, *The Man in the Making*, New York, 1934.

Campbell, Patrick H., *Scotland since 1707: The Rise of An Industrial Society*, 2nd edn, Edinburgh, 1985.

— *The Carron Company*, London, 1961.

Cipolla, Carlo, *Guns and Sails in the Early Phase of European Expansion, 1400–1700*, London, 1965.

Clarkson, Thomas, *History of the Rise, Progress, and Abolition of the African Slave Trade by the British Parliament*, London, 1839.

Clowes, William Laird (ed.), *The Royal Navy*, vol. III, London, 1898.

Coad, Jonathan, *The Royal Dockyards, 1690–1850: Architecture and Engineering Works of the Royal Navy*, Aldershot, 1989.

Colledge, J.J., *Ships of the Royal Navy: An Historical Index*, vol. I, *Major Ships*, New York, 1969.

Corbett, Julian S. (ed.), *Fighting Instructions, 1530–1816*, London, 1905.

— *England in the Seven Years War*, 2 vols, London, 1907.

— *The Campaign of Trafalgar*, 2 vols, London, 1910.

Davidoff, Leonore, and Catherine Hall, *Family Fortunes: Men and Women of the English Middle Class, 1780–1850*, London, 1987.

Davis, David Brion, *The Problem of Slavery in the Age of Revolution, 1770–1823*, Ithaca, NY, 1975.

Desbrière, Edouard, *The Naval Campaign of 1805: Trafalgar* (trans. Constance Eastwick), 2 vols, Oxford, 1933.

Donoghue, Bernard, *British Politics and the American Revolution*, London, 1964.

Drescher, Seymour, 'People and Parliament: The Rhetoric of the British Slave Trade', *Journal of Interdisciplinary History*, 20, 4 (Spring 1990), pp. 561–80.

— 'Whose Abolition: Popular Pressure and the Ending of the British Slave Trade', *Past and Present*, 143 (May 1994), pp. 136–66.

Duffy, Michael, *Soldiers, Sugar, and Seapower: The British Expeditions to the West Indies and the War against Revolutionary France*, Oxford, 1987.

— 'British Diplomacy and the French Wars', in H. T. Dickinson (ed.), *Britain and the French Revolution, 1789–1815*, London, 1989, pp. 127–46.

Dull, Jonathan R., *The French Navy and American Independence: A Study of Arms and Diplomacy, 1774–1787*, Princeton, NJ, 1975.

Ehrman, John, *The Navy in the War of William III, 1689–1697*, Cambridge, 1953.

— *The Younger Pitt*, 3 vols, London, 1969–96.

Eltis, David, *Economic Growth and the Ending of the Transatlantic Slave Trade*, Oxford, 1987.

Fincham, John, *A History of Naval Architecture*, London, 1979.

Furber, Holden, *Henry Dundas, First Viscount Melville*, London, 1931.

Gallagher, Robert (ed.), *Byron's Journal of His Circumnavigation, 1764–1766*, Hakluyt Society Publications, second series, vol. CXIII, Cambridge, 1964.

Gradish, Stephen, *The Manning of the British Navy during the Seven Years War*, London, 1980.

Haas, James M., 'The Royal Dockyards: The Earliest Visitations and Reforms', *Historical Journal*, 13, 2 (June 1970), pp. 191–215.

Hamilton, Henry, *An Economic History of Scotland in the Eighteenth Century*, Oxford, 1963.

— *The Industrial Revolution in Scotland*, London, 1932.

Harding, Richard, *Amphibious Warfare in the Eighteenth Century: The British Expedition to the West Indies, 1740–1742*, Woodbridge, Suffolk, 1991.

Harris, J.R., 'Copper and Shipping in the Eighteenth Century', *Economic History Review*, 19 (1966), pp. 550–68.

Hattendorf, John B., *et al.* (eds), *British Naval Documents, 1204–1960*, Aldershot, 1993.

Howarth, David, *Trafalgar*, London, 1969.

James, William, *The Naval History of Great Britain*, vol. I, London, 1837.

Jones, M.G., *Hannah More*, Cambridge, 1952.

Keegan, John, *The Price of Admiralty: The Evolution of Naval Warfare*, New York, 1989.

Kennedy, Paul, *The Rise and Fall of British Naval Mastery*, London, 1976.

Knight, R.J.B., 'The Royal Dockyards in England at the Time of the War of American Independence', PhD thesis, University of London, 1972.

— 'The Introduction of Copper Sheathing into the Royal Navy, 1779–1786', *Mariner's Mirror*, 59 (1973), pp. 299–309.

— *The Portsmouth Dockyard during the American War of Independence*, Portsmouth, 1988.

Lacour-Gayet, Georges, *La Marine militaire de Louis XVI*, Paris, 1905.

— *La Marine militaire sous le règne de Louis XV*, Paris, 1902.

Langford, Paul, *A Polite and Commercial People: England, 1727–1783*, Oxford, 1989.

Laughton, John Knox (ed.), *Letters and Papers of Charles, Lord Barham*, 3 vols, London, 1911.

Lenman, Bruce, *An Economic History of Modern Scotland, 1660–1976*, London, 1976.

Macalpine, Ida and Richard Hunter, *George III and the Mad Business*, New York, 1969.

Mackesy, Piers, *The War for America*, Cambridge, MA, 1964.

Marsden, William, *A Brief Memoir of the Life and Writings of the Late William Marsden, Written By Himself*, London, 1838.

Matheson, Cyril, *The Life of Henry Dundas, First Viscount Melville*, London, 1933.

McNeill, William H., *The Pursuit of Power: Technology, Armed Force, and Society since AD1000*, Chicago, 1982.

Middleton, Richard, *The Bells of Victory: The Pitt–Newcastle Ministry and the Conduct of the Seven Years' War, 1757–1762*, Cambridge, 1985.

Murray, Oswyn A.R., 'The Admiralty', *Mariner's Mirror*, 23 (1937), pp. 13–36, 129–47, 316–31 and 24 (1938), pp. 101–4, 204–25, 329–52.

Norris, John, *Shelburne and Reform*, London, 1963.

Oldfield, J.R., *Popular Politics and British Anti-Slavery: The Mobilisation of Public Opinion against the Slave Trade*, Manchester, 1995.

Ollard, Richard, *Pepys*, New York, 1974.

Oman, Carola, *Nelson*, London, 1947.

Oppenheim, Michael, *A History of the Administration of the Royal Navy*, London, 1896.

Pares, Richard, *War and Trade in the West Indies*, London, 1936.

— *The Historian's Business and Other Essays*, Oxford, 1961.

Parkinson, C. Northcote, *Britannia Rules: The Classic Age of Naval History*, New York, 1977.

Patterson, A. Temple, *The Other Armada: The Franco-Spanish Attempt to Invade Britain in 1779*, Manchester, 1960.

Phillips, I. Lloyd, 'The Evangelical Administrator: Sir Charles Middleton at the Navy Board, 1778–1790', PhD thesis, Oxford University, 1974.

Plumb, J.H., *England in the Eighteenth Century*, London, 1950.

Pool, Bernard, *Navy Board Contracts, 1600–1932*, Hamden, CT, 1966.

Porter, Roy, *English Society in the Eighteenth Century*, London, 1982.

Rees, Gareth, 'Copper Sheathing: An Example of Technological Diffusion in the English Merchant Fleet', *Journal of Transport History*, 1 (1971), pp. 85–94.

Richmond, Herbert W., *The Invasion of Britain*, London, 1941.

Rodger, N.A.M. (ed.), 'The Douglas Papers, 1760–1762', *The Naval Miscellany*, vol. V, *Publications of the Navy Records Society*, London, 1984, pp. 244–83.

— 'The Victualling of the British Navy in the Seven Years War', *Bulletin du centre d'histoire des espaces atlantiques*, new series, 2 (1985), pp. 37–53.

— *The Wooden World: An Anatomy of the Georgian Navy*, London, 1986.

— *The Insatiable Earl: A Life of John Montagu, Fourth Earl of Sandwich 1718–1792*, New York, 1994.

Savory, Reginald, *His Britannic Majesty's Forces in Germany during the Seven Years War*, Oxford, 1966.

Schom, Alan, *Trafalgar: Countdown to Battle*, London, 1990.

Schroeder, Paul W., *The Transformation of European Politics, 1763–1848*, Oxford, 1994.

Stinchcombe, A.L., *Sugar Island Slavery in the Age of Enlightenment: The Political Economy of the Caribbean World*, Princeton, NJ, 1995.

Sutherland, Lucy, *The East India Company in Eighteenth-Century Politics*, Oxford, 1952.

Syrett, David, *Shipping and the American War, 1775–83: A Study of British Transport Organization*, London, 1970.

— *The Royal Navy in American Waters, 1775–1783*, Aldershot, 1989.

Terraine, John, *Trafalgar*, London, 1976.

Tilley, John A., *The British Navy and the American Revolution*, Columbia, SC, 1987.

Torrance, John, 'Social Class and Bureaucratic Innovation: The Commissioners for Examining the Public Accounts, 1780–1787', *Past and Present*, 78 (February 1978), pp. 56–81.

Tracy, Nicholas, *Nelson's Battles: The Art of Victory in the Age of Sail*, London, 1996.

Warner, Oliver, *Trafalgar*, London, 1959.

Index

Gambier family, 117
Gambier, Rear-Admiral James, 27
Gambier, Margaret *see* Middleton, Margaret
Ganteaume, Vice-Admiral Honoré, 154
Garbett, Samuel, 62–3
Gardner, Admiral Lord James, 88n, 151
Gascoigne, Charles, 63
George III (King of England), 28, 122, 127, 128, 149; and the American Revolution, 74; and carronades, 63; and coppering ships, 50, 58n, 59n, 79, 108; on Gibraltar, 84; and Keppel Palliser affair, 88n; and porphyria, 131–2
Germain, Lord George, 36, 38–9
Gibraltar, 84–6, 116, 155
Goliath, 49
Grafton, 71n
Grant, Mr, 147n
Grasse, Comte de (Admiral François-Joseph Paul), 55, 84
Graves, Admiral, 113n
Gravier, Charles *see* Vergennes, Comte de
Great Mutiny at Nore, 110, 121
Gregson, Robert, 78
Grenville, Lord William, 133, 136
Gribeauval, Jean-Baptiste de, 62
guardships, 4, 22, 28, 98
Guillouet, Admiral Louis *see* Orvilliers, Comte d'
gunboats, 39

Hanover, 5–6
Hardy, Vice-Admiral Sir Charles, 75–8, 79, 80–1, 157
Harland, Vice-Admiral Sir Robert, 75
Harwich, 6
Hawke, Edward, 82, 127
Hawke, 48
Hawkins, Sir John, 75–6
Hébé, 68–9
Hector, 59n
Henry VIII (King of England), 29, 119
historiography, xiii–xiv
Holland, 32, 68, 109
Hood, Rear-Admiral Sir Samuel, 30, 32, 55, 59n, 75, 104
Hooke, Robert, 29
Howe, Admiral Lord Richard, 79, 85–6, 100–1, 102–3, 127–9
howitzers, and carronades, 64

Hughes, Admiral Sir Edward, 86
Huguenots, 12, 14, 139
Hunt, Edward, 31
hurricanes, 6, 8, 113n
Huskisson, William, 140, 143

Indefatigable, 108–9
India Bill, 122
Indian Ocean, 92
insurance underwriters, 36
Invincible, 50, 59n, 104

Jack the Painter, 53
Jacobs (master on the *Chesterfield*), 9
James II (Duke of York and King of England), 1, 29
James, William, 67
Jenkinson, Charles, 16, 25–6, 41n
Jenkinson, Robert (Lord Hawkesbury), 151
Jervis, Captain Sir John (Lord St Vincent), 58n
Johnson, Samuel, xvi
Jupiter, 28, 48, 108–9

Keegan, John, 156
Keith, Admiral Lord (George Elphinstone), 151
Kempenfelt, Admiral Richard, 4, 6, 55, 75, 104; and Vice-Admiral Sir Charles Hardy, 76–8, 80–2, 88n
Kennedy, Paul, 21
Keppel, Admiral Augustus: and battle off Ushant, 33, 34, 45, 101; as First Lord of the Admiralty, 84–5, 87, 90–1, 99, 100, 115, 128; Keppel–Palliser affair, 74–5, 88n
Keppel–Palliser affair, 74–5, 88n

Laforey affair, 138–44
Laforey, Vice-Admiral Sir John, 75, 88n, 139–42
Landguard Fort, and carronade trials, 65, 66
Langton, Bennet, 131
Laughton, John Knox, 5, 152
LeCras, Captain Edward, 31–2, 34, 81, 128
Leviathan, 101
lieutenants, 3, 18–19n, 31
Lind, Dr James, 16
Lindsay, Lt-General Sir David, 80
Linney, Alexander, 8

Other Titles in the Naval Policy and History Series

Austro-Hungarian Naval Policy 1904–1914

Milan N Vego, *US Naval War College, Newport, Rhode Island*

'... a welcome addition to the literature of the field.'
The Journal of Slavic Military Studies

'... readers interested in the Austro-Hungarian navy and the naval balance of power in the Mediterranean on the eve of World War I will welcome the appearance of Vego's book.'
The Journal of Military History

This unique and comprehensive account describes the interplay of internal and external factors in the emergence of the Austro-Hungarian Navy from a coastal defence force in 1904 to a respectable battle force capable of the joint operations with other Triple Alliance fleets in the Mediterranean by the eve of World War I. The book describes the relationships between naval leaders, the heir to the throne Archduke Francis Ferdinand, and the Parliament in shaping the dual Monarchy's naval policy. It also shows how the changes in foreign policy in Italy and underlying animosities between Rome and Vienna led to a naval race in the Adriatic that eventually bolstered Germany's naval position in respect to Great Britain in the North Sea.

240 pages   1996   0 7146 4678 4 cloth   0 7146 4209 6 paper
Naval Policy and History No. 1

FRANK CASS PUBLISHERS
Newbury House, 900 Eastern Avenue, Newbury Park, Ilford, Essex IG2 7HH
Tel: +44 (0)181 599 8866 Fax: +44 (0)181 599 0984 E-mail: info@frankcass.com
NORTH AMERICA
c/o ISBS, 5804 NE Hassalo Street, Portland, OR 97213 3644, USA
Tel: 1 800 944 6190 Fax: 503 280 8832 E-mail cass@isbs.com
Website: http://www.frankcass.com

Far Flung Lines

Studies in Imperial Defence in Honour of Donald Mackenzie Schurman

Keith Neilson *and* **Greg Kennedy,** *both at Royal Military College of Canada (Eds)*

This book shows how the British Empire used its maritime supremacy to construct and maintain a worldwide defence system that would protect its vital imperial interests. By combining a number of different historical threads – particularly imperial history, naval history and military history – Neilson and Kennedy rebut the idea that British defence policy in the late nineteenth and early twentieth centuries was primarily concerned with maintaining the balance of power in Europe. They thus directly challenge the view advanced by Sir Michael Howard in *The Continental Commitment* (1972), who argued that British defence policy in this period could best be explained in terms of a response to threats from the continent of Europe.

240 pages 1997 0 7146 4683 0 cloth 0 7146 4219 9 paper
Naval Policy and History No. 2

Maritime Strategy and Continental Wars

Rear Admiral Raja Menon

This work contends that nations embroiled in Continental wars have historically had poor maritime strategies. After an analysis of existing literature on this subject and a discussion of case studies, Rear Admiral Menon develops the argument that those navies that have been involved in such wars have made poor contributions to the overall political objectives. Menon argues that current technological trends are likely to lead to fleets' re-exerting their lost superiority against land-based means of conducting warfare, so long as the navies involved rebuild their structures to speed up the battle, since faster battle is the current strategic trend. Littoral superiority then becomes a naval objective on which to construct joint warfare.

232 pages 1998 0 7146 4793 4 cloth 0 7146 4348 3 paper
Naval Policy and History No.3

The Royal Navy and German Naval Disarmament 1942–1947

Chris Madsen, *University of Calgary*

This book examines the formulation and implementation of the Royal Navy's policy towards German naval disarmament after the Second World War. The British sought no less than the complete elimination of German naval power through a comprehensive programme of control, disbandment and demilitarization. Madsen details how the Royal Navy approached the disarmament of the *Kriegsmarine* with passion. Showing a remarkable level of cooperation with allied navies, particularly those of the United States and the Soviet Union, the Royal Navy controlled and disbanded German naval forces; participated in the division of the German surface fleet and merchant marine vessels in accord with the political decisions made at the Potsdam Conference; sank German submarines in deep water; supervised the clearance of sea mines off the coasts of north-west Germany; took full advantage of German technology and scientific knowhow; assisted in the prosecution of alleged war crimes; and demolished naval establishments.

288 pages   1998   0 7146 4823 X cloth   0 7146 4373 4 paper
Naval Policy and History No. 4

Naval Strategy and Operations in Narrow Seas

Milan N. Vego, *US Naval War College, Newport, Rhode Island*

A comparative analysis from Salamis to the modern day of the tactics and strategies employed by naval commanders in narrow seas. Although many books and articles have been written on wars in narrow seas, none deal in any comprehensive manner with the problems of strategy and conduct of naval operations. The aim of this book is to explain in some detail the characteristics of a war fought in narrow seas and to compare and contrast strategy and major operations in narrow seas and naval warfare in the open ocean.

256 pages   1999   0 7146 4870 1 cloth   0 7146 4425 0 paper
Naval Policy and History No.5

The Italian Navy and Fascist Expansionism 1935–40

Robert Mallett, *University of Leeds*

Challenging the views of Benito Mussolini's Italian biographer, Renzo De Felice, *The Italian Navy and Fascist Expansionism* argues that for the *Duce* aggressive war against the predominant Mediterranean powers, Britain and France, was the only means whereby Italy might secure access to the world's oceans. Following Hitler's rise to power in 1933, Mussolini actively pursued the Italo-German alliance which he believed would enable him to conquer a Fascist Empire stretching from the Mediterranean to the Indian Ocean. In the wake of the burgeoning Rome-Berlin alignment which took shape from 1935 onwards, the Italian fleet duly underwent a substantial quantitative expansion. By the eve of Italy's entry into the Second World War the Fascist administration had commissioned substantial new capital ship programmes, and created a major surface and underwater fleet that seemed to pose a serious challenge to the strategic position of Great Britain in the Mediterranean and Red Sea.

272 pages   1998   0 7146 4878 7 cloth   0 7146 4432 3 paper
Naval Policy and History No.7

FRANK CASS PUBLISHERS
Newbury House, 900 Eastern Avenue, Newbury Park, Ilford, Essex IG2 7HH
Tel: +44 (0)181 599 8866 Fax: +44 (0)181 599 0984 E-mail: info@frankcass.com
NORTH AMERICA
c/o ISBS, 5804 NE Hassalo Street, Portland, OR 97213 3644, USA
Tel: 1 800 944 6190 Fax: 503 280 8832 E-mail cass@isbs.com
Website. http://www.frankcass.com